Young Life

The Adventures of
an Ex Staffer

By Richard T. Bond

Rick Bond is a Certified Life Coach.

Email: connectdcoaching@gmail.com
Web site: www.connectdcoaching.com

Cover Photo by David Herrera
Protected under Creative Commons
https://creativecommons.org/licenses/by/2.0/

Other books by the same Author, also available on Amazon/Kindle: **Little Brown Eyes**. The story of raising, and losing our disabled child.

Foreword

You youngsters don't know how lucky you got it. Why, back in my day we had to walk to the Young Life office barefoot, in three feet of snow, uphill both ways. We had to fill out our monthly green sheets with dull pencils. We had no fancy computers. The lucky ones had Seven Star Diaries. Our idea of Young Life camping was a pup tent on the hard ground in the middle of an empty field. We had no budgets. We got paid once a year if we were lucky, in war bonds. I've been busy since those days, doing things like inventing the Internet and discovering global warming.

My spiritual journey began in Young Life, in 1963. My official relationship with Young Life lasted for 25 years, including 20 years on staff. Young Life's influence on who I am as a Christian and as a person has lasted a lifetime. Even though I haven't been on staff for 27 years, it's like the mafia; I could never really "leave", not that I wanted to. If you cut me today I still bleed Young Life. And this, from a person who most definitely does not live in the past or relish the "Glory Days," as Bruce Springsteen would sing.

I'm old enough and got in early enough to know or at least to have met a few of the first generation guys, but not old enough to have lived the first generation. I knew a lot of the second generation Young Life leaders, and younger. To all of these men and women-it's on their shoulders that I and so many of my generation stood. Their legacy was to have built a ministry that lasted, and lasted. With some, I was fortunate enough to actually become friends; with a few, very close friends.

Here are some of their names...broad shoulders: the founder, Jim Rayburn of course, Bob Mitchell, Bill Starr, Bob Reeverts, Ad Sewell, Phil MacDonald, Dick Lowey, Tom and Recie Raley, Jay Grimstead, Annie Cheairs, Roy Revere, Ken Wright, Bud Bylsma, George and Martie Sheffer, Marilyn (Horton) Dimmock, Bill Milliken, Frog Sullivan, Co Koppert, Rod Johnson, Charlie and Mary Scott, Verley Sangster, Mary Stam, Jack and Reid Carpenter, Jerry and Essie Johnson, Chuck Reinhold, Bo Nixon, Rog Harlan, Hal Merwald, Doug Burleigh, Neil and Margie Atkinson and Mal and Wanda McSwain.

I remember camps like Star Ranch and Silver Cliff. I read *He That is Spiritual*, by Lewis Sperry Chafer. I can picture the old Young Life Headquarters on Monument Street in Colorado Springs, and the Young Life Institute. In fact, because of Young Life the whole state of Colorado became a hallowed place of memories for me, which have lasted a lifetime. I remember the telling of stories of Ole' Club 37, and of Rayburn calling every staff person in the country to stop what they were doing and get out to Frontier Ranch for prayer. I recall the fascination of first hearing the stories of the purchases of Star Ranch, Silver Cliff, Frontier and Malibu camps. I hated doing Winter Work.

I have my own copies of: Carl Nelson's *Just the Greatest*, Char Meredith's *It's a Sin to Bore a Kid*, *Back to the Basics of Young Life* by John Miller, *Tough Love* and *So Long Sweet Jesus* by Bill Milliken, the granddaddy of them all, *Young life* by Emile Calliet (and his brother Yippie) and my personal favorite, *Dance Children Dance*, by Jim Rayburn III. I still have a few copies of J.B. Phillips New Testaments with the cookbook covers. I'm old enough to recollect the first Young Life

16 millimeter promotional films, like *Time for Living* ("Hondas in Young Life, just for the fun of it!")

I remember the national ban on the weekend camp game called "Wells Fargo" and then headquarters anticipating our cleverly rebellious natures and revising the prohibition to, "No use of the Wells Fargo game, *under any name*." I envision Jay Grimstead doing "The Movie Skit" and, try as we may, none of us could ever come close to his rendition. I hated doing Winter Work. I know I listed that already, but I really disliked it. I can still picture the raspberry songbooks, and the ones before those, and Johann Anderson's after those. I fondly remember the stars of the Operas (and played a few over the years), like Dudley Do-Right and Clementine Shovelful. I recollect Dirty Burt and the Trapper. I can still hear "Mockingbird Hill" and "It had to be you." I can hear Mitch's talks, and I'm just old enough to have heard Jim Rayburn speak to staff, but not old enough to have heard him speak to kids. I wish I could have heard that.

Well, you youngsters out there have no idea what I've been going on about, do you? For those of us still around from our generation, this was our history. This was our inheritance. These are our memories, our personal Ebenezer Stones, written in our hearts as of stones of remembrance. For the Gen-Xers and Millennials out there, you will have your own inheritance with Young Life, and maybe it will be greater than ours. Time will tell. This book isn't about the complete history of the Mission. It's about one guy's life as it related to Young Life: mine. And for me, it was all about some extraordinary relationships.

Contents

Part One: Maryland

Part Two: Connecticut

Why We Did What We Did

Part One

Maryland

Chapter 1

Beginnings. I Was Born at an Early Age...

"...in a hospital, so I could be close to my Mom. When I was eight I ran away with a circus, but my parents made me bring it back. My parents were in the iron and steel business. My mother would iron and my father would steal. One day, Mom wrapped my school lunch in a roadmap. I was basically an unwanted child. Now I'm wanted in several states." Corny, yes. But we used to say, "An 'ugh' is as good as a laugh."

Ok, for you nosey ones: I grew up in Baltimore, Maryland in a lower middle class home. It was a neighborhood like so many in and around Baltimore, consisting entirely of row homes. Some would say living in a row home categorized us like living on the other side of the tracks. I wouldn't go that far. Maybe on the tracks?

We moved out of the city when I was entering the fifth grade, so I spent the last two years of elementary school and all of junior and senior high school in the suburbs, but not far from the city.

Although we didn't have a lot of money I grew up in a

pretty healthy family situation. My parents never got divorced. They weren't alcoholics and they weren't abusive. That's gotta count for something. Seriously, there was a lot of love in my home, more expressed by my Mom, but certainly present with Dad...except for the second hand smoke. My father was one of ten siblings who grew up on a farm and as an adult moved to the city. Can you imagine his dinner table growing up? That's where he learned to fight.

Dad was a self-educated hard working man who began in a blue collar job and eventually worked himself up into a fairly significant executive position with a large company, The Baltimore and Ohio Railroad. But, having grown up in the Great Depression, he always carried with him a fear of losing his job (he never did, thankfully) and not being a proper provider for his family. But that didn't stop him from reminding us at least once a day of his impending doom. He was like the father in *My Big Fat Greek Wedding*, except instead of spraying Windex on cuts and sores, he sprayed caution on frivolity.

Dad had a strong work ethic which he tried to instill into my brother and me. It "instilled" a lot more on my brother. He was very frugal. He rode a bus to work every day. We didn't even own a family car until I was in the fifth grade, and that was a used car. We weren't exactly Mercedes Benz material.

My mother was a first generation American born from an Italian family. My Grandparents and the older generation on her side of the family would speak Italian to one another. I'd yell, "Speak American dammit!" I'd yell that to myself. My Italian grandmother actually had one of those moles on her chin with hair growing out of it that would poke at me when she tried to kiss me. I'd try my hardest to get my required kiss over with without hitting that dark hairy protuberance. The extended family was very close and spent a lot of weekends together. Heaven help us the few times we got my Mom's and my Dad's families together. Farmers and Paisanos.

My only brother, Jack, was almost seven years older than me. We were never really close growing up primarily because of the age difference. I was the snotty nosed little brother who took his possessions and messed with his room. By the time we reached early adulthood we grew to be very close friends, and have remained so to this day.

School and Friends

While I was never a hardcore reveler or hell-raiser, I was at times on the fringe of the social network. I starting smoking in seventh grade, mainly because I and my friends thought it was cool. I used to keep a pack of Pall Mall unfiltered cigarettes in my locker in junior high school. As a habit it lasted until my junior year of high school.

Some of the crowd I hung out with in my junior high years was pretty rough. Two memories stand out, among others, maybe because they affected me in a life shaping way, leading into my high school years. One, a friend of mine, Eddie, died from a gunshot wound to his head in an accident at home. This was my first exposure to death of someone close. The other memory was more subtle. Well, most memories would be more subtle than a gunshot wound to the head, but it had a bigger effect. It happened in the seventh grade, but to explain it I must go back earlier.

Fourth grade was a bad year for me. I got into a lot of trouble at school. My teacher, Dr. Evil, said I was "insolent and ill-tempered." By fifth grade we had moved, and in the new school system I was able to have a fresh start without any negative history or reputation. In the elementary school I attended students were placed in one of four classes depending on how smart they were.

3

As a young person, I just assumed that this was normal operating procedure. But looking back it's not hard to see that being placed in one of the lower classes (in fifth grade I was second to last and in sixth grade I moved up one level) can send a pretty crummy message that becomes a self-fulfilling prophecy: "If the school thinks I'm only this smart I guess that's what I must be." In those years of self-discovery and self-image formation, that little slice of their opinion of reality wasn't so nice.

By seventh grade I moved up to junior high school. New building, a lot of new kids around. It began well. In fact, I even got elected as president of my homeroom class. I know. It ranks right up there with being the valedictorian of summer school. As the year went on and as I got involved with some less-than-stellar kids, I could feel that my credibility was sliding downhill. One day I and two other students got caught by our math teacher in some fairly minor altercation. One of the two guys was a pretty ordinary guy. The other was a good friend and a nice guy, but pretty much a degenerate. In fact, about a month before this incident, he and two other friends of mine had been arrested for allegedly raping a girl. It later was revealed that it was consensual, but at this point Jerry was an accused rapist. Sex in the seventh grade. That was some pretty crazy stuff, for back in the 60's.

The math teacher, Mr. Laraske, yelled at us for whatever infraction we had committed. He then took the three of us aside and said he was going to give each of us his personal assessment. About my accused rapist buddy, Mr. Laraske said, "You're basically a good guy who occasionally gets into trouble. You need to watch your behavior more." Good talk, coach. Then he turned to me, and he said, "You are a complete loser and failure, and if it weren't for your parents I don't think you would even be in school." And if you don't think that made an impression on me, here I am over 50 years later and can still hear that malevolent cretin saying it pretty much word for word. Fortunately for me, messages from other people, in time, and because of what was to happen related to Young Life just a few years down the road, would have a much bigger and lasting impact in my life. But for that age and that time, it was devastating.

My family was nominally Christian. My mother sang in the choir weekly at a Methodist church. Choir robe, the whole nine yards. My brother and I were required to attend in our early years, and sometimes we actually enjoyed participation in activities such as the youth group. But mostly we thought church was a drag. My Dad was a "Creaster" Christian, that is, he only attended church at Christmas and Easter. By the time I reached high school, my mother's attempts at keeping me interested in church were losing momentum. I rather preferred my Dad's program.

Before I got involved with Young Life, in my sophomore year and in the fall of my junior year of high school, I hung out mainly with a crowd that didn't even go to my school. I had fallen in with a Catholic crowd who all attended various parochial schools. Back then many Catholic churches ran dances on weekends. In Baltimore those dances were one of the more popular social scenes, whether you were catholic or not. So my social life was more centered on that crowd, and as a result I always felt a little bit like a fish out of water in my own high school.

When I began high school as a sophomore (this was in the days when high school was 10th through 12th grades only) I was probably viewed by others as a fringe person at Woodlawn High School. I wasn't involved in anything athletic, or any social group at school. I smoked. I didn't have a lot of friends, and the ones I had at school also seemed more fringe than mainstream. Without any sports or afterschool activities, when the final bell rang I just headed for the school bus and went straight home.

My social involvement at school was with friends I had met in class, and at lunchtime in the cafeteria. It was a little intimidating being a sophomore in a large (2,000 students) school with all those upperclassmen, but there was also an excitement about it too. Woodlawn was practically a brand new school, having only opened just a few years before my arrival. It was one of the newest schools at that time in Baltimore County, and it had a good vibe. But my circle of friends at school was fairly small.

I used to see a man around the school a lot, especially when I was leaving in the afternoon. He caught my attention because every time I saw him he was talking with a student or a group of students. At first I thought he was a teacher or a coach. But I never saw him during school and after a while I realized that I would have known if he was a teacher.

Then one day after school as I was shuffling out to catch my bus, this guy came walking right past me. It was the first chance I had to look at him close up. It was only a moment, since we were both moving in opposite directions. Although he was prematurely balding, he was a good looking guy, wiry and athletic. As he passed, he totally surprised me by smiling and saying a quick and warm "Hi!" This guy didn't know me from a sack of potatoes. Why would he say hi to me? Just seeing him talking with others, he came off like a pretty cool guy. I'd see him smiling, and maybe shaking a guy's hand or patting another guy on the shoulder. But why on earth would he say "hi" to me?

Chuck Reinhold

Over the next few weeks it seemed like he was around a lot. A few more times he walked past me, and each time he would smile and say hi. I can't exactly recall how long it was after the initial contact I had with him, but one day he stopped me and said, "Hey, you're Dick

Bond, aren't you?" Well, if I was surprised the first time he said hello, I was totally shocked when he said my name. I said yes but before I could ask him how he knew my name, he anticipated the question and then revealed, "My friend Newt Hetrick told me you were going out for the baseball team."

The interesting thing is, the only reason I knew this other guy, Newt Hetrick, was due to the fact that I had signed up for baseball tryouts, and he was on the varsity team. So I assumed it was one of Newt's responsibilities on the team to learn which students were going to try out. I said before that I wasn't involved in any athletics. But I did play little league baseball when I was in junior high, and my signing up for the high school baseball team was a half-hearted attempt to at least try and fit in. It was the one sport I had played before.

Once this guy explained how he knew me, he introduced himself. "I'm Chuck Reinhold. Hey, good luck with tryouts. They're next week right?" He even knew that! It was all of a ten second chat and he was off with a wave and a "Good luck." I was not only surprised, but I actually felt pretty good about this interchange. He was an adult, though maybe not too far beyond college age. Based on a lot of previous sightings, he was popular among a lot of other students. And...he knew my name! Not only that, he knew something about me. I thought that was pretty cool.

The next week I did try out for baseball, and in about as short a time as possible, I was cut from the junior varsity team. That was a fairly forgettable part of my early high school experience. But I tell you what was memorable. That guy I mentioned before, Newt Hetrick, came up and talked to me, and said he was sorry to not see my name on the baseball roster, and what a bummer it was that I got cut. He then walked with me from the athletic field, across the street to a gas station where we each bought soft drinks and sat down and drank them together. This was all Newt's doing, and yet it seemed so natural. He was full of empathy for me having to endure the humiliation of being cut from the team. And he tried his best to put a good spin on the whole thing, and to generally be positive and upbeat.

All of this happened in the spring of 1964, my sophomore year at Woodlawn. Because Newt, a junior, had reached out to me, a sophomore, I found myself looking for him to say "hi", around school during the day, in the halls, or in the cafeteria. We didn't have any classes together, but whenever I did see Newt, even if he was around his upper class buddies, he never failed to say hello and sometimes even stop and talk. In that way he even reminded me of that guy, Chuck.

I later learned that Newt used to be friends with some of the rough guys at school. We had our share of preppy suburbanites. But there was also a bit of an underbelly of tough guys, gang members and even some greasers. Insert mental picture of Arthur Fonzarelli. One of the toughest guys, who had a reputation as a great street fighter, was Earl Crown. That Newt and he were good friends was a bit disconcerting to me. How could this really nice guy, Newt, be good friends with a guy like Earl? I didn't understand that God had gotten hold of Newt, and later on He would be doing the same with Earl Crown, in a big, miraculous way.

All during the springtime I kept running into Chuck Reinhold, mostly leaving school at the end of the day, but also at athletic events that I'd occasionally attend with friends. And whenever he saw me, from the first time he called me by name and introduced himself, he always used my name. He asked how tryouts for baseball went. And when I told him I got cut he gave me a painful look and said, "Man, that's a shame." But he didn't act that surprised. I wondered if it was because I didn't look very athletic, or maybe his friend Newt had told him.

I had no idea why Chuck was around school all the time, or even if there was any kind of connection between him and Newt other than him meeting and knowing Newt as he had met me. I really didn't have any curiosity about who Chuck was, or what he did. He was just a popular guy who, for some reason, liked me. I never heard of Young Life, and if I had heard it mentioned, I would have had no idea what it was. I still primarily hung out in my social time after school and weekends with the parochial school crowd, going to CYO dances, riding around in their cars like the movie *American Graffiti*, and wearing English Leather cologne. Just listen to *Keeping the Faith* by Billy Joel. You'll get the picture. Except he used Old Spice. We smelled better.

Band Room

My one enjoyable elective class in my sophomore year was band. I played trumpet in the concert band and was pretty good for a sophomore. I also played in a local "garage" band with some friends, although I don't think that term was used in those days. Our band actually was very good. We played at a number of local venues, and sometimes even the CYO dances, the same ones I attended with friends. We had a great horn section and an excellent vocalist. I was the youngest guy in the group. The singer looked positively old, although he was probably only about 25. We were called "The Rhapsodies," but I digress.

Because I was in the concert band, sometimes I would hang out with some of my friends in the band room after school, especially as it got towards the end of the year. Mr. Hardy, the band Director, was pretty cool about us hanging out there. And we learned that he never checked in on the boy's bathroom, so we could sneak smokes whenever we wanted.

One day, very close to the last day of school, I and my buddy Don Newhouse, a drummer, were sitting around talking and generally killing time. I looked up and saw a girl walking into the band room. As she got closer, I realized that she was absolutely beautiful. The closer she came the more I was thinking, "She is the most beautiful girl I have ever seen at school!" She was one of those girls who turned heads and dropped jaws. Long blonde hair. Beautiful, athletic figure, and a smile that just melted me. And, with no one else around, she walked up and starting talking to us! I was in a bit of a fog at first, trying to sort out why this beauty would talk with us "lowly" band guys. Don was pretty cool, and it seemed like he either knew this girl, or at least knew about her. I mentioned that our high school had about 2,000 students, but I had never laid eyes on her before. I know, because I would have remembered. After we talked for a few minutes, I began to come out of my fog and tried to be friendly and show her my best self. She said, "By the way, I haven't met you before. I'm Kathy Schilling." I told her my name, as did Don.

Kathy hung out with us for a while. All the time I was still trying to work out why she was being so friendly. Although the movie *The Breakfast Club* would not come out for another 20 years, I felt a bit like Anthony Michael Hall, the geek, talking with Molly Ringwald, the beauty. Eventually I loosened up and she and I began to engage in friendly banter, back and forth. Meanwhile Don went over and was packing up his drum kit, which left Kathy and me one-on-one. The more I relaxed (Kathy had a way about her that was so down to earth and unpretentious) the easier it was to talk with her. At one point I actually found myself trying to flirt with her! She was funny, and she had such a great laugh. And I was a sixteen year-old with raging hormones. Yet, at the same time, her openness and friendliness all had such a wholesome quality about it. All the time I was thinking, "This girl is way out of my league. This can't go on much longer. She's going to realize it too, at any minute." But she never backed away or lost interest.

I don't recall exactly how the conversation got to dating. Because it was the end of the term, we were all heading off for the summer. We had been talking about missing some of our friends even though we all lived within a few miles of the school. So in a flash of brilliance or bold stupidity, reaching far above my social level, I jokingly said to Kathy, "I just met you and now I won't see you again until school starts in the fall. So how about if we go out on a date this summer?" I quickly checked and sure enough, that had been my outside voice. What did I just do? Do I want the shock and awe of falling back into reality, that his girl was a rock star and I was, at best, a groupie?

So, you can imagine my utter astonishment when I heard these words coming back to me, "Sure I would love to go out with you this summer!" Because much of our conversation had been fun, joking and laughter, my first reaction was, "She must have thought I was joking and she was playing along with the joke." Still, in that bit of ambivalence in my mind, I proceeded down the rabbit hole. "Great. When do you want to go out?" Kathy: "How about this weekend?" Me: "Ok, where do you live, I'll come pick you up," and so on.

Kathy was a 17 year old junior, soon to be a senior. I was a 16 year old sophomore. I didn't have a car. I didn't even have my driver's license! I had *no* idea how I was going to pull off this date, even if it was serious. I thought, "Just keep talking because sooner or later it's going to come out that this whole thing is a joke. Then I won't have to admit I don't have a license or a car." Finally after a while, Kathy had to leave, and said her goodbyes to me and to Don, who by that time had wandered back into our conversation. The last thing Kathy said was, "See you next Saturday night!" I was such an idiot that I was still wondering what had just happened and if I did actually have a date with this girl. I'm telling you (if you haven't realized by now) I was not the sharpest tool in the shed.

11

Don had overheard the part of the conversation about the date, so as soon as Kathy got out of earshot he was all over that. "Are you kidding me? You actually asked her out? And she said yes?" I was too shocked myself to act cool about it. Don went on, "You *do* know that she is, like, the most beautiful girl in her entire class." Side note: back in those days they had what was called Senior Polls, where students actually voted on different categories, like: most popular, most beautiful, and most likely to succeed. And sure enough, in her senior year, Kathy would be voted the most beautiful girl in her senior class at Woodlawn High School.

If you think I have lingered too long on this part of my story, before I go on, let me just state: the three new and "unusual" friends in my story so far, Chuck, Newt, and Kathy, all were highly instrumental to my hearing the Gospel and trusting Christ. Of those three, Kathy had the most impact in terms of getting me involved initially. She was also the cutest of the three, although Newt had his moments. So, my story continues.

I know this part of the narrative will sound silly to the point of suspicious, but in spite of all that took place, as the week went on I managed to somehow convince myself that the whole "date thing" had been a lot of friendly flirting, and Kathy didn't really expect me to show up Saturday night. I know. Weapons grade stupidity, right? As you might guess, I never showed up for the date.

Flash forward to September. Summer break was over. I hadn't thought much about Kathy that summer, other than a beautiful apparition that appeared in my life for an hour and was forever gone. On the second day of school, who walks right up to me in the hallway; Kathy Schilling. A big smile, and even a friendly half-hug, then..."You stood me up! I can't believe you stood me up! We were supposed to go out this summer!" I almost fell over. Suddenly reality struck me like a ton of bricks, and although I tried to act cool (what else do high school kids fall back on in situations like that?) I was definitely back pedaling as fast as I could.

I was also mumbling, stumbling, stuttering and trying to regain equilibrium. In the midst of all this, I slowly realized that Kathy was disappointed that I stood her up, but she wasn't really upset either. It was almost as if she was enjoying putting me on the spot. It didn't take long for me to ask her if I could make up for my indiscretion, and she graciously said yes to another date request. But she couldn't resist a parting shot. "Just don't stand me up this time."

For the first date, and for others that followed (yes, we actually started dating that fall. Jackpot!) I worked it out with a friend who did drive, to double date. Not as good as being alone, but beggars can't be choosers. Also, back in school again, it wasn't long before I ran into Newt Hetrick. It turned out that he and Kathy had been friends and neighbors since childhood. And I also began to see Chuck Reinhold around school again, *and*, he had remembered my name from last spring.

My First Club

One day, not long after our first date, Kathy told me about this "youth thing" that she liked to attend. Thinking of my own church, which by that time I had long since abandoned in spite of my mother's protestations; and thinking about CYO dances, I was curious to hear what kind of "youth thing" would interest such a popular girl like Kathy. She said it was called Young Life. It wasn't affiliated with any particular church, but was open to anyone and everyone, whether they went to church or not. And the best part was, they met on Wednesday nights. This meant, if I went, I could get out a night in the middle of the week and see Kathy. And because it was sort of like a church thing, I was pretty sure my folks would let me out.

The next Wednesday after Kathy told me about Young Life, I went to my first-ever club. Since this book is all about my years in Young Life including the 20 years I was on staff full time, I think we all know where this story is headed; but bear with me while I try to describe some of those first impressions.

There were people everywhere when we pulled up; out in the driveway, on the lawn, on the porch, inside... everywhere. It was noisy and boisterous. People were yelling and greeting each other, and some people were greeting me. Most of them I didn't know, although I recognized some of the faces from around school. And from the ones I recognized there were many of the A-listers. There were the jocks and cheerleaders, the "in" crowd and popular kids. Also there were students from the band and theater crowd. Just think of Ed Rooney's secretary, Grace, listing all of the cliques that liked Ferris Bueller: sportos, motorheads, wastoids, dweebies, and there were a whole lot of people, well, like me. And we all thought Ferris was a righteous dude.

It only took a moment before I got a slap on the back. I turned around and there was Newt. "Glad to see you Dick! Glad you could come." I guess I should have been surprised, but although I hadn't yet worked all of this out in my mind, somehow I wasn't startled to see him there. I was just beginning to get the notion that something unique and different was going on. I was far from being able to articulate it, but I thought, it just felt good to be there.

At the front was the guy I had been wondering about since last year. There he was, Chuck Reinhold. So *that's* what he does. He leads this thing. Chuck was starting to get everyone to sit down. He looked over and noticed me. Right away a broad smile widened on his face and he yelled out, "Dick Bond. My man! Good to see you!" That simple gesture had an immediate effect on me. Walking into that room was, to some extent, intimidating. Chuck's greeting put me at ease. There must have been between 150 and 200 high school kids there. It wasn't anything like a high school assembly or pep rally. It wasn't like any youth group I had attended either. It was more like a party than anything I could reference. It was definitely stretching my comfort zone big time, even though it sure didn't hurt that I walked in with the most beautiful girl in the room, Kathy. And by the way, she seemed to know *everyone*. They all wanted to say hi to her, and her to them.

The second effect from Chuck's greeting was that it gave me credibility. I noticed a few students follow Chuck's eyes and saw that it was me he had singled out with his greeting. "Yeah, that's me Chuck singled out. We hang out all the time." That made me feel welcomed and accepted. And I barely knew that guy.

Chuck finally asked everyone to sit down. I was thinking, "With all of these people here there is no way there's going to be enough chairs for everyone." But everyone just sat on the floor. I followed suit, along with Kathy next to me, and Newt was not too far away. As I looked around I began to recognize a few more familiar faces, which also helped put me at ease.

Everyone got settled, although at no time, at least early on, did it really quiet down. It was more like controlled semi-mayhem. A few of the students, seniors, got up and started tossing little books out into the crowd. And it wasn't polite tossing, it was more like overhand throwing. Some guys starting throwing books to each other, or more precisely, *at* each other. One came close to me and I grabbed it and opened it. It was a song book. "Ok, I can sing. I'm not a great singer but in this crowd I won't stick out."

I noticed over in the corner there was a piano, and a lady (not a student) who began playing. I later learned that Chuck was a Young Life leader and this lady was called the "girl-leader." Chuck yelled out a number, and everyone turned to the corresponding page in the book and we all started singing. These songs sounded sort of religious, but they were nothing like songs I had sung at church. And on top of that, Chuck was leading them in a way that almost seemed irreverent. One song was called, "Joshua Fit the Battle of Jericho." I had heard of this song and was thinking it was some kind of spiritual. Not the way we sang it. It was more like a combination of a rock and roll song arrangement and a cheerleading chant.

The Minutes

After a few songs, Chuck said it's time for the weekly minutes. Although this seemed a bit tame compared to the agenda so far, it did make sense. It was called a Young Life *club*, after all. I thought this meant that he would read the minutes of last week's meeting. Not! If you are reading this and are familiar with Young Life, you may know that way back in the day, the skits were first called "minutes." And the reason, I later learned, was to have terminology that was familiar among school social clubs, the kind that met after school.

I also later learned that the man who started Young Life, Jim Rayburn, held the first Young Life clubs after school, at the school, patterned after high school social clubs that met in the 40's and 50's. There were French clubs, science clubs, cooking clubs, and oh yes, suddenly the Young Life club. It was only later that Rayburn moved the Young Life club to the evening and into homes of students. It made me wonder what it would have been like to be in high school back then, to pull a Marty McFly and go back and check it out.

At about that time I was expecting a book with actual minutes to be read, but instead Chuck asked for a volunteer out of the crowd. When a guy got up there, Chuck had him help out with a skit. It was called "The

Honeybee Skit." It ended with a really funny surprise ending. Everyone was howling. I was thinking, "Man, this isn't anything like a youth group. What was Kathy thinking? I'm not telling my parents about all of this when I get home, not the way I sold them on getting out of the house for something religious."

Later on I'll jump into the whole topic of humor in Young Life in much more detail, but for now I'll just say that the skits in particular, and the general light hearted and often downright funny atmosphere, headed by Chuck and filtering down to everyone, was a big surprise for me, and a refreshing one. All of my, admittedly, limited experiences around churches and youth groups were serious business. Jimmy Dugan once said, "There's no crying in baseball!" I always believed, "There's no laughing in church." I had never seen a skit other than on TV, and certainly not in church. But it was more than that. The times I saw and spoke with Chuck and also with some of the student leaders and other adult leaders, there was always a lot of laughter going on. And it wasn't, as far as I could see, for any particular purpose. These people just loved to laugh, and loved making each other laugh. And often they would try to outdo each other trying to make their friends laugh. There was such a positive and unique sort of energy and flavor.

After the "minutes" a.k.a. skit, the songs' tempos slowed down a bit. I surreptitiously looked around and couldn't help but notice that kids were really getting into the singing. Were these the same students that I passed in the hallways and who sat in classes with me? After another song, Chuck interrupted the singing again. This time he actually had a few serious announcements to make. One of them was about a weekend retreat that Young Life was holding over the upcoming Thanksgiving holiday weekend. Except, he didn't call it a retreat. He said it was Young Life's "Fall weekend camp to Natural Bridge." Everyone started cheering. Why would people cheer for a weekend retreat? Wouldn't this involve vows of silence and self-flagellation? Maybe that was just Methodist retreats. I looked over at Kathy who was also cheering and gave her a look, like, "What's up?" She said, "We're going to Natural Bridge. You *have* to go!" Well, I didn't know Natural Bridge from a bar of soap, but when that smile of Kathy's hit me, I was ready to go even if it was for a weekend root canal. I was to learn a lot more about that weekend camp in the near future.

Chuck's Talk

Finally, the last song was completed and by this time I actually did figure out that there must be some sort of sermon. Sure enough, Chuck put down his songbook and started talking to us. Except, something was odd about his talk. At first it was so casual I thought it was going to be more announcements. But he was telling a story. Chuck had played football in college. I later learned that he was a star halfback at the University of Pittsburgh. I knew that Pitt was a big-time football school. Chuck didn't go into all of that, but instead he told a story about one of his teammates. It wasn't all that serious. In fact, parts of it were really funny. At the very least, it was entertaining and not boring.

The other thing I couldn't help but notice while he was talking: virtually everyone I could see was listening, and I mean *really* listening. Years later I was to learn all of the factors that lead to this intensive connection. But at this, my first-ever club, I was just trying to take it all in. After Chuck finished the story about his teammate, quick thinker that I was, I realized it wasn't just a story but it was an analogy. But an analogy for what? He then reached over and picked up a book. I strained to see the title but couldn't. As he began to read it, I realized that it was a Bible. But, it didn't look like any Bible I had ever seen. It wasn't big and it wasn't leather bound. Maybe they couldn't afford regular bibles in the Reinhold family? It looked more like one of my Mom's cookbooks than a Bible.

And another thing; it didn't sound like any Bible I had ever heard read before. I spent enough of my younger years in church, and I had clearly remembered Bible reading sounding a lot like Old English, sort of Shakespeare stuff. A lot of "thee"s and "thou"s, and "thou shalt"s. Chuck was reading a story about Jesus, and in it Jesus was healing a guy. But what he read sounded like normal everyday language, not some special "spiritual" language. And also, it was about then that the story he had told about his football teammate began to make sense as the illustration. Oh, I'm quick.

Chuck would read a few lines, then he would stop and explain it. And again, it was nothing like any speech or lecture I had heard before. It was more like a friend sharing or telling a story to me. At one point he put the Bible down and actually acted out a part of the story. At times he was really funny. But then he had this knack of going from momentary hilarity to total seriousness in a flash of a second. But everyone, myself included, seemed to follow along and not get lost or confused. It just felt natural.

After Chuck finished the Bible story, he started casually giving us a few points about the story. He talked about how Jesus cared about not only the man he healed, but that today, 2000 years after this story took place, he still cared about us personally. Another distinctive difference from other speakers I had heard was in Chuck's delivery. Everyone I had ever seen give a speech read or at least glanced at notes. And where was his podium? At no time did Chuck even pull out a paper from his pocket, and for sure there wasn't a podium in site. Chuck never faltered or stuttered or seemed lost in his talk. It all just flowed out of him so naturally that, after a while I forgot all about it being a speech and even forgot about the people around me. I know he was looking at everyone in the crowd, but it felt more like he was just speaking to me.

I don't recall all the particular points he made about this story, but it surprised me that there was not one sound coming from anyone. From my field of vision, there wasn't a person looking anywhere but at Chuck. I snuck a look at others and I was the odd one for looking around. I had been in enough classrooms in my life to have mastered the art of appearing interested in the teacher while my mind was a million miles away. This wasn't happening during Chuck's talk.

Finally Chuck was finished and closed with a short prayer. Here again was yet another surprise in a night full of surprises. The prayers I had heard until that night sounded...spiritual. And by spiritual I mean, like, with King James English, flowery and poetic speech. When Chuck prayed it was more like he was talking to God and God was sitting right in front of him. He was totally respectful, but it was like a conversation. Maybe I had expected something like the pope out on his balcony? I think I liked Chuck's prayer better.

And that was it. I thought the whole club was about half an hour. It went by so quickly. I was even a bit disappointed to see it come to an end. I was shocked when my watch told me we had been in that room sitting on the floor for a whole hour.

After Chuck finished his prayer everyone got up, and the noise, laughter and mayhem picked right back up where it had started. Some people were talking in groups, just as if we were at a party. Some were running around being social butterflies, again just like a party, come to think of it. And there were also some people who looked like they were locked into serious conversations.

Kathy grabbed my arm and took me around introducing me to a whole bunch of people, most of whose names I promptly forgot. But everyone seemed friendly. I had never been in a group of peers that seemed so "un-cliquey." Everyone, popular and unknown, it seemed to me-one of the unknowns-to be comfortable there. Finally, we made our way out the door, and Kathy turned to me and asked me how I liked it. I wanted to come off cool but by this time in our dating she knew me well enough that I couldn't fake it. I just let go, gushing, "That was so much fun! I can't believe anything like this even existed! Let's come back next week!" She just gave me one of her warm smiles, and said, "Hey, I want you to go to that weekend camp. Everyone's going."

Over the next several weeks I looked forward to Wednesday night and didn't miss a club. Kathy was always there, as was Newt, and of course Chuck, and the lady who played the piano. I finally met her. Her name was Anne, and like everyone else, she was friendly. In the weeks that followed I noticed there were a lot of people who remembered me and even remembered my name. Each day at school it seem like I'd run into someone I had met at Young Life. I knew it wasn't really a club, like I was used to using the term. It was, however, a really cool bunch of people, from all different crowds at school, who shared the common interest of going to Young Life.

My First Weekend Camp

As November approached, each week at club the enthusiasm for the upcoming weekend camp was building. I picked up a flyer and took it home and asked my folks if I could go. By that time my parents were fine with my Wednesday night outings, with me going to something that sounded as if it might be religious, or at least a positive influence. Back in those days "B.I.", Before Internet, how did they check out organizations? I think my mother asked around to some of the other parents in the neighborhood, but I'm not sure. I was allowed to go on this weekend camp. I got my $25 and took it to club the next week and signed up. Yeah, I know. You can barely have a Starbucks date for that kind of money these days.

On the day we were to leave, we all met at the high school parking lot. Two huge blue, very old Brill coach buses pulled up and we all piled in. There was a lot of excitement and energy. I had been on bus rides before, and even a few youth retreats. Still, this felt different. I think it was because there were all of the kids from school I had known or met and really enjoyed being around. It wasn't exactly a Kum Ba Yah crowd.

Natural Bridge, Virginia was a few hours bus ride from Baltimore. The time passed quickly on the bus and when we arrived we found a tourist kind of hotel and entertainment area: a gift shop, an ice rink, playground, but no mud wrestling ring. The centerpiece, hidden from view and down a winding path and beyond a gate where we had to ante up some money for admission, was the semi-famous (I had never heard of it before, but what did I know?) natural rock arch known as Natural Bridge.

By now I was used to expecting the unexpected, and the weekend didn't disappoint. There seemed to be non-stop games, mixers, events and activities. Everything was planned around four "clubs" throughout the weekend: one on Friday night, two on Saturday and the last one on Sunday morning. They were very much like the Young Life clubs I had been going to back in Woodlawn, except these had several hundred kids from a lot of different schools, and different Young Life clubs from around Baltimore. There was a feeling of unity though, as everyone seemed to get with the program, know the music and was ready at the end to hear a talk, similar to the ones that Chuck had been giving at our Woodlawn club. The speaker for that weekend was a guy named Harv Oostdyk. He was from New Jersey and he worked with Young Life with some inner city kids. He had a rough edge on him but yeah, he could communicate to a large group of high school kids.

It was during those first three club talks that, for the first time I really heard about Jesus, and began to understand what the Gospel was all about. I had listened to Chuck's talks back home and was beginning to get a picture of Christianity that was new and refreshing. Maybe those talks were preparing me for this weekend.

At the Saturday night talk Harv explained that to be a Christian a person can invite Christ into their lives personally, and when we make that decision we can begin a personal relationship with Him. This was something I had never heard or had explained to me before. I never considered myself philosophical or a deep thinker, but Harv really got me thinking about my life, and about Christ, in a way that was fresh. And I could tell there were a lot of other kids in the room feeling the same way.

At the end of the night we all headed back to our rooms. Chuck led us in a bit of a discussion in one of the rooms, about Harv's talk. After that, people split up and were talking, and a lot of guys were getting ready for bed. I walked outside and ran into a guy named George Johnson, who I had met earlier on the weekend. George was a cool guy. He was a senior and the fact that I could tell he enjoyed talking with me had already made an impression in my mind. He was into the theatrical crowd, which in our school at that time was a pretty big deal. He also had known Kathy for a long time and knew we were dating.

As we stood on the porch, George started asking me about Harv's talks and what I thought about them. Then he asked me if accepting Christ into my life was something I wanted to do. As long ago as that was, I can still remember thinking, "The only time I can ever think of talking with another student and using the name of Christ, in my entire life, was as a cuss word. Here is this cool senior talking about Him, in a serious way. If he thinks this is cool and acceptable, I need to reconsider my whole religious experience paradigm." Ok, I didn't use that exact wording. But George wasn't talking religion anyway. He went on to tell me that asking Christ into my life was simply a matter of prayer, "Just tell Him that this is what you want."

Funny how I can still feel the emotions from that night. Part of me was embarrassed talking about Christ in that time and place, but another big part of me was interested and curious, and wanted to give this whole thing a try. I don't think I had worked it out at this point that Newt, and Kathy, and George, and a whole bunch of other kids had made this decision about inviting Christ into their lives. But George explained enough to me that I decided I was going to pray that night and ask Christ into my life.

Gonna Try It

By the time I got back to my room the lights were out and the other guys had gone to sleep. I got into bed and thought, "Ok, I'm going to do what George said. Here I go..." And I started to pray. I said very quietly, "Dear God," and all of a sudden I stopped. "Wait, am I supposed to pray to God or Jesus with this request? I mean, all my life I've heard about God. But Young Life seemed to talk as much or more about Jesus. And it's Jesus I'm supposed to ask into my heart, so maybe I should be praying to him." After thinking about it for a while and still not sure what to do, I finally started back with my prayer, and I actually said, "Dear God and/or Jesus." I went on. The rest of my prayer was something like this: "I've been hearing about this 'asking Jesus into my life' this weekend, and George said I should pray and ask you, so that's what I'm doing...Amen."

What happened next? I opened my eyes and looked out, and there, standing at the foot of my bed, was Jesus, beckoning me with his hand................................... Naaaaa. I looked and saw...nothing. The guy in the next bed rolled over and belched. That was it. Was that a sign from God? There was not one piece of evidence that anything happened. I thought I must have done it wrong, somehow messed up the prayer. So, I gave it a second try. This time I threw in a few "thee"s and "thou"s, thinking, maybe Chuck's casual prayer style at the end of his weekly talks had thrown me off. The second time I finished the prayer and opened my eyes, and still...absolutely nothing. I was getting a bit frustrated.

I did try a third time, and it went something like this, "God, I really don't know if I'm talking with you, or just to the ceiling. But this is something I really would like to get in on, and if it's real I pray you do it to me." I later learned that it wasn't so much about the words I used as it was about the attitude in my heart. I said "amen" and rolled over and eventually went to sleep.

The next morning I got up, still feeling nothing. I hadn't developed any Super Powers overnight. I didn't feel relieved, or healed, or forgiven, or holy, or anything. I felt just like I had felt the day before. After breakfast we had the last club, and I soon discovered that a whole lot of kids had come to the same decision I had come to the night before. And some had very different reactions. Some were really happy and smiling. Some were crying, as in, tears of joy. Others were talking about being sort of overwhelmed. And some had reacted more like me, with little or no emotion.

We were offered a few different discussion groups after the last club, and I picked the one for people who had made a decision to invite Christ into their lives. It was a large group and it was run by a guy named Jerry Johnson. I didn't know it at the time, but this man would play a huge role in my future. In this meeting, Jerry explained that asking Jesus into one's life was an important, life-changing decision, but everyone's experience is a little different. Whether we feel great emotion or no emotion at all, that didn't measure the reality of Christ coming into our hearts. He also explained a Bible verse that I never heard before. It was as if it was written just for me, for that day: Revelation 3:20, "*Behold, I stand at the door and knock. If anyone hears my voice and opens the door, I will come in and dine with him, and he with me.*" Jerry explained that the "door" was the door to my heart, and the prayer I prayed the night before was opening my heart and inviting Jesus to come in. I still didn't have any emotional reaction, but I had an explanation of what I did, and what Jesus did. And it all started to make sense and to get clear for me.

On the bus ride home something else had changed. Kids were still loud and having fun. But there was also an underlying kind of...peace...about the ride. Kathy and I talked a lot about the decision I had made the night before. And sure enough, it was a decision she had made for her life a few years before. And she confirmed what by then I had suspected, that Newt and others all had come to the same understanding and acceptance of Christ at some point in their lives. So this wasn't something I did on my own. A lot of people helped me get to Young Life and to the trip, and to hear the Christian message. And now I was going home with a lot of those same people who already made the decision I had made, like George, Kathy and Newt. They had been down this road before me and were there to help the rest of us understand what was going on. It was a pretty amazing, totally surprising, and literally a life changing experience for me.

In the days and weeks that followed Natural Bridge, I began to notice some changes going on with me. I seemed to be more at ease with life. I definitely felt very accepted by a huge crowd of sharp people, and that felt really good. My mother could sense that something was going on, but I was too unsure of myself to try and explain what happened. I could tell she was happy about it. When I took out the trash after only being asked three times, I thought she was going to faint. I know, baby steps.

It was also great to see some of my own classmates and friends changing, knowing they had made the same decision in their lives. One was a guy named Duke VanSant. We had been friends, and he had been elected as our class president. So, he was a pretty popular guy. He was also a fun guy and had been a bit of a hell-raiser like me. Having a guy like that experience what I had done helped me think about starting off in some new directions.

Another friend who accepted Christ at Natural Bridge, and who was to later become part of my life was Joni. She was a year behind me, and was a fun, positive person, the kind you wanted to hang out with. She was also an amazing athlete, and played varsity field hockey, basketball, and lacrosse. She will come up again later in my story.

Campaigners

Kathy told me, now that I accepted Christ, I'd want to go to something else that Young Life held that was designed to help Christians grow in their faith. It was a weekly Bible study and it was called Campaigners. I never knew back then why they called it that, but it turned out to be more important in helping me grow in my new found faith than going to club. Chuck ran that too, but it wasn't like club. It was Bible study and fellowship, and prayer.

The first Campaigners I went to was held in my friend Joni's house. She lived pretty close to the high school in a house that her Dad had built. Chuck would ask different kids to host Campaigners at their houses, so it moved around during the year. The second Campaigners I went to was held at Kathy's house. Something happened to me that day, painful at the time, but very significant.

After the Bible study was prayer time. I had never been in a group of peers who could just take turns praying out loud, without a script or something written out, but who could pray as easily as talking, having a conversation with God. Everyone else would be listening in; then another person, and another would pick up when the previous person was done. This went on for several minutes, and in the midst of that I started to feel something I had never felt before. No one made me feel bad or guilty. But I think for the first time, around all of these people my age, who had their faith, I felt so far behind. And I felt shame. I felt for the first time aware of my sin, and how unworthy I was for the lavish gift I had received. It was that day that I really began to understand how earth shattering it was to be able to have a relationship with the God of the universe.

Much later I learned about the first time the apostle Peter had met Jesus, when Jesus helped Peter and his friends catch a huge pile of fish. Rather than yell, "Jesus, you're the man!" or "Let's you and me open a fishing business!" He said, "Stay away from me. I am a sinful man." What Peter felt was sort of what I was feeling that day at Campaigners. Peter suddenly realized that the guy at the other end of the boat wasn't just human. Peter found himself in the presence of God. And that closeness shamed Peter. That's how I felt that day. I could sense God in the room as I watched all of these high school kids who were serious about Jesus and whose lives were just incredible in my eyes. It wasn't any longer about who was cool, and who was popular. This was *real* like I had never experienced *real* before.

After the meeting broke up and everyone was making their way out, I stayed behind. Kathy and I were going out that night anyway, so she didn't think anything was unusual. And I hadn't told her what I was feeling. After everyone left she finally came in and noticed that I hadn't moved an inch from where I had been sitting. She didn't say anything, but she just sat down beside me. It was then that she noticed tears streaming down my face, crying quietly. And she understood before I even had to explain it to her.

Weeks turned into months and I could see my faith growing, as I was around such a great group of Christians. Club and Campaigners were a regular part of my life. Newt and Kathy and many more friends were part of my life: like Harry Perrine, Betsy Sandbower, and Linda Carroll. Linda would eventually, several years later, wind up being Mrs. Chuck Reinhold. Both she and Harry became not only good friends, but also role models for me.

A New Sport

I noticed that several of the guys in Campaigners were also on the lacrosse team. In Baltimore lacrosse is hugely a popular sport. My only exposure to it was back in junior high PE class. I really liked it, but we didn't get to try it much. Baseball had been a bust the year before, but I figured, with all of my Christian buddies playing lacrosse, maybe I'll give it a try. I was a junior and maybe I could make the junior varsity team.

The two biggest stars on the varsity lacrosse team were Doug Holladay and Roger Eggers. And they were both in Young Life. Doug was close friends with Chuck and was one of the real student leaders at club and Campaigners. He too was to have a big influence in my life in the years to come. He was already having an impact.

The day I went out for lacrosse, I was such a nonathlete, that I literally had no idea what I should wear to practice. You'd think I could have at least known enough to wear gym shorts and a tee shirt. I can still picture what I wore that first day because of guys making fun of me. I wore a pair of Bermuda shorts, and a shirt that buttoned down the front. I could have been a nerd in a John Hughes movie if he had been around in those days.

Lacrosse for me turned out to be one of those rare undertakings in life where it just fit perfectly. I took to it like a duck to water. I fell in love with it and couldn't wait to go to practice and play in games. In my spare time at home I would go find a brick wall and throw a ball against it, practicing my stick skills. I wound up being one of the leaders on the JV team that year. Plus, I got to hang out with so many of my Christian friends who played. This had all happened within months of first going to Young Life and then receiving Christ into my life. Lacrosse was to have a huge impact on my life, for my entire adult life and that of my own children many years later. I had no idea at the time. It just felt right to do and it was fun. I got really good at it, but for me at the time it was part of the much bigger picture of fellowship with Christian friends.

I was experiencing a multitude of blessings from God. Up until that time, my life was like an old black and white TV. From the end of my sophomore year, when it all began, and then Natural Bridge, my whole life had changed...to color...high-definition if it had existed back then. Kathy was my girlfriend, but much more. She was a confidant, a friend, a fellow Christian, and someone who was further down the road and who helped me grow. Plus, she had pursued me when I didn't believe enough in myself to think I was pursuable. Kathy was a blessing from God. And there were so many others.

I got to know Chuck more and more. He was a big part of my life now, as was Doug and a whole bunch of guys. Newt was a very special friend in many ways. One story stands out about Newt. His job was to call every person on Sundays to remind us to come to Campaigners. We used to meet Sunday afternoon at 4 o'clock. Every Sunday for the entire school year I got a phone call from Newt. In December of that year our much loved football team, the Baltimore Colts (not that traitor team out in Indianapolis), had made it again to the NFL Championship game. This was before Superbowls. Everyone I knew was a rabid Colt fan. They had won the NFL Championship in 1958 and '59, and were poised to win it again in December of '63. The game was Sunday afternoon, against the Cleveland Browns, led by the great Jim Brown. But, the game started at 4 o'clock, and that was Campaigners time. But...*no* one missed the Colts when the Colts were playing, much less for the championship. And on top of that some of the Colt players were Christians. Chuck even had eventual Hall of Fame wide receiver, Raymond Berry come speak at club one night. Didn't we have to support the team?

Newt called at his usual time, about 3 o'clock, and said he was reminding me about Campaigners. Knowing I didn't drive, he always asked me if I needed a ride. And the times I did, he either picked me up or had someone else do it. That day when he called, I said, "Ah, Newt, you do realize that the Colts are playing the Browns at 4:00 for the NFL Championship." Newt didn't hesitate. He replied, "Yeah I know, but what's that have to do with us? We have fellowship together and that's what's important. See you at four!" And you know what? With peers like that, modeling that Christians are committed to fellowship, that was strong leadership and I followed it. By 4 o'clock that day I was at Campaigners, and so were a whole room full of kids. Oh and by the way, the Colts lost to the Browns. Where was TiVo when I needed it?

The more involved I got with my new Young Life friends, the less I saw of my parochial school crowd I used to hang out with. On a typical weekend night, as often as seeing Kathy, I'd go out with guys like Doug and Roger and others from the lacrosse team and from Young Life. And I began learning more as a young Christian with their role modeling. For example, no matter how late we were out, (and those guys always had to drive me), whenever they dropped me off at home, before I got out of the car, Doug or one of them would say, "Hey, let's have a word of prayer before you get out." Let me tell you, when those guys, who were not only seniors, but were also the coolest guys in my school and the top athletes, would pray with me in the car, that made a lasting impact. In so many ways my life was being turned upside down, in a good way. I was blessed, and the blessings kept coming.

Doug Holladay was part of that senior group of role models that I looked up to, and probably the one I looked up to and admired the most. He was overflowing with relationship skills and leadership skills. And he was just crazy-funny. Maybe because of lacrosse, we seemed to hit it off particularly well. He was the big star on the varsity team, and eventually I became the star on junior varsity. So not only did I look up to him and admire him as an older Christian brother, I also did because of his amazing skills on the lacrosse field. When he graduated he went to the University of North Carolina and played lacrosse there. I made sure I inherited his jersey number, 22. Doug wore it because it was the jersey number of the greatest player any of us had ever seen play, the Naval Academy attackman and winner of three consecutive National Championships, Jim Lewis.

Number 22 stuck for me and I wore it all through college and every year after that, playing men's USCLA lacrosse. And when my own sons started playing one or both of them wore the same number. Of course they didn't know it began out of admiration for Doug, but I never forgot. Doug's role as a mentor for me was to continue well beyond high school and even college. Our paths and spiritual journey would cross many times over the years to come.

Chapter 2

Onward and Upward

One day near the end of the lacrosse season, Doug arrived for practice and he stopped by my locker with a paper in his hand. He handed it to me and said, "Chuck and I have been talking, and we think you should apply for Work Crew at (Young Life's) Frontier Ranch out in Colorado." Young Life owned ranches out west and had an extensive program where thousands of high school kids from all over the country would spend a week at camp. The idea was like the Natural Bridge weekend, but much more advanced in that Young Life owned the properties and could design a great program from top to bottom. Plus, in Colorado you didn't have to pay to see their bridges. I later learned that Young Life had one of the premier camping programs in the country, and the properties were considered more like resorts than camps.

When I looked at the application, I had never heard of Frontier Ranch, and for sure I had never been to Colorado. Doug and Chuck said I should apply for something called Work Crew. As the name would imply, this was a group of people who worked at the camp while high schoolers would attend the camp as guests. The Work Crew commitment was for a month.

At first I was impressed that Chuck and Doug thought of me. Then I was a bit unsettled, thinking I would be spending an entire month away from home, two thirds the way across the country. I was no Momma's boy, but a year before, I wouldn't have had the confidence to say yes. I could see that my personality was evolving, and there was a transformation going on inside of me because of my growing relationship with Jesus. I filled out the application and was accepted.

Work Crew

When the day came to leave we joined a busload of campers heading for camp. We all drove cross country to Chicago, where we took a train to Colorado Springs, then a three hour drive up into the mountains to Frontier Ranch. A few years after that the buses started taking campers all the way from the east coast to Colorado, eliminating the train ride. But since my Dad was a railroad guy and I had been on trains since I was a child, I really enjoyed that part of the trip.

When we arrived at Frontier Ranch it was like stepping into another world. If I could have created a resort designed exclusively for high school kids, I couldn't have imagined a more perfect place. It was nestled in the side of Mt. Princeton in a beautiful spot, with the mountain behind us and the Arkansas River Valley below us. All of the buildings were rustic and western. Much later I was to learn the stories about how Young Life acquired each of the camps. Every story was as much miracle as it was a story. At this point, as a high school student arriving, the *wow* factor was off the charts.

A group of teenagers formed two lines as we exited the bus and they became the welcoming committee. I soon discovered that this was the Work Crew greeting us. The atmosphere was party-like. Everyone was excited and that excitement became contagious. The Work Crew was made up of mature Christians from around the country who were selected because of their maturity and leadership skills. When I learned this I was even more gratified that Chuck and Doug thought enough of me to ask me to go.

The campers who arrived each week were very much like those who I had met at Natural Bridge; a number of Christian kids who brought their non-Christian friends to camp to hear about Jesus and to learn how they could have Him in their lives. Back at Natural Bridge, Kathy, Newt, and George, and a bunch of other Christians were on the bus with guys like me, and Duke, and Joni. Now I was one of the Christians, helping new kids who came to camp to experience what we had experienced.

The campers got right into the program. Because I was on the Work Crew, I went straight to work. Hence the name: Work Crew. I was assigned in the kitchen to wash dishes. We can't all be Gandalf. Some of us have to be Hobbits. We washed dishes for 350 campers, plus staff and Work Crew, three meals a day, seven days a week, for four straight weeks. Didn't Colorado have any child labor laws? We were called the Pit Crew, not without a good deal of pride, I might add. Our boss was the head of the food services, and also the head cook. He was a very big African-American man named Andrew Delany. But everyone just called him Goldbrick. He was a character, and in the course of a month we came to love this guy. He cracked the whip when he had to, but we knew he really cared about us.

One morning some of us guys were a little late getting up for breakfast duty. I knew we were in trouble when our cabin door flew open and in strode Goldbrick with his booming voice, "Come on gang, time to get up!" And with that announcement, in one motion he reached up and grabbed a guy around the waist and pulled him out of the upper bunk, onto the floor, with one hand. His other hand was doing the very same thing to another guy in the bunk across the aisle. We were never late getting up after that.

Being responsible for the food that was served to everyone at Frontier, Goldbrick represented one of the most unique and distinctive core values in Young Life camping. Reflecting the value and commitment of Young Life's founder, Jim Rayburn, the camps were committed to excellence in food preparation. Anyone who had ever been to a youth camp knew what institutional food was like: second rate. It was expected. But Rayburn believed otherwise. He felt that everything should be done with excellence, and the quality of the food had a direct impact on how kids would be open and receptive to hearing the Gospel. One of the distinguishing features of all Young Life camps was high quality of food, and plenty of it. And Goldbrick made sure that mandate was fulfilled. There was also a commitment to excellence in serving the food as well. The Work Crew who waited on the tables were carefully trained to exhibit a "servant's heart" attitude. There was great attention to detail, from the spotless look of the dining room right down to the way the salt and pepper shakers were aligned.

Every now and then Goldbrick would let me get in on food preparation. My favorite job was breaking eggs. No fake eggs for this place. But in order to break 400 eggs and have the job done before the Second Coming, required great dexterity and skill: one egg in each hand, crack them open, dump them in (without the shell please) and grab for the next two eggs. I mastered this skill. It turned out to the least useful talent I ever learned.

One month at Frontier Ranch did more for my faith than a year would have done at home. The fellowship was intense and positive. We were 50 students from all over the country. We worked like crazy, but we also learned so much, and we got to be part of a team that had a life-changing impact on the hundreds of campers that came through Frontier in August of 1965. Being together for a month produced some amazing friendships, and to be honest, a few summer romances. 'Nuf said.

The Staff

The person chosen to speak at the nightly clubs that summer was Bob Mitchell. The guy who ran the program was Jay Grimstead. The Work Crew boss was Bob Reeverts. There were several others I came to know. It was an interesting month as it related to the staff of men and women. Interesting in that when I arrived I had no clue who I was dealing with; no idea of the caliber of talent and leadership that was before me each day. The talent just blew me away, but it wasn't until after a few years with Young Life that I fully came to appreciate what a special and unique group I had been around. These guys were rock stars.

Bob Mitchell, or Mitch, was an extraordinary speaker. Every night he could hold 350 high school kids spell-bound. And he could make the Gospel message incredibly clear and inviting. It was something to marvel at, to be around every night for a whole month. In the years to come I would learn that this man was one of the best speakers there ever was in Young Life.

If Mitch was like Sinatra, Jay Grimstead was like Robin Williams. Jay's specialty was running the program. The program at camp covered virtually all of the activities except for the nightly club talks. This included events like swim meets, volleyball tournaments, mountain climbing, river rafting, horseback riding, rodeos and the occasional curling matches. Each evening there were social activities and the ever-present Young Life skits and humorous entertainment. Jay Grimstead was both funny and over-the-top talented. I was told that he had been offered a job to write for a comedy TV show. I have never asked him if that was true, but it wouldn't have surprised me. He just oozed with talent. People wanted to be around him and wanted to be like him.

Perhaps the greatest contribution that Jay brought to Young Life was the formation of what was to become the program structure for all Young Life camps for many years into the future. Program activities at Young Life camps are like nothing I've ever experienced, before or since. That summer in 1965 was my first exposure, and I had no point of reference. It was amazing, but I couldn't fathom how unique it was until later.

Traditional thinking at camps, Christian or otherwise, was to provide activities and options for campers that, essentially, filled out the week. A good camp had lots of activities and strong programs. (A bad camp had a bookmobile.) Indeed, if you attended a Young Life camp it would appear traditional just in that same way, at least on the surface. However, Jay saw something different. If you start with the premise that the greatest good coming from camp is that kids hear about Jesus, how you run the program takes on a whole new light. If, on one hand, just hearing about Jesus is the main goal, why not just make that the agenda each day? Just have talks and seminars about Jesus. Why even have program at all?

One obvious reason is that no one would come. Duh. No one wanted religion jammed down their throats. The only kids who would show up would be the same ones who went to summer school...voluntarily. But Jay was the one to understand that program wasn't just to fill the week. Rather, it could be used to enhance the presentation of the Gospel message. So instead of program for program's sake, or instead of competing with the spiritual message, Jay designed a program that would complement the message and help make people more receptive to it. I was to learn that a key to Young Life ministry was that everything worked together for the Gospel, but you didn't always have to speak the

Gospel. The gospel could be in the sense of humor, the program, the servant attitude of the Work Crew and staff, and right down to how a dinner table was set.

The first night's entertainment, for example, was specifically designed to help break the ice, as well as to create a few other outcomes. Jay spaced events and activities, all with the greater goal of the Gospel in mind. I barely understood any of this. Later as an adult on Young Life Staff I had the privilege of spending time with Jay and came to understand the "whys" behind his program designs, on which I will elaborate in a later chapter. Back then I just marveled. Jay, as well as Mitch and the other staff were all friendly and approachable that summer, which was a bonus for everyone.

Meeting the Man

There was another highlight for me, one which I will be grateful for as long as I live. At the time Young Life owned three properties outside of Buena Vista, Colorado. Two were camps; Frontier Ranch and Silver Cliff. The third was a resort for adults, called Trail West. It was often used for conferences, but also for adult guests to be entertained and to have to opportunity to go visit the two camps and to see the ministry "up close and personally." It was one evening while those of us on Work Crew got to visit Trail West that I got to meet the man himself: Jim Rayburn, the founder of Young Life. Even then, at that young spiritual age, I had a sense that I was in the presence of greatness. In the years to come, and especially after Jim passed away, I came to cherish the few minutes I had to speak with him. He truly was one of the giants of the faith and great evangelists of the 20th century. He was the Michael Jordan of Christian outreach.

Jim gave a talk to the group of us and the guests staying at Trail West. He spoke about the Young Life philosophy, using the Bible text, I Thessalonians 4:12,

"Walk in wisdom towards those who are without." He took each word and explained it and how Young Life's blueprint was taken from this passage. Walk - reaching out to kids. In Wisdom - Young Life had a strategic plan to reach lost kids. Towards - going to wherever kids congregated. Those who are without - Young Life's commitment to kids who haven't heard the Gospel.

I also got to meet Bill Starr, who was Young Life's president at that time. He was Scottie Pippin to Rayburn's Michael Jordan. I was to get to know Bill for many years thereafter, as he was still the president when I eventually graduated from college and went on full time staff.

Just one year before, I had barely known anything about Christianity and nothing at all about the ministry that would so strongly impact my life. And in one short summer, I was able to meet all of these amazing and talented men who made a huge and lasting impression on me and shaped my understanding of Jesus and ministry.

I started a habit early in my month of working at Frontier; a habit that also shaped me. I would get up an hour before Goldbrick wanted us in the kitchen and would hike up to a ledge far above the swimming pool area, overlooking the valley. It was there that I had morning devotions, or quiet times; reading the Bible and praying. This became part of my Christian life, and like so many things, it sprang from the spiritual foundation that was forming while I was on Work Crew. When I got home it wasn't easy replicating the view from that ledge back in Colorado. I had to settle for looking out of my bedroom window at cars passing on the street.

Leaving

After a month of what I thought was living "heaven on earth", we all had to leave, as it was the end of the summer. That was one of the saddest days of my life, saying goodbye to all of those people with whom I had gotten so close. And to think, just a month before I was worried about being so far away from home for longer than I had ever been away in my life. One situation Work Crew did not prepare me for was leaving that place. I just had no clue how to understand or process the pain from separating from the place and the people. We were from all over the country and when left Frontier Ranch we scattered everywhere. I'll never forget sitting on the bus pulling out of camp, overwhelmed and out of control, crying like a total baby. The two thousand miles of bus and train rides home was painful and sorrowful. It was hard at that point to imagine going back and adjusting to "normal" life ever again.

But of course, I did. Over time the pain of separation faded and what was left were the good memories, and more importantly all that I had experienced and learned; and most importantly, how much I had grown in my faith. School soon restarted, along with Young Life and Campaigners. And now I was a senior. Kathy and Newt and Doug and all of my older brothers and sisters in the faith had graduated and gone off to college. I, along with my peers like Duke and Joni had their large shoes to fill. We were the ones inviting our non-Christian friends to club, and getting them to Natural Bridge. The mantle had been passed. How were we going to handle the responsibility? We were scared, but we were also excited. We were standing on the shoulders of some pretty incredible Christians before us. But we were prepared to carry on. I was learning the one of the best ways that kids were discipled wasn't just Bible study and fellowship. It was the challenge of leaving our comfort zones and reaching out to our non-Christian friends. Years later I was introduced to Sam Shoemaker's poem, *I Stand by the Door*. If there ever was a poem that captured the heart of Young Life's posture towards lost kids, this is the one.

Chapter 3

High School Senior

A change took place over the summer that very much rocked my world. Chuck left. He was scheduled to be in Baltimore for a limited time to work under and to be trained by Jerry Johnson. After that, because Young Life was trying to expand across the country, guys like Chuck were called upon to open new areas and new cities. In Chuck's case he was asked to move to Rochester, New York.

Those of us left behind were devastated when we heard the news. Some were hurt. "Why would he leave now, when we are seniors? We really need his leadership now." But as I had learned from Work Crew, (aside from cracking open raw eggs) we can't keep things as they are, change will inevitably happen, whether it's leaving "heaven on earth" to come back home, or losing our leader.

Young Life replaced Chuck with another guy for Jerry to train, Dick Eckhardt, and he wound up leading our club as Chuck had done. He was a great guy but he suffered through no fault of his own: he wasn't Chuck. Dick was new and wound up leaning on us, the remaining seniors. Even then I could see one positive side of Chuck leaving, because it forced us to help Dick and to take on more of a leadership role.

In addition to missing Chuck, we really missed our seniors. That was a very special group. Years later I could track a large number of them who had gone on into Christian work and who had made huge impacts and contributions in ministry. Some, like I eventually did, worked for Young Life. For years after that class of '65 graduated, the faculty at Woodlawn would say there had been something very unique about it. I believe that God had His hand on that group and Chuck in a very special way, and for as long as I live I will be grateful to have been drawn in by them, loved by them and nurtured by them. Personally I've always had a sense that there are times and places in our history where God specifically touches and blesses people and ministry in a unique and very special way. It may be a church, or a Christian movement, or in the case of the Woodlawn class of '65, a particular part of a Christian movement. It doesn't mean God will chose to bless every school in every year in the same way. The Holy Spirit blows where it will.

Club was good in my senior year. It wasn't monstrously large like the year before. But that was to be expected. I'm not sure Young Life at Woodlawn was that good for the next twenty years. And that includes five years later when yours truly, then a senior in college, would be the leader. But I will say this: we saw a lot of friends go to weekend and summer camps. And we saw a whole lot of kids come to faith and begin to grow, just as we had done.

Connecticut

An experience I had in winter of my senior year was especially memorable, not only because of its spiritual impact on me, but also due to its prophetic nature. Young Life's growth in the 50's and 60's was dramatic. By the time I arrived on the scene it seemed like it was in just about every major metropolitan area of the country. In some places, like Baltimore, for a whole lot of reasons I was yet to understand, rapid growth came easily. In New England, Young Life's expansion wound up taking a bit more time. In Southern Connecticut there was an Area Director (the same position as Jerry Johnson held for Baltimore,) named Jack Carpenter. Jack ran clubs in the wealthy New York City bedroom communities of Greenwich and Darien, Connecticut, and oversaw several other clubs in his area.

Jack got an idea that the Christian high school kids in his area could benefit from exposure to Christian kids from other Young Life areas along the Eastern Seaboard. So he created a program that he called "Host a Campaigner Weekend." He contacted Area Directors in neighboring states, inviting them to send some of their mature Christian students to Southern Connecticut for a weekend. They would stay in the homes of his Christian kids, and he planned a whole host of activities. I was one of the students invited to go.

Bo White was already out of high school and one of the many volunteer leaders in Young Life. He was to become a very close friend. He was the leader who drove us from Baltimore to Connecticut, via New York City. We stopped there to visit the place on the Lower East Side where some of the great pioneer Young Life urban ministry was going on. At that time it was led by Bill Milliken. Working with him was a man who was to also become a very good friend and co-worker in a few short years, Bo Nixon. Bo grew up on the streets of New York and had come out of a gang life when he and his brother, Tap, met Christ through the Young Life Inner City ministry. Their headquarters was on the Lower East Side. When we arrived we were ushered into a Chinese restaurant on Mott Street, where we met Bill, and Bo, and Bo's wife, Mary.

From there we headed up to Connecticut and met Jack

Carpenter along with his female coworker, Co Koppert. At that point there were groups of other students arriving from all over the east. Jack held a big club for all of us, basically to get to know each other and to get to know his local kids. Afterwards we were introduced to our host families, who took us to their homes.

Early the next morning we all assembled at Greenwich High School and piled into vans. Jack had planned for all of us to go skiing for the day. Off we went to a place, not in Connecticut but actually a bit south of us, in New Jersey, called Sterling Forest. This was the very first time I experienced something that would eventually become one of the great recreational loves of my life; skiing. However, anyone who actually saw me trying to ski that day would scoff at the notion that I would ever even learn to ski, much less fall in love with it. In the words of the immortal John McEnroe, "You cannot be serious!"

I skied a few yards, started to go fast, and fell over. It took forever to get back up with those two dumb sticks on my feet. Another few yards, more speed, fell over again. After several hours of this recreational activity-don't call me a quitter, slow learner maybe-I happened to notice that some people weren't going straight down the hill like sleigh riding. They were actually turning. Why didn't someone tell me! (Hand palm slap to the forehead gesture.) And they were pigeon-toed. Snow plowing, baby! Now we're talkin'. I was not alone in my mediocre learning curve. I had the company of many others in our group. Misery loves company. But we all made it through the day, and in the process got to meet a lot of new friends, including Jack's Young Life kids, which really was the main purpose of our trip.

We got back to Greenwich that evening and Jack had another club planned for us, complete with songs, skits and a talk. But instead of it being the normal Young Life outreach message, it was geared to challenge Christian students, both Jack's and the rest of us.

Sunday morning Jack took all of us to his church, Stanwich Congregational Church. It was a small church even by New England standards, and our group easily filled the first several rows. Jack and his wife Judith were members there and he introduced us to the pastor. His name was Nate Adams. When I met him, he struck me as having a bit of a resemblance to Ichabod Crane. I kept that little fact to myself. I'm glad I did because years later he was to become a great friend. He was a lovely man and he knew how to preach. Nate was on Jack's Young Life support committee. I later learned that Stanwich Church was the only church in town that really got behind the Young Life ministry.

Being in New England, and with a fellowship of so many Christians, was a moving and memorable experience for me, and I believe for everyone involved. I loved the town and the people, but little did I know that both would one day play such a huge part in my story and my life. The weekend was soon over and we said our goodbyes and Bo drove us back to Baltimore.

Friends, Not the TV Show

I mentioned Joni before, related to Young Life. She was a year behind me, now a junior. And she had a whole bunch of sharp young Christians in her class coming up behind us; Daryl Hocksra, Connie Garriet (who later married and who we still see, even to this day, when we're in town), Carol Case, who later would marry Andy Byrd. The list was long and illustrious, and I know I'm leaving out many names. I thought, "The near future, at least, is going to be in good hands when my class graduates." My good friends Ray Steckman, Diane Hidey, and Andy Byrd were, like me, among the seniors to accept the responsibility of leadership roles in club. Andy was a laid back guy with a southern accent and a pleasant disposition. If I was ever upset or frustrated, all I had to do was spend some time with Andy and he could get me to lighten up. I know we worked well together in Young Life leadership roles, but looking back, my favorite memories of time with Andy seemed to all surround something funny or nearly disastrous.

My favorite story about Andy involved the nearly disastrous. Roller skating was popular back then, and sometimes Young Life would sponsor a roller skating night at our local rink. It gave us an opportunity to invite a lot of new people, who we then could also invite to club. On the night in question Andy had managed to convince his Dad to allow him to take the brand new family car, because it was a large four-door sedan with lots of room. I rode with Andy and we piled in more kids than was probably legal, and headed to the rink. After a night of skating we all headed out to the cars and began loading up to leave.

There was a girl who was unceremoniously assigned to the middle seat in the front (one wide bench seat in those days) because she was fairly small and fit better. Andy was starting the car. Both front doors were still open at the time, waiting for more arrivals. Just as the car started and Andy momentarily gunned the engine, the girl in the front seat, who had been turned around facing us in the back seat and talking, slipped and fell backwards. As she did she accidentally hit the gear shift lever, which caused the car, which had been revving in neutral, to suddenly shift into reverse.

What happened next occurred in an instant, and was a shock for the ages. Andy's car suddenly shot backwards. Both front doors, which were wide open, came into solid contact with the cars parked on either side, and caught on them. As his car continued to move quickly backwards the front doors were leveraged and had no choice but to completely part company with Andy's car. After about ten feet Andy managed to hit the brakes and stop his car. And as we all piled out to see what happened we found ourselves staring at two beautiful shiny new car doors laying on the ground in the parking lot.

The next part of this story moves to the pay phone up by the entrance to the skating rink. This is where Andy would be calling his father and explaining exactly what happened to Dad's new car. I'll never forget listening to one side of that phone call, from Andy in that Southern drawl. "Hi Daddy! Yes, I'm ok. I had a little problem with the car though. (pause) Well...the front doors sort of came off..." it only got funnier, or went downhill from there, depending on your point of view. No one was hurt, and the doors came home, one in Andy's trunk and one in a friend's trunk. Those of us who rode home with Andy experienced a bit of a draft that night.

Chapter 4

Off to College

Andy and I and the rest of the Young Life seniors graduated that spring. Joni and her crowd prepared to take on more of the leadership roles that we were vacating, just as we had done the year before. I had had a great year in lacrosse in my senior year, and a few colleges were looking at me. At one of our games I spoke with a representative of Johns Hopkins University in Baltimore. But in my family, where not too many people even went to college, the thought of attending a high powered school like Hopkins was scary. Interestingly, it wasn't the thought of playing lacrosse at that level that worried me. It was the fear of becoming a financial burden for my Dad. So instead I made a safer choice. The University of Maryland was opening a brand new campus just outside of Baltimore, called University of Maryland, Baltimore County, or UMBC. I and about 750 other incoming freshmen made up the first-ever freshman class.

Looking back, I can see it was an unusual college experience. With no upper classmen leading the charge, we had to make our own way and create our own experiences. They planned to have a lacrosse team so I was able to continue in my favorite sport at the college level. And because the campus was located right in Baltimore, I was able to become part of Baltimore's Young Life leadership team. Jerry Johnson, who I had first met at Natural Bridge, was the Area Director for Young Life Baltimore. And as such, he ran the leadership team. This group of, mainly, local college students was to become my main source of fellowship and Christian influence for the next four years. There were also a few Young Life friends with me at UMBC, both from Woodlawn and from a few other local schools.

As freshmen, the responsibilities that Jerry allowed us to have in Young Life fell more into the "watch and learn" category, which we eagerly did. Jerry himself only ran one Young Life club in the area. But he recruited and trained leaders to run several more. Eventually there would be dozens of clubs, and all of them were run by volunteers. And almost every volunteer was a local college student that Jerry trained.

Jerry had a huge influence in my life during my college years. So many of my Christian friends and I learned how to be Young Life leaders through his training. We would regularly drive 45 minutes one way to his house, not only for leadership training meetings, but also at other times just to hang out with him. I couldn't get enough of being around the guy. The funny thing was, we all considered ourselves to be pretty cool people. But Jerry was the most uncool adult we knew. He was quirky, different. But he was sharp and insightful. He redefined cool for us.

When I began leading a club, I would call Jerry every week and get a message that I could give at my club that week. Except I would ask him for a second talk, acting like I wasn't too sure about the first one. That way I got two talks and kept one for future use. He never acted offended that I didn't like his first message idea. I think secretly he knew what I was doing and just played along.

Going from Young Life in Woodlawn to Young Life Baltimore leadership put me in with a group of people from all over the county. I met a whole lot of other guys and girls, each with their own story and background in Young Life; some very much like mine, and others unique and different. There were some sparkling personalities and funny characters. Two guys that really rocked my world at that time were Bo White (who had driven us to Connecticut) and Bill Linthicum. Bo and Bill were a few years older, and they came from the opposite side of the city. Were it not for Young Life leadership and Jerry, I never would have met these guys. Both were mature leaders with more experience than me.

But what really grabbed me was that they were the funniest and craziest two guys I had ever met. Their brand of humor was often subtle, so you thought they were being serious, when all of a sudden everyone was laughing and you'd realize they pulled off something outlandishly and wickedly funny. Whenever Bo and Bill were at leadership, or at an all-county club or all county Campaigners meeting, we all just knew something wild would eventually happen. Weekend camps during my college years were perfect platforms for their antics, from being the "stars" of weekend entertainment, to completely off-the-cuff and ad-lib hysterics. Bo was going to play a big part in my future.

The Love of My Life

Being at an entirely new school campus gave all of us the opportunity to meet new people. In addition to classes there were social events, like the popular "mixers" or Saturday night dances-any place to cruise chicks and suck face. (So sorry. Every now and then I slip into inappropriate old movie quotes). I meant, any place to get to know the ladies. But the one lady who really caught my eye, I first saw when she came walking into freshman English class that fall. (Cue saxophone music here with a slo-mo video entrance into the classroom.) She was blonde, cute and sharply dressed. She wore glasses, which made her look studious, a look I definitely did not have. I asked around and found out she had graduated from Howard High School, not too far from Woodlawn, and her name was Carol Hesson. It turned out that she ran with a pretty popular crowd at school. It wasn't long before we met at one of the mixers.

I hadn't been dating too much at that time since Kathy and I had an amicable break-up after she had graduated and gone off to college. Carrying on a dating relationship when I was a high school senior and she was a college freshman wasn't very viable. Even after breaking up, we always carried a special place in our hearts for each other. But once she went to college we were in different worlds. We kept in touch and remained friends.

While it was still warm, one day in the early autumn of my freshman year a bunch of us were invited to a friend's house for a pool party. Carol Hesson was there and I got up enough courage to ask her out. I had no idea about her religious background or faith, and I can't recall what thought process in my brain wound up with me taking her to a Billy Graham movie for our first date. Maybe it was, "What the heck, she may as well know up front about my own beliefs." We actually had a great time. She liked the movie. Go figure. Hmm, maybe she was a keeper. Maybe she thought I wasn't a keeper. Ever think of that? It eventually led to more dates and after a while our dating became regular. Before I knew it, we were a couple.

One of our dates that year was a concert at school, featuring the late, great Otis Redding. Another concert date we didn't make that year, however, was a group we never heard of and I assumed they would never make it big anyway. They were called Chicago Transit Authority. They later shortened their name to, simply, Chicago. I knew a lack of talent when I saw it back then.

Two years later, for our junior prom I could have booked a fledgling group for under a thousand dollars, but like Chicago, I didn't think they would amount to anything: Sly and The Family Stone.

Carol had grown up in a nominally Lutheran family, and had even taught Sunday school at her church. But like me in high school, she had never really heard the Gospel, at least not in a way that made sense to her. As we started dating more regularly and we got to know each other's friends, she began to hang around some of my Christian and Young Life friends. Somewhere along the line she began to suspect that there was something about them and me that wasn't quite right. Not pod people or Stepford Wives type-odd. I mean, she saw us as unusual in terms of how important and personal our faith was. Although I was learning how to work in Young Life and even how to give Christian messages, I had no clue how to share my faith one-on-one with another person, much less a woman I hoped to hang onto. So I never even tried to tell her about my faith. In an evangelistic Bizarro world, she wanted to hear the Gospel but I wasn't going to tell her. No way. Let her learn the good old fashion way, from someone else.

Some of my Christian friends were starting to say that I was "missionary dating", meaning I was dating a non-Christian instead of a Christian. I always regarded that term as derogatory, and wasn't happy about being labeled that way. But unfortunately we did know a lot of Christian friends who went off to college and got into a non-Christian crowd and eventually the faith they had in high school faded.

But I never felt in jeopardy of that when dating Carol. I guess my friends meant well and didn't want to see me stray from my faith, so some were critical of my dating choice. But all throughout my freshman year Carol was nothing but positive and curious about Young Life and my Christian beliefs. I just didn't know how to articulate my faith. Although we had dated for most of our freshman year and had gotten pretty close, neither one of us really had any plans for keeping in touch over the summer break. But that was to change quickly.

Liberty Road

On the last day of school, in June of '67, to celebrate the end of our freshman exams, Carol and I double dated with another couple and were heading out to a movie. Sheldon was driving, Betty was up front next to him in his old '57 Chevy. We were driving down Liberty Road, when suddenly a drunk driver coming in the opposite direction swerved and tried to make a turn right in front of our car. We tee-boned him at a fairly high rate of speed. Although we were all thrown around and beaten up, Carol was the only one to sustain a serious injury. When both of her legs struck the metal brace on the back of the front seats, it left her with two very nasty golf ball-sized hematomas on her shins. In addition to messing with those great looking legs, there was a danger that blood clots could form. And of course, if one of those blood clots moved to the heart or the brain, cancel Christmas.

At the time Carol's parents had just left for Nashville, where they were attending her brother's graduation ceremony from law school at Vanderbilt. With no one at home, the hospital wanted to admit her for a few days of observation until either the hematomas decreased or her parents got back to town. Hearing this news, my parents, who by this time had met and had come to really like Carol, stepped in and offered our home and our hospitality until her parents returned from Nashville.

For the next few days I became head nurse and cheerleader, waiting on Carol hand and foot, as she sat propped up on our living room sofa. The whole event was what kept us from winding down our relationship for the summer and led us to continue dating.

That summer two events stand out. Both had a lot to do with Carol learning about Christianity. The first was, out of boredom sitting on the sofa all day, I got out my high school yearbook and let Carol read it. It was common for friends to sign each other's yearbooks, and with so many Young Life friends in high school there was no shortage of salutations and well-wishing from my Christian buddies. Carol would read some of the Christian references, and positive spiritual messages, and wonder, "Who *are* these people? I've never seen students my age be so forthright and outspoken about their beliefs." As during the school year, I remained silent about telling her what had happened to me back at Natural Bridge and what had happened to so many of my friends. For Carol, reading my yearbook and meeting my Christian Young Life friends had a big impact on her coming to faith in Christ, which took place the following winter.

The other event that marked that summer happened to one of my good friends who I have already mentioned earlier, Joni. She was swimming at one of our favorite beaches on the Chesapeake Bay when she accidentally dove into shallow water, and in so doing wound up striking her head on the bottom and suffered a broken neck. Although we didn't know the extent of her injury that day, it was soon discovered that she was, and would be for the rest of her life, a quadriplegic. For Joni and her family, and also for her friends, the news was devastating. Sometimes I would take Carol with me to visit Joni in the hospital. In those visits Carol saw Christians, especially Joni, dealing with tragedy and coping in ways that she had never seen before. This, too, had a huge impact on Carol's spiritual journey.

By now you may recognize Joni's name, Joni Eareckson Tada, and know about the amazing life she has led from a wheelchair and the worldwide ministry that she has created and run so successfully, Joni and Friends. She went on to become a sought-after speaker, an author, a singer, and an artist. We have never lost touch with Joni over the years. I've always had a certain pride in knowing that Joni and I heard the Gospel for the first time at that Natural Bridge Young Life weekend camp.

A Club of Our Own

By the fall of my sophomore year, Jerry felt I was ready to be a Young Life leader with a club of my own. At that time, however, the clubs that had been started around Baltimore all had leaders. So Jerry helped a few of us to form a team and he assigned us to get a club started at a school that wasn't far from the UMBC campus, called Brooklyn Park High School.

Our team consisted of me, my high school buddy Andy Byrd, and Carol Gumph. All three of us were new leaders, and Brooklyn Park was our first experience out on our own. Long before we could ever start a club, we had to start going to the school to meet high school kids. While none of us had ever done that before, I had a great role model because I used to see Chuck do it all the time. It's called "contact work" and for anyone reading this who isn't familiar with this ministry, it's the heart and soul of Young Life.

Later on I'll go into a more detailed look at contact work. But for now I'll just say that it's not just showing up at the high school to recruit kids to come to Young Life. It's far deeper and more significant than that. It's being relational. It's initiating conversations with young people and building friendships over time. It's not easy and it's not efficient. Kids may think we're there to recruit. But contact work is about being their friend without strings attached. It's reaching out to them without a hidden agenda that would say, "I'm friendly to you because my payback is that you'll come to our Young Life club." Contact work is probably the single most difficult concept for people to understand, but it's the most important.

One of the critical philosophical differences between Young Life and other ministries is something that I hadn't even contemplated at the time. I was so close to the mission of Young Life that I never saw it or questioned it, but it made all the difference in the world. Conventional thinking was, to start a youth ministry the best strategy is to identify and recruit the Christian kids in a high school, the ones who already had a church background. The ministry known as Youth For Christ took this approach. And on the surface it sounds perfectly reasonable. However, a Young Life club is in reality a Christian club for non-Christians. When you start a club with Christian, churched kids, the entire composition, texture and atmosphere of that club is significantly dissimilar to what we were trying to accomplish.

It's more risky starting a club with non-Christians as the core participants. Sometimes very non-Christian things happen. Often there's less control. I've run clubs where, at times, I wasn't sure if or when the wheels were going to totally come off the entire evening. At one club, years after Brooklyn Park, I had an "irate neighbor" (my committee chairman) walk right into the very first club and start yelling at me that somebody ran over his kid's bicycle in the front street. It was painfully embarrassing to see this man berate me in front of everyone. To dissuade his anger I meekly offered him one of our after-club desserts, a pie, which I suddenly plunged right into his face. As he sulked away, disgraced, the place went wild. From the middle of the club one of the guys burst out, in a moment of intense, even if somewhat displaced loyalty, "Dude, I was so close to punching the s*** out of that guy!"

Non-Christian kids who became Christians through that kind of club wound up with a very different outlook and attitude. Their lives were changed by God at a time when they were not involved or even interested in Christian matters. It was loyalty to Young Life, but it was more than that. On one hand they didn't have the advantages of growing up in a church community, with all of its benefits. But on the other hand they weren't encumbered by many of the potential hang-ups that surrounded many churches at that time. Although it's a generalization, I believed that churches and Christian organizations could be described as having one of two different world views: they were either focused on grace, or focused on performance-based works. In many churches that embraced orthodox theology and emphasized evangelism, there was also a lot of legalism. And that encumbered people.

We were very careful not to devalue kids with church backgrounds who wanted to be part of Young Life. It's just that our prime focus wasn't on them. Many church kids would become vitally important to the ministry. Others struggled with our seemingly (in their eyes) irreverent approach at times. We learned that we had to be honest, and also very tactful in our relationship with local churches, defining our desire to partner with them in the kingdom work. We were clear that we were not a church and never intended to function as one, or to replace the church. Yet at the same time, being non-denominational and outreach focused, we could be specialists; outreach "arms" of the local church, who could reach out to kids with little or no church history.

Why Am I Putting Myself Through This?

But in order to start with non-Christian kids, that meant doing contact work. And for a young leader, it's the scariest thing to do. Imagine just showing up at a local high school, not knowing one person, and trying to befriend kids. Then coming back the next day, and the day after that, for days, weeks, and months. Progress is painfully slow, but necessary. In those early days of contact work at Brooklyn Park Andy or Carol Gumph and I would try to go together. Safety in numbers. I figured, if things turned ugly I could push one of them under of the bus. Although we were never in any physical danger, contact work was frightening. Here we were, sophomores in college, which made us no more than two years older than the seniors at the high school. It was hard enough to reach out and make friends at our own school with kids our own age. We were expected to drive eight miles, walk onto that high school campus and initiate with total strangers. And who knows for how long before we could expect to see progress? I believe the marketing term is "cold calling." The fear, the main fear at least, was in one form or another: rejection. What if they laugh at me? Make fun of me? Accuse me of being a drug dealer? And perhaps the worst of all, what if they just ignore me? Yeah, contact worked scared the hell out of me.

We learned to target events where kids gathered. After-school sports was one of the most accessible. Also, since I was a college lacrosse player, and by then I was beginning to be known a little bit around town, I often concentrated on meeting kids on the Brooklyn Park lacrosse team, and even occasionally volunteering to help their coach.

I say we started off not knowing anyone, but, Jerry Johnson had a longtime friend who was a PE teacher there, a guy named Rick Ulmer. Rick was instrumental in introducing us to a lot of students. Rick himself had been a Young Life leader, and was well acquainted with Young Life methods. I'm not sure he was all that impressed with these three young and inexperienced rookies that Jerry had assigned to his school. But he worked with us, and in the years that followed, Rick was to become a great friend.

We all had to find time get to the Brooklyn Park campus between our own college courses, and to balance being a full time student with starting and running a Young Life club. And we all did it. At one point Jerry's Baltimore leadership team numbered well over 50 students, and every one of us were committed to giving all of our spare time to running our clubs. It was an amazing learning and growing period for me, both in my faith and in my leadership skills.

After several months of continuous contact work we finally had befriended enough kids, and eventually shared our plan with them to start a Young Life club. They had absolutely no idea or point of reference to understand what a Young Life club entailed. Anyone who didn't know Young Life couldn't begin to comprehend our goal, or how on earth we were going to reach it; how our work could possibly pay off with a club. But we knew it would because we had seen it when we were in high school. And Jerry kept training us and encouraging us. We really felt like we were pioneers, cutting edge. Our college classmates had no idea what comfort zone-stretching we were subjecting ourselves to, and probably wouldn't have understood or even cared. Learning to do contact work as a college sophomore was important groundwork and formed a foundation for my life that reached far beyond anything I could have imagined at the time.

Getting Club off the Ground

We "sold" the concept of having a club to enough of our high school friends, and finally, at the home of one of the students, held our first-ever Brooklyn Park Young Life club. We started with about 35 kids, and by the end of the year we were up to around 50, and had even recruited a few of them to go to a Young Life camp that summer. I was learning that there was a big difference between simply sitting in club when I was in high school, and now having to prepare for club each week and try to replicate the quality program we were used to. We sought to have a weekly club that was engaging, fun, and funny. Above all, it had to be where curious non-Christian teenagers could hear about the person of Jesus in the most attractive setting and atmosphere we could possibly create.

It would be politically correct to say that my priorities that year were: school first, then lacrosse, then Young Life. But the reality was: Young Life first, lacrosse second, and schoolwork third. Fortunately, I was just barely a good enough student to make that work, but the priority was always Young Life. In fact, looking back there were times that I would get away with murder in lacrosse. I can't imagine telling a head coach in a college sport today that I would be leaving practice every Wednesday about half an hour early, because I had to get down to Brooklyn Park to run my Young Life club. But I did, and I guess because I was the captain and most developed player on the team, he let me do it. Trying that today could earn a player a fat lip, metaphorically speaking of course, unless the coach was Bobby Knight. Or Woody Hayes.

Junior Year at College

We finished our sophomore year and our first year of the Brooklyn Park club, feeling pretty good about what we had started. Andy, Carol Gumph, and I all had learned so much. When we returned for our junior year at college, Andy had moved to another club, leaving Carol and me as the only leaders. But Carol and I carried on without Andy. We had the privilege of seeing a number of kids come to Christ, especially through the camps, and we maintained club at Brooklyn Park at around 40 to 50 kids.

In my junior year at UMBC I decided to run for class president and was fortunate enough to win. At that time, in addition to being a volunteer with Young Life, I and some of our other leaders, including my now-steady girlfriend, Carol Hesson, convinced the ministry of Campus Crusade for Christ to come to UMBC. As class president, one of the strategies I was able to pull off was to have the other members of the student government sit and listen to the Campus Crusade Staff guy share the "Four Spiritual Laws" Gospel tract.

I first met Tom Pilsch because he was also in student government; freshman class president the same year I was junior class president. Later that spring he joined me on the lacrosse team. Tom was one of the guys I had arranged to meet with the Campus Crusade guy, and for the first time in his life, Tom heard the Gospel. Although he didn't accept Christ, he did take the Gospel tract home, and sometime afterwards he read through it again and decided to pray the prayer at the end. In a short time he and I were becoming fast friends, not only being in student government and on the lacrosse team together, but also sharing our spiritual journeys as Tom began growing in his faith.

By that time some other Christian friends had enrolled at UMBC, many of them from the Baltimore Young Life leadership group, some also involved in Campus Crusade. I was able to leverage my influence as class president to bring a number of Christian events to school, mainly sponsored by Campus Crusade. Also by this time Carol's growth in her faith was simply meteoric. Back in the middle of her sophomore year, without much help, she pretty much connected the dots on her own. She never had a "Natural Bridge" experience, but in the quietness of her own heart, she had accepted Christ. She got involved in Young Life leadership with the rest of us and eventually became one of the most talented leaders in our group.

Carol and my friend Duke VanSant, who I mentioned had become a Christian at Natural Bridge the same time I did, paired as leaders at Carol's old alma mater, Howard High School. Together they built that club from scratch to somewhere eventually in the neighborhood of 250 to 300 kids a week. One of girls Carol knew who became a Christian also became one of Carol's closest friends and their friendship continued after high school, Bobbi Price. Years later Bobbi had Carol in her wedding, and to this day Bobbi and her husband, Tim Smick, remain very close friends. They live in Florida and we get to see them often.

Mike Coleman, who was a year behind me and in the same class as Joni Eareckson at Woodlawn, also arrived at UMBC. He and another friend, Neil Duddy, ran a club at nearby Catonsville High School. Mike went on to join Young Life Staff after graduation and later became a Presbyterian pastor and has remained so to this day. He's also remained a special friend-for-life.

Hotel California

Between my junior and senior year of college, the Campus Crusade Staff leader challenged me to go out to Crusade's headquarters, south of Los Angeles in a place called Arrowhead Springs. At that point in my life I still wasn't sure what I was going to do after graduation, but I was thinking more and more about full time youth ministry. For me that probably meant Young Life. But a lot of us were also very involved in Campus Crusade. Young Life outreach wasn't to UMBC students, but Crusade gave us the opportunity and the means to have ministry right on our college campus. Already Tom Pilsch had come to faith in Christ through this ministry, along with several others. As Tom was a young Christian and also by then a close friend, I managed to recruit him to go with me to Campus Crusade's headquarters that summer for their two week training.

Although my involvement Crusade was important, I still fulfilled my primary responsibilities to Young Life, and that meant taking kids from our club to camp in the summer. We managed to book a week out at Frontier Ranch in Colorado that ended a week before the start of the Crusade training in California. Of course now I had Tom with me, and he was starting to get involved with

Young Life also. Tom and I left late in June with a busload of kids from Baltimore, and spent a week with them in Colorado, where we were their leaders. Well, I was their leader, and Tom was a fast learner and soon-to-be leader. In fact, after graduation, Tom also joined full time Young Life Staff, but that part of the story will come later.

We had a great time at Frontier Ranch, the same Young Life camp where I had spent a month on Work Crew just a few years before. We still hadn't worked out how we were going to get from Colorado to California. We had been hoping that there would be a busload of California kids at camp and we could hitch a ride, but no such luck.

Sometimes reality is stranger than fiction, and if I'm lyin' I'm dyin'...about half way through the week two lovely young ladies dropped into camp for a few days. (Back then you could pretty much just pop in and the staff would work out how to feed and house you). In addition to being young and beautiful, the two ladies just happened to drive a young and beautiful brand new Mustang convertible, and, they were on their way to... where else but, California. Seriously, I'm not making this stuff up.

Needless to say, we took this as nothing short of God's divine intervention and His will for our lives. Even though they were headed to San Francisco and not LA, we managed. I don't recall exactly how many hours it took to drive from Frontier Ranch to San Francisco, but in that time I think the two girls may have driven their Mustang for a total of, maybe, two hours. Tom and I finagled our way into the driver's seat for the rest of our journey. After all, we were only being gentlemen and offering to help with the long arduous task of driving.

On our way to California we did make a side trip. We had heard that there was a new Young Life camp that had opened in Northern California, and we wanted to see it. It was called Woodleaf, and the day we arrived there was a grand opening celebration and a catered luncheon, which we attended. I looked over and who was the chef? None other than the man I worked for on Work Crew at Frontier Ranch, Andy Delaney, a.k.a. Goldbrick. I was far from home and completely off his radar, so we had a surprising and happy reunion.

Tony Bennett Land

Upon arrival into San Francisco Tom and I parted company with our lovely travel companions. Seriously, they were sharp Christian ladies and we did have a grand time traveling with them. Their arrival at Frontier Ranch had really been a blessing for Team Pilsch-and-Bond.

So here we were, Tom and me, in San Francisco in the summer of 1968. If you are a student of history, or of our generation, you'll understand the implication. If not; let's just say, we were at the nexus of the universe for the youth counter-culture revolution of the late 60's and early 70's: cultural upheaval, war protest, hippies, free love, anti-establishment, flower power, LSD, The Grateful Dead, places like Haight Asbury, and Cal Berkley. Wild and whacky people everywhere. Walking down Telegraph Avenue looked like the café scene in Star Wars. I have a photo of Tom and me sitting and playing (someone's) guitar on the steps of Sproul Hall at Berkley, famous for being the scene of many political protests at the time. And exactly how we secured our housing for the night I do not recall, but I clearly remember that we stayed in a genuine, bonafide, certified, commune.

The next day we sprung for the cost of a plane ticket down to LA and were picked up by a driver who took us to Campus Crusade headquarters down in Arrowhead Springs. I have to say, the layout that Crusade had there was impressive. It had originally been a lavish resort. They made a big deal of the swimming pool which was designed by Olympic swimmer-turned movie star, Esther Williams. Crusade staff had some very sharp people, led by Bill Bright, who was at least as famous in the Christian world as Jim Rayburn, Young Life's founder. It was a pleasure to meet him and to be around him, especially as I was giving Crusade staff some serious consideration as my possible future employer. And what better way to test the waters than to spend a few weeks in "Mecca?"

The facilities were great, the people were friendly, and the training was solid and very forthright. If you are familiar with Campus Crusade, you know what I mean. Their basic evangelism strategy was to approach people with their Gospel tract, "Have You Heard of the Four Spiritual Laws?" It was very much "cold turkey" evangelism and quite different from Young Life's highly relational approach. But their tract contained solid theology and their tactics at that time were highly effective on a lot of college campuses. I knew that both from using the tract back at UMBC and also because Tom himself was a Christian because he first heard the Gospel through the same booklet.

The Beach Boys

A few times each week we took bus trips out to the Southern California beaches to share the Gospel with people. They never failed to push our comfort zones, but we did have some prior experience from back at our college campus, and also I was by then a pretty seasoned Young Life leader. That had to count for something. Tom and I paired up and made our "team." There was a third guy on our team. I say this with as much graciousness as I can muster; he was the biggest nerd and country hick I'd ever seen. He was from some school out in the mid-south, and had a southern accent and a heavy hillbilly drawl. Tom and I considered ourselves pretty cool, so we weren't real happy that we had to have Jed Clampett with us.

Our instructions were to wander up to people on the beach and just start a conversation by asking if they had a few minutes to talk and if they had ever heard of the Four Spiritual Laws. Tom and I struck out a few times, but Clem (I think that was his name) wasn't deterred. He walked straight up to the coolest group I'd seen on the beach. The girls were Photoshop-good looking, and the guys were absolute studs, six pack abs, well-tanned, and very *Magic Mike* fit. Clem walked up to the coolest guy and asked him the big question. To our absolute shock, the guy started listening and interacting. Clem proceeded to share the Four Laws with the guy. When you've seen this process happen enough times you begin to get a feel when someone is just being polite. But you can also sense at times when the Holy Spirit has just arrived. You could see it on a person's face, and how they would start to listen. And man, this big stud of a guy had that look.

After going through the Four Laws, we saw the guy's head bow, right in full view of all his buddies, who by now were rather dumbfounded themselves. He prayed to receive Christ right there on the beach with our team's new MVP, Clem. Tom and I tactfully came closer and in time Clem turned and introduced us to his new friend. His name eludes me, but this I do remember; he was a starting wide receiver on the USC football team. Go Clem! Tom and I will have another piece of that tasty humble pie now.

Chapter 5

College Senior

The two weeks at Arrowhead Springs passed quickly and before we knew it we were back in Baltimore. Soon after that I began my senior year in college. School began well, and I was enjoying the feeling of being a senior. I decided not to run again for class president, which was fine. I gave 'em the ole LBJ: "I shall not seek, and I will not accept, the nomination of my party for another term as president." I felt I had had a good experience, met a lot of people, and was able to use whatever influence I could muster from that position to develop ministry opportunities.

The whole climate and culture of school was going through incredibly radical and rapid changes that year. Some of what I had seen at Berkeley in the summer had come full-force to UMBC. There were anti-war protests, and, to be honest, "anti-pretty-much-anything" protests. There were more and more radicals on campus, and these guys were the ones who actually led a takeover of the college administration building, something that was being copied in several college campuses across the country.

Many of my friends who had left school for summer

69

break just a few months previously had returned in September shockingly changed. Preppy clothes had given way to hippy garb, tie dye tee shirts, grungy jeans...anything that screamed counter-culture or anti-establishment. Getting drunk and partying on weekends gave way to weed and harder substances almost overnight, or so it seemed. LSD, the hallucinogenic drug, became popular. Music changed. Gone were the days of weekend "mixer" dances. The music was replaced by protest songs, much darker hard-core rock, and something called psychedelic music, featuring groups like *The Strawberry Alarm Clock*. Just a quick look at the change in the Beatles music style during this period would be a convenient way to envision the change in the music culture at the time. I linger on the music because I believe that art in general and music specifically is a reflection of the values of a culture; and as that related to my world it helped me to understand the changing youth culture.

Racial Landscape

On top of all of this, a new racial climate was emerging. And in my opinion, crucially, away from one of the more tragic elements of American history. I am speaking of both personal and institutional racism. Even 100 years after the Emancipation Proclamation, deep seeded racism was still thriving in our culture. We had more recently gone through and were still going through the vast and historic transition in the form of desegregation. History books tell the story in much greater detail than I need to state here. But what impacted me that was going on in the late 60's on college campuses and indeed in cities everywhere, was a new Black empower-ment movement. While history shows that people like Dr. Martin Luther King had the most powerful and lasting impact, at the time there were alternative voices, whose prophets were people like Malcolm X, Dick Gregory, Huey Newton, Bobby Seale, and Angela Davis.

Young Life: The Adventures of an Ex Staffer

I generally tended to come down on the more conservative side of political opinions. But at the time I felt that much of what Black Power was about was actually progressive, even though there were a lot of threats and posturing in their public rhetoric. I read books like, *The Autobiography of Malcolm X, Manchild in the Promised Land,* and *Invisible Man,* and they had a huge influence on me. But I didn't share my opinions with many people. When the Black Power movement hit our campus, it shouldn't have surprised me, but it did, that I was cast in with everyone else whose skin was light in color. I was whitey, and I was the enemy. In what was my first experience of reverse racism, it apparently didn't matter that I was sympathetic with the cause. Since I was white, I was automatically in the wrong.

When I was growing up, before we moved to the suburbs, we lived in a neighborhood that started out all white. Even though I was young, I remember realtors going door-to-door trying to get people to sell their homes. They used a scare tactic: "Negroes are starting to move in!" I'll always appreciate that my parents, although probably holding some racist attitudes that were holdovers from their own upbringing, would not acquiesce to the realtors' tactics. However, most other neighbors did, and as a result we found ourselves living in a largely Black neighborhood. For a time in my younger years a majority of my friends were African Americans. Because this was all pre-adolescent for me, I think I was very fortunate to have learned at a young age not to judge people on the basis of skin color.

However, in my senior year of college it was as if none of my history and background mattered. I was considered one of the ignorant ones and was part of the enemy because of *my* skin color. For me it was all discouraging and troubling. Over time, though, I learned to see that it was just part of the fallout of our history and if that's the price I had to pay at that time, so be it, especially if we were ever going to see the end of racism in our country.

All of these transitions I've been describing are in many ways generalizations and they are very much from my own personal perception. Clothes styles, political unrest, Vietnam, race riots, music changes and recreational drugs; it felt like some malevolent master had taken over and our world was slowly being turned upside down.

All of this change also brought on incredible polarization. It had the tendency to force people into an "us or them" mentality. If you weren't radically embracing whatever cause someone or some group was pushing, you immediately became labeled as their enemy. And it seemed like everyone was just angry, or at least very serious. In that cultural scene it became much more difficult to try and relate to people who believed differently about Christianity or about anything. It was a world of extremes and of non-stop confrontation. And even if you had no desire or passion for one stance or another of a particular issue or cause, you were forced into taking sides.

For many of us, for me at least; I spent a lot of time scratching my head, thinking, "This is crazy and it's changing so fast. It's like we're careening down the road out of control and nobody's got their hands on the throttle anymore. It reminded me of the lyrics from a Jethro Tull song, "Old Charlie stole the handle and the train it won't stop going, no way to slow down." It was disconcerting and anxiety producing. Yet at the same time there were parts of it that were exciting. Exciting in the same sense that running down a street in Pamplona being chased by bulls would be exciting. But whatever it was, it was not business as usual, and it sure wasn't boring.

When we look back on the 60's, and early 70's we have

the great advantage of historical perspective. We know now that it was an exceedingly turbulent time, unprecedented in my lifetime. Everything, all aspects of our culture and life went through vast changes. But living right there in midst of it, with no idea where we were going and how it would turn out was, as the Grateful Dead sang, "What a long, strange trip it's been."

Having enjoyed the benefits of some moderate popularity up until that time as one of the better athletes on campus and as class president, all of a sudden in my senior year these markers of credibility and popularity became liabilities rather than assets to a whole lot of people. No individual or group was beyond the ever searching eye of Sauron, or in our case, the protestors. The student government was protested, because we were "in bed with the man." Translation: we worked too cooperatively with the faculty and the administration. The lacrosse team was protested. In that case it was probably justified because one day our whole team trampled a tent that housed political propaganda and destroyed some of their protest flyers. Crazy times. Dark times. We had friends who had dropped out of school and headed to Vietnam. We lost friends in that war, people we had known and had gone to high school or college with.

Almost Drafted, and Not by the NFL

The government instituted a draft system during the war that was based on a lottery. Everyone was given a number from 1 to 365, corresponding to a randomly picked day of the year. Your birthday was your number, and the lower the number, the more likely you were to be drafted. My number was 68. Not good. Full time students enrolled in colleges were given draft deferments regardless of our draft number, but only if we remained, not only full time students, but also on schedule to graduate in four years.

In my freshman year I was mistakenly placed in a Spanish course which I discovered was far too advanced. Instead of transferring to a lower level Spanish, I simply dropped the course, which changed my credit level and therefore enrollment status. Within a few weeks I received the letter from my draft board telling me I was to be drafted into the U.S. Army and to report to Ft. Holabird for registration and a physical. That was one scary experience, and seemed like the longest day of my life. It felt like the evil twin of *Private Benjamin*. Afterwards I had to appear before my draft board and appeal my case to have my student status reinstated. Fortunately my appeal was accepted, otherwise it may have been *Good Morning Vietnam* for me.

Previously I mentioned war protests. There was a group called *The Catonsville 9* who caught national attention by breaking into the Selective Service Offices in Catonsville, Maryland where they destroyed several hundred draft records. That was my draft board. Unfortunately, they missed my records. Opps, I didn't mean that. (Yes I did.)

When I and many Young Life leaders did graduate and wanted to join staff, our draft boards would receive a personal letter from the Senior Senator from Oregon, The Honorable Mark Hatfield. Mark was on the Young Life Board of Directors. This was during the escalation of the Vietnam War. In my freshman year of college, 1967, Muhammad Ali went to prison for refusing army induction based on religious grounds. Draft boards soon became suspicious of anyone seeking a deferment. For us, it wasn't an issue of dodging the draft. We just wanted to be on Young Life Staff.

Back to Woodlawn

In the midst of all this craziness, we got up every day, went to classes, ran our Young Life ministries, and tried to live life as normally as we could, even when it seemed the whole world was crashing around us. Carol and I had both declared our majors earlier, psychology. So that meant we were in a lot of classes together. Except for a brief period of time, (I call it our *Annie Hall* period. Carol refers to it as our *Dumb and Dumber* period) we had basically been dating steadily since our freshman year. And although we didn't really talk about it, I think by that time we both had a good sense of where it was heading. Carol was by then as deeply involved and successful in Young Life work as any of our other top leaders in Baltimore. I mentioned before how she and Duke VanSant went back to Carol's old high school and together built that club from nothing to a massive ministry in a relatively short time. I was so proud of her.

As for me, Jerry Johnson had called me one day over the summer and said that although the Brooklyn Park club was doing well, he had a problem and needed my help. One of the largest clubs in the area had lost its leader and they needed someone with more experience to run it. I was the person Jerry wanted, and the club was none other than my old high school, Woodlawn. I was honored to be considered and readily agreed, even though it would mean leaving Brooklyn Park. The opportunity to be back at Woodlawn, and it being one of the crown jewels of the Young Life clubs in the area, was tremendously attractive.

For the previous few years the Woodlawn club had been run by a couple, Larry and Diane Bonney. Larry was a big, scrappy athlete, great looking, and very popular. It also didn't hurt that his wife was a sharp, experienced leader with a great personality. I knew them from leadership. Larry had decided to sign on for the FBI and was about leave for Quantico for training. Larry did leave me with one very helpful gift. Because of their schedule and housing, Diane would remain in the area. So she stabilized the transition with her presence and experience as I replaced Larry. It was a thrill working with her. Together we ran the Woodlawn club, and I had what was to be one of the best years of running a club that I ever had.

Doing contact work at Woodlawn was surreal. Just a few short years before, I was a high school kid in those halls, acting cool and sneaking smokes in the boy's lavatory. And it was on that walkway out front that I first met Chuck Reinhold and he learned my name. I was meeting kids now and trying to learn their names and get to know them.

The club year went by in a blur. The two years I had spent starting and running the Brooklyn Park club (now under new leadership) served me well. By then I had the kind of experience necessary to keep this large and growing ministry on track. Diane had already been used to large numbers and the challenges they imposed, so I leaned heavily upon her expertise. There were no houses large enough to hold a club that regularly exceeded 250 kids. We had to find an alternative meeting place, which we did. Campaigners, the weekly Bible study, regularly exceeded 50 students. This meant that we had to find someplace other than a home to meet, which we did. When it came to the Fall and Spring weekend camps, we didn't take a busload a kids. We took, busloads, plural.

Club that year was so much fun. In fact, Young Life was going well not only at Woodlawn but at several high schools, including Howard High where Carol was leading. We all felt like rock stars. Interestingly, of all of those clubs run by college students, the smallest club in the entire area was led by the only fulltime Young Life employee, the same one who trained all of us how to do Young Life, Jerry Johnson. I knew he must have had a great deal of pride in us. There wasn't a week that went by, however, that we didn't tease him about how much bigger our clubs were than his.

Eric Clapton Time

One event happened that year that didn't seem that significant at the time, but in retrospect it marked a rather important turning point in leading a club. I was at home, sitting in my parent's basement, studying for semester exams. It was getting close to Christmas. Our next door neighbors, the Fioretti's, used to store their kids' unwrapped Christmas gifts, which always included toys, in our basement. On Christmas Eve they would retrieve and wrap them for Christmas morning. There was always an assortment of toys, like a Red Ryder BB gun for Ralphie Fioretti. One night I looked over and noticed that one of the gifts was a six string guitar. Back in junior high I had a cheap little four string baritone ukulele that I used to play. That was back in the days of folk songs, Peter Paul and Mary, Dylan, and hootenannies. (If you aren't familiar with the latter, grab your phone and Google it. I'm not taking the time here.) I reached over and started fiddling with the guitar.

Since I had been involved in Young Life as a leader, now in my third year, one part of club that had begun to feel dated was the music. We used to sing some hymns, just like in church hymnals. We would doctor some of them to make them more upbeat, but still, they weren't anything like music on the radio. I kept thinking, "What's wrong with singing some more popular songs, and why do we have to continue using a piano?" Besides, it wasn't easy finding a piano in every home where we wanted to have club back at Brooklyn Park. "Wouldn't it be a whole lot easier if we could just take a guitar with us?" Little did I know, but at the same time all over the country there were other Young Life leaders asking the same questions.

I went upstairs and said to my parents, "Is it too late to make a last minute Christmas gift request?" When they responded favorably, I told them I'd really like a guitar. My parents were not always the hippest or most youth-insightful people, but they knocked the ball out of the park this time. When Christmas morning came I realized that, given their limited budget and time, the guitar they picked couldn't have possibly been a better choice. It was a Yamaha FG300 with a jumbo body. That guitar became part of me. For the record, it was in every Young Life club I ever led for the next 20 years, served me for eight more years when I became a youth pastor, and was eventually used by my son when he became a youth pastor. It's finally been retired and is sitting in a closet. But other than some very tired strings, it's still ready and willing.

After Christmas I gave it a try; and as far as I knew, at the time I was the first guy to lead club music with a guitar. I felt like the *Lewis and Clark* of club work. When I shared my discovery at leadership, I realized that some of the other guys had been having the same thoughts. Jerry was pretty old-school when it came to some things, but with music I'm sure he could see the handwriting on the wall, and readily agreed to our suggestion of going full-out with guitars at the upcoming spring weekend camp, to be held in Ocean City, Maryland. One of the other leaders, Dick Rohlfs, and I led the music, exclusively with our guitars. There wasn't a piano in sight. Kids loved it. Leaders loved it, and from then on everyone started using guitars.

At Woodlawn, Diane and I had a great core of Christian kids, all very committed to getting their non-Christian friends to club and to camps. One enthusiastic young lady and a good friend of Joni's, especially after Joni broke her neck and was paralyzed, was Sheryl Liphard. She was the little sister of one my classmates, Bob Liphard. So when I first met Sheryl, knowing her older brother, we hit it off instantly. She was the kind of person who just exuded Christ-like enthusiasm; the kind of student whose positive nature was contagious and who you wanted in Young Life. The reason I mention Sheryl at this point in my story: years down the road she would be playing a major role in my life, and Carol's life, and the life of my brother, Jack. Eventually I'll get to that story, but for now, spoiler alert: she was to become my sister-in-law.

Regarding Diane Bonney and I working together, for those familiar with Young Life today, it may be hard to comprehend, but Jerry Johnson's philosophy was, if you had a girl leader and a guy leader, go start a club. If you had another girl and guy leader, don't waste them on club number one, go start another club! So, much of the work of running the Woodlawn club was on Diane's and my shoulders. Back then we didn't know it could be done any differently. We did cheat a bit and would recruit some other "helpers" from time to time, like when we had a few busloads of kids going to camp. In the years to follow, the philosophy of "two leaders, one club" would change dramatically. But not at that time.

As my senior year progressed, I thought a lot about what to do with my future. At times when Doug Holladay was in town I spoke about it with him. Someone once said that the three biggest decisions in life are: master, mate, and mission. The first, I decided back at Natural Bridge in high school. In my senior year of college I was about to decide the other two.

Engaged

In February, 1970, I made a quiet decision that I wanted to ask Carol to marry me. By then Mike Coleman and I were very close friends and there wasn't much I didn't run past him. When I shared my intentions his response was something like, "If you don't marry that girl you are the biggest idiot in the world!" Mike was that kind of guy. Mike, why don't you tell me what you really think?

By this time in my life I really had grown to love skiing in spite of my shaky start in high school. There weren't a lot of great places to ski near Baltimore, and certainly nothing like the years to come when we would be living in New England. But one place I liked was called Seven Springs, located in western Pennsylvania. Some of us would go there from time to time when we could afford it and could get away. I managed to rally some of the troops and a bunch of us headed off for the weekend. It was late Saturday night, standing on the balcony outside of the restaurant that I asked Carol Hesson to marry me. After a lot of begging and some money changed hands, she finally said yes.

We hustled back to Baltimore the next day because our leadership met on Sunday nights and we wanted to be there to tell everyone the good news. They weren't just Young Life leaders, they were our closest and most valued friends. Everyone, of course, was excited for us. Looking back, we really were a bit of an incestuous group, as so many couples met and began dating and wound up marrying from that fellowship of Young Life leaders. Jerry's only rule was, you couldn't be dating if you were working in the same club. Carol and I soon set the wedding date for a few months after graduation, September 20th. That left the last of the three "master, mate, and mission" questions to be answered.

Mission

While I certainly had a lot of involvement with Campus Crusade, and enjoyed ministry with them, at the end of the day I made a decision, one that deep down I really knew all along. I wanted to be part of the ministry that reached me when I was a disinterested, turned off, tuned out non-Christian high school kid. I spoke a lot about it with Jerry Johnson, along with Doug and Mike and my other closest Christian friends. Everyone I spoke with, and especially Carol, confirmed my feelings.

Jerry told me about an exciting opportunity available with Young Life Staff, if I was interested. In fact I had already heard about it from because Doug Holladay, who had graduated from the University of North Carolina the year before, was now on Young Life Staff and part of this new program. Instead of having scattered Area Directors, like Jerry, each train a new recruit, Young Life wanted to select one city and make it a training center, where a whole group of new staff recruits could come and be trained. Doug was in the first year of that training, held in nearby Washington D.C. Not only that, but the person selected to be the Training Director was none other than Chuck Reinhold. He had been the Area Director in Rochester, NY since leaving Baltimore, and accepted the position in D.C. I was ecstatic at the possibility of being trained by Chuck, especially since I had always felt somewhat shortchanged when he left Woodlawn at the end of my junior year. Being part of that training program was an option that had my attention.

Air Young Life

By my senior year in college there were three of us who were on the lacrosse team who were also running clubs. The other two were Tom Pilsch, who was a starting midfielder, and Neil Duddy, who was our starting goalie. Both were not only club leaders, they also were very close friends. Tom was to be in my wedding and to this day, remains a close friend.

Every now and then our involvement in lacrosse conflicted with our first love. The Spring Weekend Camp that year took place right in the middle of lacrosse season. As a senior I was a candidate to become the first All American athlete in the (short) history of UMBC. While that certainly mattered to me, it didn't matter nearly as much as my Young Life commitment. There was no way I, or the other two players were going to miss that weekend camp, and we told the coach. With the other two players, Tom and Neil, also being starters on the team, having us miss the game placed our team in a real bind. I shudder now to think how audacious our demand was to our head coach. But I had an idea.

The Spring Camp was a few hours' drive to the east, in Atlantic City, New Jersey. The game scheduled on the Saturday of the camp, was against Western Maryland College, and located a few hours' drive west of UMBC. There was obviously no way we could drive to the game from the weekend camp, and back. However, we were not to be deterred. We knew that the weekend camp schedule had a big chunk of free time in the middle of Saturday afternoon, which was when the game was scheduled to be played. We figured if we flew, we could get to the game, play, and get back by dinnertime at the weekend camp. I'm not talking about commercial flying, as the only airport near where the game was being played was a private strip that had a grass runway. "Roads? Where we're going we don't need roads."

Terry was one of my club kids, and even though he was only 18, he already had his pilot's license. Imagine this idea coming to life in my head, then convincing this student to fly me and two leaders from Atlantic City to western Maryland, and back. Then I had to sell the idea to Tom and Neil. Finally, I had to convince our coach to let us fly in for the game. But that's exactly what we did. Teleportation wouldn't be invented for a few hundred years. (Even then, it didn't end well for the Fly.)

Terry had gotten his pilot's license less than a year before. His lessons were taken while flying a Piper Cherokee, which is a low wing plane, that is, the wing is located below the fuselage as opposed to above it. But because we were departing from Atlantic City, we had to rent a plane that was available there. And the only four place single engine plane available was a Cessna 172, which is a high wing plane-not a plane that Terry was certified to fly. No problem. Tom, Neil, and I, along with Terry, had taken our buses full of our club kids and had arrived in Atlantic City Friday night when the weekend camp began. We drove Terry to the airport in Atlantic City early Saturday morning.

In order to get certified to fly the Cessna, Terry had to go up with an instructor and pass a flight test. And if he didn't pass, the whole plan would be a bust for us in terms of ever getting to our lacrosse game. Fortunately, Terry passed.

By lunchtime Terry and the three of us were at the airport and took off for western Maryland and the lacrosse game. My parents planned to meet us at the Western Maryland airport with all of our equipment so we didn't have to take it on the plane. We got to our destination with just enough time to land and get a ride to the game. However, we encountered a slight problem. We couldn't find the tiny airport! There was no "tower" per se, but just a small office at the strip. A grass landing field in the midst of rolling hills and pastureland isn't exactly the easiest thing to see. Several times we thought we saw it, only to get close and realize it wasn't the airport. Terry started to get frustrated, and smooth flying slowly deteriorated into, "Darn, that's not it," a sharp yank on the controls and a steep turn to get over the next hill and look more. By the time we finally found the runway, not only were we late, everyone except Terry was about to lose their lunch from the up, down and twisty flying.

My parents were relieved to have us finally arrive and whisked us off to the school and the game. But because we were late by then, we only arrived as the team was heading out to the field for warm up. No problem. We rushed and got our equipment on and ran out well before the game started. Yes a problem. Our coach, whose tolerance was already stretched to the limit in the first place, had become further irritated by our tardiness and decided to impose a penalty. All three of us had to sit on the bench for the entire first quarter. Not only did this give our team a distinct disadvantage, with three of the ten starters out, it also didn't exactly ingratiate us to our teammates.

I don't recall the score that day, but I know that we won the game. I scored a fair number of goals, and every one of them was an "angry" goal. I was angry that we had to sit on the bench for the first quarter, and yet had gone through so much trouble, not to mention personal expense, to get to the game. So, I was going to take it out on the other team. By the end of the game all was forgiven by both our teammates and the coach. Winning can do that for you. Had we lost it may have been a different story altogether.

The Return Trip

We didn't have much time to get back to the weekend camp, so my folks drove us right back to the little airport. We all jumped into the plane and in short order Terry had us rolling down the runway for takeoff. Except that we began to encounter one slight difficulty; we weren't taking off!

Tom and Neil were in the back seats, and I was next to Terry in the front. I should tell you that by this time I had done enough flying with some other friends in small planes, to at least have an idea what was going on most of the time. So while Tom and Neil in the back really didn't understand our take-off trouble right away, I did. Remember I said that Terry had to be checked out that morning in the Cessna? This story is going to get a bit technical, both in takeoff now, and later on when we were landing, so pay attention. There may be a test at the end. And besides, it's necessary in order to appreciate all that happened that day.

About half way down the runway Terry and I exchanged concerned glances, and at about the same time we realized the problem. The Piper plane, with which Terry was familiar, required a certain degree of flaps for takeoff. So when we started down the runway that day, Terry lowered the flaps. But what the instructor failed to communicate earlier was that a Cessna's takeoff with the degree of flaps we were using would inhibit the forward speed of the plane. On top of that, we were on a grass runway, and one where there had been a lot of spring rainfall which made taking off more sluggish and slow. We were rapidly running out of runway!

There was another design difference between the two planes which worked against us. The Piper's flap release, with low wings, was mechanical, very much like a hand brake in a car. However, the flap release on the Cessna was electric, and that took painfully longer to get the flaps retracted. More time…less runway. At the very end of the runway the ground dropped away sharply. We were so late lifting off that our plane literally dropped below the horizon and out of sight, before reappearing in a distance, climbing out. My parents, who were witnessing this entire take off, and having no idea what was going on in the cockpit, had a real moment of panic. My Dad had suffered a heart attack the year before. When I finally got back home after the weekend camp and we were talking about that takeoff, my Mom told me that Dad had to take one of his nitroglycerin pills.

Finally, we were in the air and headed back to the camp. With the earlier problem of not being able to find the airport on arrival, and then the problem with the takeoff, we thought we had seen the last of our troubles. We were wrong. All day we had enjoyed beautiful weather. But wouldn't you know it, the closer we got to Atlantic City, the storm clouds began to close in and the visibility dropped. We tried staying above the clouds for as long as we could. By the time we were close to the airport we couldn't see the ground, so Terry descended fairly rapidly in order to get under the clouds and to get a bead on the runway so we could land. This brought on a pilot error, perhaps simply from Terry's inexperience. It could have been as disastrous as if we had run out of runway earlier on takeoff.

When small, piston engine planes with carburetors descend rapidly, especially in changing and cooling weather, condensation can form inside the carburetor that can actually wind up freezing, which then causes the engine to stop running. Not good. So the plane was equipped with something called "carb heat" which was described to me as a sort of shield to slow cold air flow over the air intake of the engine. A similar principle is used in school buses. Maybe you've seen them with a zippered cover over their radiators, which are used in severely cold conditions to keep the engine heat in. At any rate, Terry never activated the carb heat that day. With losing altitude at a rapid rate, and with the dropping temperature from the rain, just as we crossed the threshold (the end) of the runway, the engine conked out completely. Terry and I exchanged a glance that looked like the two guys in the crow's nest on the Titanic when they first saw the iceberg. We were looking at the propeller. Shouldn't that thing have been turning round and round? Instead it was just sitting there smiling at us.

Fortunately we did have enough momentum that Terry executed a perfect "dead stick" landing. In spite of multiple, potentially fatal errors, Tom and Neil, in the backseat were, for the large part, blissfully ignorant. Terry and I on the other hand, could have used one of my Dad's pills. It made for fun story telling when we got back to the camp, and the next week back at school, but it always reminded me of the old saying, "Our guardian angels had tattered wings." The Lord covered our backsides that day in several huge ways.

Saranac Opening

One other notable event took place in that spring of 1970. Young Life had purchased a camp in upstate New York, in the Adirondacks, and named it Saranac Village.

It was located right on Upper Saranac Lake, not far from Lake Placid. It was originally built as one of the great summer homes, similar to those built for families like the Rockefellers and the Carnegies. This one housed the Adolph Lewisohn family, the mining magnate and multi-millionaire. Later on it was sold off and eventually became a very exclusive summer camp for girls. It was about to be repurposed for a much greater cause.

Before Saranac, there were no Young Life camps in the east. To go to summer camps meant for us to travel all the way to Colorado. But Saranac changed all of that, and we were going to be part of it. Jerry Johnson had told us about its purchase and imminent opening that summer. We were all excited because it meant getting our kids to experience summer camp without that long cross country bus trip. Jerry wanted our entire leadership team to help get Saranac opened in time, by taking a busload of us and drive up for a long weekend and become a work force. Road Trip! We loved it. One weekend in the spring, we all piled aboard one of the old blue Brill buses, owned and operated by a Christian man in Baltimore, Bob Kirkley, who was the Pastor of Mt. Washington Methodist Church. These buses were used every summer, all summer to transport kids from the east coast to Colorado for camp.

I don't remember a whole lot about that weekend at Saranac. It was an impressive place, although it needed some work and sprucing up before it would be ready for the loads of kids who were signing up to go that summer. We worked hard and helped to make it happen. But my favorite and craziest memory was the bus ride home, and not for the right reasons at all. In all of Jerry's leadership and mentoring, there were times when, although we loved him dearly, we were just out of control in terms of doing some things he definitely would not approve of. Carol and I were engaged. There were several others who were dating and more would wind up marrying each other. Other couples started pairing up on the ride home and making out in the back of the bus, like it was the Hindenburg on its way to mooring and we were getting in our last flings. Jerry was at the front of the bus. I never really knew how much he was aware, but I knew this: even Stevie Wonder could have seen there was a whole lot of face-sucking going on in back.

By the time Carol and I graduated from UMBC, in June, we had had a pretty amazing last semester together, even more exciting because we were engaged. In lacrosse, I was, in fact, selected as the first-ever All American at UMBC after a strong senior year where, at times, I led the nation in scoring. Carol and so many friends were always on hand, along with my Christian teammates like Tom, Neil, and Jim Cross. Also that spring the craziness at school continued. In fact, radicals managed to get the school closed down towards the end of the semester so that we couldn't complete the last week of classes. But our graduation, the first-ever graduating class, did take place on schedule. A lot of firsts for both Carol and me.

Graduation and Transition

Graduation also meant winding down our respective Young Life Baltimore responsibilities, which, with Jerry's supervision, meant turning over our club leadership responsibilities; Carol with Howard High, and me with Woodlawn. I decided to join the D.C. training program, so that process was underway, along with preparing for a wedding and a move to D.C. On top of all that it meant starting graduate school, a requirement for all Young Life Staff.

Because of the nature of Young Life work, it normally wouldn't be possible for staff who work in the field ministry to attend graduate school at the same time. But Young Life had a program that worked in cooperation with Fuller Theological Seminary, in Pasadena, California. Great school. Lousy football team. Our degrees would be from Fuller, but instead of attending classes out there, Fuller sent professors to a temporary summer "home", just for Young Life Staff. This summer location, the Fountain Valley School, was just outside of Colorado Springs and conveniently located within a few miles of Young Life's Headquarters. The plan was for staff to attend summer classes, taking either one or two, four-week semesters, depending on the extent of staff responsibilities back home and how long people could afford to be out of their areas. It was whole lot easier to leave our local areas during the summer months when clubs did not meet and our schools were on summer break.

For me, back in the summer of 70' (Message for Brian Adams: you were only off by one year, dude.) it meant the month of August would be spent in classes in Colorado, leaving Carol to plan our wedding and prepare for our move to D.C. I'm not sure which of us suffered more during that long month: me, two thousand miles away and missing my fiancé and desperately wanting to be around for all of the upcoming excitement, or Carol for having to deal with the hundreds of details of a wedding and a move out of town without my help. September couldn't arrive soon enough.

Chapter 6

Young Life in Bowie

We got news that Carol and I would be assigned to a new neighborhood in suburban D.C. out in Prince George's County, east of the city. The town was called Bowie. It was a pleasant community developed post-WWII by a huge housing development company called Levitt Homes. Bowie High School was to be the site of our new club, in a town that had never seen Young Life before. Early in July Carol and I made the short 45 minute drive from Baltimore to Bowie, and met the parents that Young Life had recruited who would form the first Young Life adult support group, called the Committee. They turned out to be a wonderful group of Christian parents, but they were as new at being committee members as we were at being on staff. Over the next two years we were to learn a whole lot together, share a lot of joy, and, I'd like to think, make a bit of Young Life history. We met many people, including the Patti's, Don and Jean Grove, Walt and Nancy Pitzenberger and their appointed committee chairman and his wife, Tony and Bette Ketchum.

These folks were not only enthusiastic and motivated, they had the resources to fund the ministry, something I never had to deal with while a volunteer leader in

90

college. Before we even met them they had undertaken the purchase of a home in Bowie, and the plan was to charge us rent, very inexpensively, to help pay the mortgage. That way our housing needs were met right from the start. Carol's Dad was glad to know that. I'm not sure he was all that enthusiastic about his little girl being married to a guy who worked for an outfit that depended on donations for a paycheck. In his mind I'm sure he pictured us eating government cheese and living in a van down by the river.

In the weeks before the wedding Carol and I would drive down and work on our new place, transferring our clothes and some of the furniture we had bought, and also doing some cleaning and painting. We also found some time for licky-face. Has anyone used that expression In the past 30 years? At least we never called it "necking". Ever. By September 20th we were not only ready for our wedding, we were ready to move into our new digs and new place of ministry, right after our honeymoon.

Wedding and Honeymoon

Ah yes, our honeymoon. The question was, where were we go on a honeymoon when we had such a tight budget? I was swiftly learning that God delights in finding ways of surprising us and at the same time using people in the body of Christ to bless each other. I had heard about a man named Francis Gosling. Everyone called him Goose. Get it? Goose? Gosling? He was a bachelor, in his 50's, who devoted a lot of his free time coaching youth soccer. At one point someone told him about Young Life and when he investigated it he liked what he saw. So he recruited a bunch of his soccer players to travel to Frontier Ranch in Colorado, where they heard about Jesus and many of them trusted Christ. Back home Goose started the first Young Life club, which, over time, grew to many clubs, and the hiring of a full time National Director. Goose wasn't an

American. He was a former Olympic diver from the nation of Bermuda.

Goose had a great home in Bermuda, high on a hill that overlooked the Atlantic. He also had a studio apartment that he enjoyed letting friends use for vacations and, in our case, a honeymoon. I wrote to Goose over the summer, introduced ourselves and asked if we might be able to use his apartment for our honeymoon, and he readily agreed. Without Goose it would have been impossible for Carol and me, not to mention a large number of other people, especially Young Life people, to ever enjoy the beauty of Bermuda. We had no idea when we arrived in Bermuda and got to know Goose that we would wind up becoming lifelong friends. I also had no idea that I would be invited back to speak for Young Life weekend camps, that I would take many groups there from Connecticut with Young Life, and that Carol and I would get down there as often as we could afford, to celebrate anniversaries over the years.

Finally September 20th rolled around, the day of our wedding. Carol was a bit anxious about my showing up on time and in one piece. It's not what you think. I had been playing semi-pro football with a team In Baltimore, living out an unfilled dream of playing that sport. Baltimore County had banned high school football for many years. It was finally reinstated but not until the year after I graduated from high school. UMBC didn't have football, so when I got out of college I promised myself I would try to find some place to play, and pro football was out of the question. Well, not for me, but the NFL had these silly standards. Apparently you had to actually be good, or something. The semi-pro team I played for had a game on the morning of our wedding. I played (we won!) and didn't injure myself in the process, and when Carol walked down the aisle she was relieved to see me waiting at the altar.

Young Life: The Adventures of an Ex Staffer

I don't know if there was such a thing as a Young Life wedding, but if there was one, I suppose it would have been ours. Our attendants included Jerry Johnson, Mike Coleman, and Doug Holladay on my side of the altar; and the ladies on Carol's side were: Linda Perrine, who later married Jim Cross, Betsy Sandbower, and Linda Holloway, Doug's girlfriend and our close friend. Tom Pilsch, who had a great voice, sang a solo. (Side note: Years later Tom became Godfather to our second son, Adam. Twenty-nine years after that, Adam asked Tom to also sing in his wedding, and Tom sang the very same song he had sung at our wedding. You'd think he could have learned a new song in all that time.)

While the reception was limited, the wedding itself was open to all friends and relatives. With Carol having run the Howard High Young Life club, and me at Woodlawn, our wedding had about 500 guests, and high school kids easily made up over half of that crowd. Carol's parents hosted a fantastic reception at Baltimore's Martins West, complete with a well-known band called the Admirals. And I had to admit, they were better than either band in which Tom or I had played.

Our honeymoon in Bermuda: yada yada yada, sorry no details. That will be in my sequel, *Fifty Shades of Bermuda*, coming out soon. The week passed all too quickly and before we knew it we were home and living in Bowie, Maryland, ready to start Young Life. But first I had to get acclimated with the Young Life D.C. training program and reunite with my Young Life leader, Chuck. The Young Life offices were on the other side of Washington D.C., and also housed the offices of the Divisional Director, another great man in Young Life who was to have an impact on my life, Tom Raley. The U.S. was divided into three divisions, so Tom was in charge of one third of the country and was also Chuck's boss.

D.C. Training Program

There were four guys in the first year of the training program, one year before I arrived. The only one I knew was Doug Holladay. I soon met the others, every one of them, very sharp. It was impressive to see the quality of the people that Young Life attracted and it was a confirmation that I had made the right decision to join the staff. Skip Ryan was from New England and had just graduated from Harvard. The last two guys came from the Rochester area and had known Chuck when he was working there, Brad Smith, who went to Roberts-Wesleyan College and Greg Kinberg, who attended Rochester Institute of Technology (RIT). Before moving on, it's worth noting that in addition to all of them being great Young Life leaders, all but Greg (who remained on staff) eventually moved on to other careers and all had great ministries. Brad became a pastor, as did Skip. Skip started Trinity Presbyterian in Charlottesville, Virginia and later was called to Park Cities Presbyterian in Dallas, which was one of the largest PCA churches in the country.

Doug went on to do so many things it would take a whole chapter just to cover his accomplishments. He was the one who got me involved with Doug Coe and The Fellowship, a group of Christians who had (and still has) an incredible ministry with politicians on Capitol Hill. They also sponsored the annual Presidential Prayer Breakfast, among other great ventures. At one point Doug actually worked in the White House where he was Under Assistant to the Secretary of Education, and worked in mediation for South Africa as a "Special Ambassador." Yes, Doug was a rare breed and an amazing guy. I felt privileged to be a friend. Lastly, Greg Kinberg wound up staying in Young Life for his entire career. After the training program he moved to North Carolina, and advanced from an Area Director to a Regional Director and eventually became a Divisional Director. In later years he moved to Colorado Springs where, among other positions, he served as a special assistant to the President, Denny Rydberg, and was Young Life's first Chief Operating Officer. At the time of his retirement he had been the longest actively serving Young Life Staff person in the country. Yes, these were all pretty amazing young men.

My class of recruits also had some pretty impressive guys, and like Doug's group, we were all pretty much diamonds in the rough at that point. Only time would tell how and where we would all wind up. There were nine of us altogether. When I was reunited with my friend I mentioned earlier, Bo White, I knew that no matter what, we were going to be having some fun. Dave "Tuck" Knupp, like Brad and Greg the year before, was down from the Rochester Area, Tuck had been in Chuck's Young Life club in that city, and arrived in D.C. via Duke University where he had completed his undergraduate work. The others were: Don Lemons, Bill Reardon, Steve Oliver, George Kennedy, Ray Steckman (my high school buddy) and Gary Treichler. I haven't done as well keeping in touch with the careers of all these guys, but to my defense, I had been doing a lot of weed. Just kidding! Sheesh, lighten up Francis.

Gary and his wife Kim were on staff for many years and later served in church ministry. They were to remain lifelong friends and our paths crossed many times, including a number of years when they lived close to us in South Florida. Steve Oliver came to D.C. from University of North Carolina, a year behind Doug. Steve bypassed medical school to come into the training program. He wound up serving on staff for many years in Hingham, Massachusetts, and later went into finance, becoming a very successful financial manager.

Don Lemons was a graduate of University of Virginia. After serving in Young Life for a number of years he went into law, eventually becoming a circuit court judge. Today he is the Chief Justice of the Supreme Court of

Virginia. Tuck Knupp served Young Life for most of his career in many capacities in Virginia. He and his wife, Cindy, were in Prince George's County during the training program, and therefore close to us. In more recent years Tuck has gone into church ministry and is currently the pastor of Swift Creek Presbyterian Church in the Richmond area. We don't see them as often anymore but we've remained friends over all these years. And last but not least was my buddy, Bo White. Telling his stories would take another chapter alongside those of Doug Holladay.

The third year class of the training program saw the entry of even more talent, not to mention guys who were very special to me. Among them were Tom Pilsch and Mike Coleman.

Bo White

Bo and I had lost contact with each other for a few years, and only re-connected during the month in Colorado at seminary just before Carol and I got married. Being out there alone afforded me the opportunity to do some serious hanging out with Bo. It was good seeing him again after the time apart. Initially I was surprised by his serious demeanor. He had had an interesting few years. After going to college in the Rochester, New York area, (so he could continue to work with Chuck Reinhold,) he got a position traveling overseas with the great Methodist missionary E. Stanley Jones. Coincidentally the little Methodist church in Baltimore that I grew up in (and eventually avoided as best I could) was the very same church in which Jones grew up; Memorial Methodist Church. I remember as a youngster, once a year a famous man would come and preach. I remembered that he was really exciting to listen to. Only much later did I really learn about E. Stanley Jones.

I don't know if it was the missionary work he had done, or being in the academic atmosphere of seminary, but Bo just seemed very "un-Bo" like. It soon became my mission to find the Bo I had known before. I saw myself like Tinker Bell (not with the leotards) trying to get Peter Panning to remember when he was Peter Pan. It didn't take long. It's time for a Bo White story!

One of Bo's favorite styles of comedy was "pull your leg" humor. I enjoyed it most when I wasn't on the receiving end of one of his tricks, but even when I was, it was like a compliment to get pranked by Bo.

One evening at seminary, Tuck Knupp asked Bo if he would like to go into town for the evening. Unlike most of us, Tuck had a car with him, so Bo said yes and he and Tuck took off. One of Bo's favorite pranks was to station someone (on this night he persuaded Tuck), on a crowded street corner. Bo would walk up, pretending to be a plain clothes policeman. He would flash his wallet as if it was a badge, and then proceed to pat down his suspect, lean him against the car, and eventually push him into the car and speed away. While this was taking place people would gather and watch, assuming they were witnesses to an arrest. It never bothered Bo that he didn't go back and tell people. For him, the fun was pulling peoples' legs. He and Tuck just drove off and laughed about it.

Eventually they got back to the seminary. Tuck went to his room and Bo came and found me. He quickly told me what had happened, then said, "Bondo, I have to use your phone." I knew right away Tuck was in trouble. He called over to the dorm where Tuck was living, knowing in all likelihood at that time of night that Tuck would be answering the phone. Tuck did answer, and in a very official voice Bo said, "I am looking for the owner of the car with the license plate (and gave Tuck's plate number). Tuck replied, "That's my car." Bo: "Are you David Knupp?" Tuck: "Why yes I am. Why?" Bo: "This is the Colorado State Police. Were you driving your car tonight in Colorado Springs? (Yes) Where are you located right now?" I could almost see the blood draining from Tuck's face. Tuck gave him the address and Bo ended the call with, "Stay right there. We're on our way," and hung up.

Now, most "normal" people would go tell Tuck what they had just done, and everyone would have a laugh. Not Bo White. He just looked at me with a sly grin and picked up the phone again. His next call was to the Colorado State Police. "Hi, I'm sorry to bother you, but I'd like to report a trespasser. I think he's gone but it's been kind of scary. I'm over here at the seminary and was wondering if you would mind just sending a police car to the campus. Everyone is jittery and I think it would help if you just drove through...Fine, I'll come meet you when you get here."

When he hung up, he looked at his watch and said to me, "Another few minutes and Tuck should be here." Sure enough, a few minutes later Tuck came busting in, out of breath and scared, and told Bo about the phone call, completely convinced that it was triggered by their police impersonation earlier that night. It didn't matter that Bo had been the one pretending to be the cop back in town, of course. The only connection the police could possibly have was through the license plate number, and that was on Tuck's car, not Bo's.

The masterful part of Bo's humor is that he could be so believable. I sat there in wonderment while Bo listened to Tuck and acted completely innocent of the entire scam. He even sympathized with Tuck and tried to calm him down.

Bo wasn't finished. Trying to judge when the police would actually show up, Bo suggested that they walk down to the main entrance of the seminary and then just confess what they had done, offering to Tuck,

"Since it had been my idea all along, I will take the heat from the police." So, off we went to the main entrance to wait for the police to arrive.

By this time of the evening a lot of other people were returning from a night out, and word soon passed that the police were on their way. Sure enough, not one but two State Police patrol cars drove up the main road and into the entrance. People stopped to watch, and I could tell that Tuck's legs were getting wobbly. At that point Bo turned to Tuck and said, "Tuck, just stay here. Let me go speak with them. I'll take care of it." Tuck was only too happy if Bo could somehow extricate them from this frightening police encounter. Bo calmly walked out to the two cruisers.

It was too far away to hear what he said, but Tuck and I, and a gathering crowd of students all stood by and watched. Later, I asked Bo what he had told the police. It went something like this: "Officers, thank you so much for driving by. By now the trespasser is long gone, but just by coming by here, I know everyone appreciates your presence. I've been asking around and things are pretty calm now. If we hear of anything more I'll call you right away." Apparently the police bought his story and before long they made a U turn and were on their way.

Bo walked back to Tuck and me and the rest of the crowd. Besides Bo, I was the only one who knew the real story. But by now virtually everyone had heard Tuck's version of the story, and were expecting Tuck, or Bo, or both of them to get arrested; and were relieved to see the police cars turn and drive off. Bo never made a big announcement. He just pulled Tuck aside while I waited. It was absolutely priceless watching Tuck's face. I just told everyone who was straining to hear what Bo was saying to wait and watch Tuck. Very soon the cry came, "Bo! I can't believe you did that to me! You are absolutely crazy!" The real story passed quickly. By the next day it was the buzz of the seminary. Bo was an instant celebrity, although that wasn't even remotely why he did it. It wasn't Bo's style. Interestingly, Tuck was a bit of a celebrity too. Welcome to the world of being friends with Bo White.

Back in D.C.

Back in the D.C. training program Chuck turned out to be quite the taskmaster. His background in competitive sports, i.e., football at Pitt, gave him that competitive desire and it carried over into how he trained us. I should actually have seen this coming. Back in my high school days, before he left for Rochester, he used to run a special discipleship group that was open to kids who wanted more in-depth teaching than was offered in the weekly Campaigners Bible study. He held us to a rigorous standard. One of our assignments was to memorize a Bible verse each week. If you showed up without a Bible verse ready to recite, you were in trouble. A private joke among us students was asking each other, "What's your verse this week?" and the stock answer, rather than get Chuck on our backs, was "John 11:35." As you may know, that's the shortest verse in the Bible, "Jesus wept."

Chuck's training regime in D.C. was much more strenuous than that. And it wasn't always learning about the X's and O's of doing Young Life. One of the biggest influences in Chuck's life had been the ministry known as Navigators. We all came to appreciate that great ministry as Chuck enthusiastically would incorporate some of the Navigators best discipleship material into our training. Chuck was hard on us, but we loved the guy and had total respect for him.

Then there were the touch football games. For a break after lunch when the weather cooperated Chuck managed to make time for a bit of friendly touch football among all of us trainees. By this time everyone was aware of Chuck's athletic prowess and his success at Pitt. I also learned that he played on the same team with a guy who would become a legendary player and coach, Pro Football Hall of Famer Mike Ditka. Being a competitive guy myself, I always wanted to be on the team that played against Chuck. After all, I had just graduated as an All American. UMBC lacrosse was not exactly Pitt football, but it was not too shabby either. Also, I'd been blessed with speed and quickness; and in lacrosse, as well as most any sport, that can be a great advantage.

But the first time I lined up opposite Charles Emerson Reinhold, I was in for a surprise. I had never seen quickness like that. I had never seen a human being elude three and four guys at a time while running a ball, all in the space of a few yards. Forget tackling him. It was touch football. To stop him all we had to do was just touch him, with one hand! And more often than not, we couldn't even do that. He already had my admiration and respect on a spiritual level, but he quickly earned my respect also as an athlete. It's a guy-thing.

Settling In, in Bowie

Meanwhile, back on the home front, Carol and I were beginning to settle in as newlyweds into our new home. The house that the committee purchased was absolutely lovely, and huge; four bedrooms, two baths, a full garage. It was bigger than the house I grew up in. Carol was the perfect homemaker, transforming our house into a home with all of her personal touches. But keep in mind, she wasn't just a pretty face. I was moving in and setting up shop with one of the most talented Young Life leaders from the Baltimore leadership. Plus, I thought she made a wise choice in not bringing all of her books on Scientology. We really looked forward to getting started.

It wasn't long before we located the high school and started "contact work," Young Life's term for exactly how I described my observations of what Chuck was doing at Woodlawn High School back in the first chapter. Except it wasn't Chuck from Pittsburgh doing this in Baltimore. It was Carol and me from Baltimore, doing it in Bowie. Also, this was in the fall of 1970, long before the fiasco of the early 80's when the when the Establishment Clause and the Free Exercise Clause in the US Constitution were diabolically reinterpreted to create a strict separation of church and state. That spelled the end of Young Life leaders' access to many schools. Don't get me started. But at Bowie High school we made our way to the administration and let them know why we would be around, and that we wouldn't be high profile or interfere in anyway. We were welcomed with open arms. How times have changed.

For anyone who knows Young Life and contact work, it's an ongoing process. Back then very few people or Christian organizations really understood what we were doing. And hardly anyone we told, even if they were interested, wouldn't have the patience to continually go back to a high school, day after day, week after week, and month after month. Once I tried to explain contact work to a youth pastor. After a while he reluctantly said that if he really worked on his schedule he might be able to squeeze in a visit to the high school about once a month. Others also couldn't understand that we were not there to recruit kids to our youth group. And if we weren't doing that, they would see the hours upon hours of time used as inefficient at best, or a complete waste of time at worst. But it had been the same foundation back at Brooklyn Park and Woodlawn. Contact work was vital there and we had confidence it would be fruitful in Bowie. Inefficient maybe. Effective definitely.

At that time most Young Life leaders were people who had been the recipients of the benefits of contact work when they were high schoolers. They received unconditional love by adults who had stepped out of their own comfort zones and wandered into the sub culture of young people. They were Young Life leaders who had no agenda other than to be a friend, with "no strings attached"; non-judgmental and focused on reaching out and initiating with high school kids. Carol was one of the few exceptions. She never did have that experience when she was in high school. But she understood all of it at the deepest level, which is one of the things that made me so proud of her.

Up until we got to Bowie, Carol and I had always worked separately. We were about to combine our forces: Stanley and Livingston, Lennon and McCartney, Batman and Robin, Bert and Ernie, Abercrombie and Fitch, DiMaggio and Monroe, Anne Boleyn and King Henry... opps, maybe not.

In the first few days we began to meet kids. The first girl we met was named Jill Rothgeb. A "Where are they now?" comment: 45 years later, we're still friends with Jill, and still try to see her when we return to Baltimore, where she and her husband live not far from my brother, Jack. We met Martine Mundy and Cindy Slepitza, who were also to eventually have a part in our future, even beyond Young Life. We met Candy Collins, Tom Mulrenin, Vicky Kinney, Joey Palumbo, Jimmy Green, Bob Dalton, Ronnie Plummer and so many other great kids also.

I eventually made my way to the football field. I had introduced myself to the coach so he didn't think I was spying on his practices or selling steroids. I got hold of a roster and began memorizing names at home. I met Tommy McMahon, and Terry Terrell and his brother Brett. I met Jim Bachelor, Jim Critchfield and a whole bunch of other guys. I'd talk with them at practice, and eventually would see them at their games. At first they wondered, as kids do and as I did when I first met Chuck, "Why is this guy hanging around?" I just gave them a fairly innocuous explanation; that Carol and I were new in town and were eventually going "to do some youth programs," and just wanted to meet people. My explanation seemed to be accepted, and over time they stopped wondering and we slowly became friends.

One day Carol and I were sitting at one of the football games. We noticed that one of the cheerleaders seemed to be particularly friendly to everyone, and had even given us some eye contact. During halftime we decided to see if we could meet her. It wasn't difficult to start a conversation. Her name was Kathie Epstein. She was not only a very popular kid, but as soon as she got wind that we wanted to meet kids, she would take it upon herself to march us up to friend after friend to, "Meet my new friends, Dick and Carol Bond. They're new to town and are really cool people!" I can't tell you how many kids Kathie introduced to us in those first few months. She was amazing. "Where are they now?" You'll know Kathie Epstein as Kathie Lee Gifford. One and the same, and we have remained friends all these years. She now lives in the same town where we used to live in Connecticut, and whenever we go back, we catch up with her. Kathie's parents, Joan and Eppie, became not only committee members and great friends, they were one of the first married couples who were role models for Carol and me. They were committed Christians, and loved us and opened their home to us. Kathie's sister, Michie, was two years younger than Kathie and also got very involved in Young Life. We had missed their older brother Dave, who had graduated before we moved to Bowie. But eventually we got to know him when he was home from college.

We did contact work almost daily in one form or another, from just walking around the halls around dismissal time, to watching team practices and games, to even chaperoning events like dances and football after-parties, something which ingratiated us to the people on the faculty whose job it was to maintain a healthy supply of volunteer adult and parent chaperones. We began at Bowie at the end of September, and by early December we had befriended enough kids that we could begin to tell them about this new club we wanted to start. Because we were friends and they trusted us, it was all very natural and organic, and not in the least bit contrived. Anyone reading this who knows Young Life understands exactly what I'm talking about. For anyone else, please know that what I'm describing has worked in thousands of high schools and towns and cities in all corners of the country and around the world.

We began to take kids to Chuck's club at nearby DuVal High School, to give them a sense of what we had in mind, and also to expose them to other high school kids who were friendly and interested in spreading the excitement and fun. Like me at the first club I attended, the Bowie kids had very little idea what they were getting themselves into. But they trusted Carol and me, and it was fun.

When I stop to think about it, taking kids to Chuck's club was a bit of a mind-bender for me. Here I was in a whole new city, taking kids to see a Young Life club for the first time, and the club was being run by the same guy who was there at my high school and the first club I ever saw, just a few years earlier when I was in high school. How cool is that?

Our First Bowie Club

After a few weeks of driving over to Chuck's club, Carol and I casually started asking our kids what they would think about Bowie having its own club. By then enough of them were sold on the idea and it was just a matter of putting together the logistics. One of them volunteered their home. We spread the word. We had songbooks, and the kids we had been taking to club even knew some of the songs. And by then we were using guitars and singing a lot of popular songs in addition to some of the ones we used to sing when I was in high school. We had skits prepared and I had my talk ready to go.

The big night finally arrived. Our committee people all knew about it and were praying for us. We were about as ready as we could be. About 30 kids showed up. Even though it was a lot smaller than what Carol and I were used to in our senior year in college, we had anticipated that. In this case it was beginning from scratch, much like Brooklyn Park HS back in my sophomore year of college. In fact, it felt very much like that beginning. Kids were all excited and the night came off well.

Jerry Johnson once said, "The main goal of that first club is to get kids to come back for the second club." Jerry was full of little gems of wisdom like that. But return, they did. All of the people I've mentioned before, and a whole lot more. Within a few short months club was approaching 100 kids each week. If the phrase had been used then, I would have said it "went viral". It became the place to be and the thing to do on Wednesday nights if you went to Bowie High School. Another Jerry Johnson saying: "You know you've made it when kids go from saying, 'Where is everyone?' to 'Man, everyone is here!'"

Pretty soon we outgrew kids' homes and found a local church that met in a former model home, right on the main street running through Bowie and almost across the street from the high school. It looked exactly like the home it started out to be, but once inside you could see that the back wall was extended. We could easily fit over 200 kids in that room, and by our second year in Bowie the club at times approached 250 kids. One night, the Pastor of the church stopped by to see club. I held my breath. His lovely church had been transformed into a setting that looked like a mob of shoppers on Black Friday at Macy's. Part of his beautiful little altar had been transformed into a Laugh-In wall. I said to Carol, "I'm afraid to look. Is he laughing?"

Our own home also became one of their hang outs, and it wasn't unusual to have kids over anytime day or night. I had one of those Bobby Hull table hockey sets and guys would come over and we'd beat up on that thing for hours on end. The girls and Carol would do, I don't know, whatever it was that girls did. For Carol and me it was a dream come true. Ministry, relationships, and a great committee of adults supporting us both financially and spiritually.

Chuck continued to train and challenge us. The other staff guys, scattered all around the D.C. area, were experiencing similar success in their own ministries. We joined together for all-county clubs, fall and spring weekend camps, and summer camps. The training program was intended to be for two years, so the older guys, Doug, Skip, Greg and Brad were, by their second year, already looking to be shipped out to start Young Life areas around the eastern part of the country. But all during our first year they were very visible and available to our group, and provided some great role modeling and encouragement to us slightly younger guys.

Some Sunday Afternoons

Sometimes Tom Raley would host Sunday afternoon gatherings for committee and donors at his large home in the D.C. suburb of McLean, Virginia. All of us in the training program were required to attend, something that wasn't one of my favorite pastimes, especially in the fall when, for me, Sunday afternoons were football-on-TV times. I never had a great attitude about putting on a jacket and tie and driving cross town.

At one particular gathering I was bored but also feeling a bit roguish. "Let's see what kind of trouble I can get into." I looked around and spotted the back of Greg Kinberg's head. He was standing with a few donors and talking animatedly. I thought, "Isn't that just like Greg, doing just what Tom wants all of us to do." Greg was actually a really good guy, but I wasn't in the mood. I decide to knock down Greg's enthusiasm a peg, and embarrass him for being so darn polite and proper. So I very casually moved over behind him and gave him a very soft "goose."

If you don't know what a goose is, I would say stop right now and Google it. It should pop up under the urban dictionary. But please do not do that. I don't know exactly when or how the definition changed, but back in our day goosing was no more than poking someone in the butt with your finger. I know, very mature. But I wanted to make Greg jump and be embarrassed. The problem was, when I goosed him, he didn't respond at all. In fact, he didn't miss a beat. He just kept politely talking to those people. So, I waited a few minutes, came around and goosed him again, this time a little harder. Still absolutely nothing! All the fun in goosing someone was seeing their shock of surprise, and Greg wasn't reacting. By that time he really had me aggravated. I wasn't going to quit until I got a jump, or a yell, or something.

I waited a few more minutes, circling out of his peripheral vision in case he could see me coming and clench his butt cheeks. And then the last time I tried, it was so hard that I'm pretty sure I saw his heels slightly lift off the ground. That did it! He didn't yell, but he stopped talking, and very slowly turned around and as he started to face me...I am telling you the God's truth here...with a stab of absolute panic I suddenly realized...it was NOT Greg Kinberg! It looked just like him from behind, but when he turned, I saw a young man who I had never laid eyes on before. And he glared at me with such a malevolent look; as the saying goes, if looks could kill I would have been a dead man right then and there. And I don't care what anyone says, there's no coming back from that. There was absolutely nothing I could say to even begin in some small way to rectify what happened or to justify my actions. I started..."You aren't Gre!...I thought you were someone el..." I just stopped mid-sentence and slid away.

I never learned who he really was. I never saw him nor wanted to see him again. I found Bo shortly afterwards, who shared my dislike for Tom's Sunday parties, and pulled him aside to tell him what I had just done. Bo didn't miss the opportunity. He smiled and said to me. "I got you Bondo. I spent two hours dressing that guy up to look like Kinberg!"

Summer Assignments

During our first summer in Bowie I was very fortunate to receive one of most the prized assignments available. I was asked to be on staff for one month at one of the Young Life camps. Barely anyone my age and with such little experience was asked to take a camp assignment back in those days. First of all there weren't even that many camps. Secondly, the assignment spots were almost always filled by seasoned veterans. However, because Young Life had just recently opened Saranac, there was a shortage of personnel. Not only that, there was an opening for one of the most prestigious assignments at camp, the Program Director. That position usually took years to get. Short of being the camp speaker that was the job requiring the most skill and experience. It also was the most demanding job at camp. I mentioned earlier that I met Jay Grimstead, who was the Program Director at Frontier Ranch when I was on Work Crew. I was going to have his job, at Saranac.

Remember my high school friend and mentor, Newt Hetrick? Newt had graduated from college and had gone on staff in suburban Baltimore, actually opening an entirely new area in Anne Arundel County under Jerry Johnson's supervision. By then Newt had married Claire Nethen, who had been in Baltimore Young Life a few years behind us at Milford Mill High School. Even though

Newt and Claire were associated with Baltimore Young Life and Carol and I were attached to D.C., because our counties bordered each other, it was convenient and fun for the four of us to get together pretty often.

Like me, Newt loved the challenge of running a camp program. His only experience, also like me, was at weekend camps. Neither he nor I had the kind of raw talent that a guy like Doug Holladay had. Very few people did. Doug already had been assigned for one month at Saranac. Newt was not only funny, he was a great planner and organizer. So Young Life decided to have the two of us run the program together, a strategy that I hadn't heard used before. We loved the challenge. We were combining our talents, like Starsky and Hutch, Turner and Hooch, Calvin and Hobbs, or Han and Chewbacca. I was Han.

When we arrived at Saranac we met the rest of the team, all prepared for their various responsibilities. Newt and I had already spent months in preparation for all of the various program events for which we would be responsible. We may as well have said, "Goodbye, Carol and Claire." About the only time we weren't working, day or night, was for a few hours on the afternoon of day six. And because this was our first assignment we were always playing catch up. But we absolutely loved what we were doing. It was like being in a movie, a Broadway play, in the best lacrosse game ever, and a huge non-stop Young Life club, all rolled into one. Day seven would end with the buses of kids pulling out of camp in the morning, and by 3 o'clock in the afternoon the next group of campers was arriving. Four straight weeks, 28 straight days. 250 kids each week.

For a whole month we didn't even know what day of the week it was. Our life was, "Day One, Day Two" and so on. At least no one ever said to us, "Somebody's got case of the Mondays." Newt and I loved working together and had great chemistry. We didn't know it at the time, but that was to be our last program assignment together. In the years to follow, we each got our own assignments as Program Directors, each with our own assistants. Our timing couldn't have been better, because the window for program assignments had only opened briefly, and then the positions over the next few years were again filled. Aspiring Program Directors had to again wait their turns. But by then Newt and I had experience and seniority.

We had a great fall season when we got back to Bowie after our summer camp work. By springtime of our second year, club was huge and very exciting. Everything Carol and I were doing in Young Life was fulfilling but very time consuming. We didn't have a whole lot of time for personal things. But I did make one big exception. I wanted to continue to play lacrosse.

Chuck's Got My Six

For those unfamiliar with lacrosse especially back the 70's, for most college players their lacrosse careers ended at graduation. But for those good enough or lucky enough, there was the possibility of playing for one of the top Club Lacrosse teams. There was no professional field lacrosse like today. But there were plenty of club lacrosse associations and leagues. The very top league, somewhat like the Premier League for soccer in England, was where the best players in the country got to play. After graduation I was fortunate enough to be recruited by one of those top teams, called Carling Lacrosse Club, sponsored by Carling Brewery, back in Baltimore.

By national standards UMBC, my alma mater, was a small program; certainly not like the traditional national powerhouse teams. So, even though I was an All American, I was sometimes referred to as a "big fish in a little pond" because I hadn't really competed at the top level in college. When I was recruited by the Carling Club, I was eager to prove myself at the highest echelon of the sport. So it was with the greatest sense of satisfaction at the end of my rookie year, I was the top scorer and named the Most Valuable Player in the nation. In addition, our team made it to the semi-finals of the National Championship. In my second year we won the whole thing. It was such fun, and in Baltimore in those days our games were covered in the news-papers almost as much as the Orioles and the Baltimore Colts. So we were minor celebrities too.

In my second year in Bowie, during the springtime, which is lacrosse season, a very powerful National Lacrosse Team from Australia was on tour in America. By the third week of their tour my team, Carling, was scheduled to play them. In the first two weeks the Aussies beat every team they played, from the top college teams in the country to the top USCLA Club teams. The more they won and the closer they got to their date with us, the pressure mounted. Was anyone capable of beating these guys?

The week before our scheduled game it was decided that the game would be moved to a bigger venue, anticipating the crowds. Fun! But they also changed the date to Wednesday night. Not fun! That was our club night. I could not miss that game. There was so much hype and press, and my teammates would have lynched me if I wasn't there. But neither could I miss club. I was between the proverbial rock and a hard place.

The one guy who really understood my predicament was also my boss. I've mentioned before how much people loved and respected Chuck. What he did for me that week was quite possibly the best expression of caring I ever experienced from him since I left high school. He said to me, "Dick, you can't miss that game. I'll cover your back and come over and run club for you." My boss was giving me permission to miss the most important part of my job. Not only that, he was offering to take my place so I could do something that had nothing to do with Young Life. He understood. He cared. And oh, by the way, the only game where the Aussies were defeated in America was against Carling Lacrosse Club that Wednesday night.

Leaving the Nest

Near the end of the second year in Bowie, like everyone else in the training program, we were looking, praying and wondering where we would go next. Tom Raley had been anticipating our moving on as part of Young Life's expansion and growth plan. He had places in mind for each of us to consider. The first place we looked was out in Suffolk County on Long Island. Although it didn't work out, we did meet the couple who wanted to sponsor our move, and they wound up later becoming lifelong friends; Shelley and Mary Ellen Ivey.

Our next stop was in upstate New York in a small town called Kingston. We met a lovely group of parents who had already formed a committee, and they even showed us a nice home that was available. But at the end of the day there just wasn't a sense from Carol and me that we should be there. Then, almost as an afterthought, Tom Raley told us that since we were in that part of the northeast, maybe we should have a look at Greenwich, Connecticut. Because of my high school experience in Greenwich, I was immediately interested.

When we got to town we were met by the very same Jack Carpenter who had invited me to come to his area seven years before. Carol and I felt almost right away that this was the place where God wanted us to be. I'm not sure how Jack felt, but he was the same warm and friendly guy I had met when in high school, and I was glad for Carol to get to meet him. We stayed with the committee chairman and his wife, Bart and Joan Swift. We also interviewed with another committee couple while we were there, George and Pam Klein. They were to become very close friends in the years ahead. George was a guidance counselor at the high school. And we still see them from time to time when we visit Greenwich.

I don't recall any deep and labored discussion or prolonged praying about whether to go to Greenwich or not. It felt good having visited. On the other hand we didn't come away dancing like Carlton either. But it just felt right from the very beginning. When we got back to Bowie we called Jack and said that if he'd have us, we would like to come. We began to make our plans to move. In neither Carol nor my families, immediate and extended, had anyone ever left Baltimore that we could recall. Moving to Bowie was a big step for Carol and me. The thought of moving to Connecticut felt like we were about to move to Mars. I don't know whether it was just our family, but I always had the sense that Baltimore people enjoyed staying in Baltimore, and didn't move away as much as people from other cities. At any rate, we were leaving the Baltimore/Washington area and everything that was familiar. Looking back it doesn't seem like that big of a stretch, but back then it was an enormous step for us.

In the process of moving it meant saying our goodbyes and bringing closure to many relationships: friends, leaders, committee, and of course, the kids. I'm not sure if our leaving was harder on the kids or on us. I never forgot how unprepared I was for leaving Frontier Ranch at the end of Work Crew. I believed, and still believe that there are three things we can easily take for granted as leaders in Young Life, and we never should: intimacy, confession, and separation. At Frontier, the staff had no problem saying their goodbyes to each other. I later wished some of them had helped me with that closure, or separation. They were used to the "mountain top" experiences and coming down the mountain because they had done it often before. But for me it was new and it was frightening.

Regarding intimacy; with kids, over time we experienced

a kind of spiritual intimacy with a lot of them. But we should always keep in mind that many of them have never been as open spiritually, and maybe even emotionally, as they are with their Young Life leaders. We need to be very careful with other people's feelings. And the same also applies to confession. Any Young Life leader I know could tell story after story of kids who have opened parts of their lives that for them were shameful, and were able to confess. Just because we've heard it many times from many kids, we must never take it for granted. Rather, we have to remind ourselves that for some kids, they've never opened up to an adult like that in their lives.

While I'm on my Dennis Miller-ish rant, I'll add just one more point. Being involved with people relationally and incarnationally sometimes translates into "getting our hands dirty in their lives." That is, we sometimes found ourselves involved with the messy, the dysfunctional, the embarrassing, or the depressing parts of a kid's life. Now and then we may have been involved in counseling situations related to family crises, or abuse, or dependency issues. Occasionally some of us were called to hospitals, police stations, and sadly, funeral homes. It's the price we paid for where God had placed us.

That was a little mini-sermon, but my point is that bringing closure to our dear friends, both adults and students, in Bowie, was important to us. We spent a lot of time and energy to give people the opportunity to say goodbye to us, and us to them. Some we would see in the future, and we would get back to Bowie to visit with them. Our friends Martine and Cindy were going with us, and I don't mind admitting, that really helped Carol and me, not only with our own feelings of separation but also with our impending move to Mars. With them, we got to take a little bit of Bowie with us. They had just graduated from Bowie HS, and had the enthusiastic support of their parents to take a year off and live and work with us in Greenwich.

We were also naturally concerned about the Bowie club carrying on after we left. When any leader starts a club from scratch, it's as if it's his or her "own baby." There is a deep sense of ownership, and a desire to see it continue effectively once the leader leaves. Certainly Carol and I felt like that about Bowie. Fortunately Young Life had a plan and a person. A man named Lee Patkus did a great job taking over for us for one year. After that, another young and talented guy was scheduled to take over for Lee. We hadn't met him before, but we heard good things about him. His name was Lee Corder. And from all reports, he also did a fantastic job and the ministry in Bowie continued to flourish under his leadership. His only shortcoming was that he was considerably taller than me, but other than that he checked all of my other boxes.

Where are they now, you ask? Anyone even remotely connected with Young Life knows that Lee Corder, like Greg Kinberg, went on to be an Area Director, then a Regional Director and then one of the Senior Vice Presidents for Young Life. In more recent years he has overseen the Northern Division of the international arm of the ministry. His resume is impressive to say the least. He also married one of Doug Coe's daughters, who by then had become friends with Carol and me, Paula Coe. Paula was (and is) every bit the talent that Lee became. And we're happy to say, although we no longer get to see them often, we still do connect from time to time, and still consider them great friends.

In the summer of 1972 I once again was enrolled in Young Life's seminary program in Colorado Springs. This time, however, I was able to have Carol with me. We spent a great month, me studying, and both of us having close fellowship with staff from all over the country. What was very much on our minds was getting back to Bowie, packing up and moving to Connecticut.

Look out Greenwich, here we come! I got a fever, and the only prescription is more Cowbell!

Part Two

Connecticut

Chapter 7

New State, New Beginning

The moving van arrived in Greenwich with all of our worldly possessions in September of 1972. Bob and Bonnie Caie had been the staff representatives who ran Greenwich Young Life at the time. Prior to our arrival they moved from Greenwich to nearby Mt. Kisco, New York, just across the state line from Connecticut. We were filling the vacancy they created. We were also filling the vacancy in the house they had been renting. One of Greenwich's committee members, Mary Jackson, had a large property which included the main house, a carriage house, and a third, guest house. Bob and Bonnie moved out of the guest house to make room for us. If they tell you we kicked them out don't believe them. When we arrived, I felt sorry for the movers because the house was located on the side of a hill and access was only via some very long and very old stone steps. Hey, better them than me, right? But there was plenty of room inside for Carol and me and for our new house mates. Martine and Cindy had graduated from Bowie High (taking a year off) and were ready to come live with us in Connecticut.

The local committee had been active for a long time. That's not code for saying they were old. They weren't.

Ok some of them were. Jack Carpenter had originally run the club in Greenwich, and a few years before we arrived he had handed it over to Bob and Bonnie. However, as they had already transitioned up to Mt. Kisco, there weren't many kids around. It was almost as if we would be starting again from scratch. At least Carol and I had experience with that just two years before, when we moved to Bowie.

The first several days were used to move in and get acclimated to our new home and new surroundings. Greenwich is a beautiful town, with tree lined streets and manicured lawns. Mary Jackson's property was located in what was referred to as, "back country" or "back Greenwich," far away from town and the beaches on the Long Island Sound. Back country also had a lot of four- acre zoning on which stood some of the biggest mansions we'd ever seen, Mary's being one of them. It didn't take us long to realize that there was a lot of wealth there. Everything was so different from our past. It definitely felt like New England, or as we had imagined it. We were glad to have Cindy and Martine with us to share our new experiences.

Greenwich High School was located close to town. It was nearly brand new, designed by a California architect and had an open, airy feel to it. It really was a beautiful school. The first student we met had heard about us from Bob and Bonnie and he came out to our house to introduce himself, Tim Ficker. Tim was an incoming sophomore. Like the schools in Maryland at the time, Greenwich High was just three grades: 10th through 12th. It didn't take us long to start contact work. Tim would eventually become a key person in getting us introduced to a whole lot of other kids. But at this point, as an incoming sophomore he felt about as new as we did to the high school. Fortunately, as with Bowie, the vital people in the administration welcomed us. Moving slowly and with inconspicuous style, in a very short time we became part of the landscape at Greenwich H.S.

Carol waited at least six months before offering to volunteer giving pole dance lessons for the faculty.

As with Bowie, we found as many ways as possible to be in and around the school and to get to know kids. Some would say that kids are pretty much the same anywhere you go. I guess on some levels that's true. But the more we got to know students, we began to see some subtle differences; nothing earth shattering, but some variations. Oddly though, they all had a third eye right in the middle of their foreheads. But seriously, over time we learned that the differences were far more substantial than we ever could have imagined. That took time, and the learning curve was steep. Martine and Cindy were able to get part-time jobs to help with their expenses. No freeloaders in our house. They did some contact work with us, but, being just out of high school themselves, we weren't in too much of a hurry to drop them into the deep end of the contact work swimming pool.

Another important piece of news about us, which we already knew but we started sharing with our new Connecticut friends, was that Carol arrived in Greenwich with a "bun in the oven," pregnant with our first son and due in April. Of course this was very exciting for Carol and me, and Martine and Cindy got caught up in our enthusiasm. They even helped us decorate a new baby's room upstairs.

One of my fondest memories during Carol's pregnancy was definitely not her fondest memory. But it's notable to me because of what it said about Carol's character. It probably also gives a clue to my own warped sense of what constitutes someone's character. Carol had terrible morning sickness. In fact, sometimes it wasn't only in the morning. The further she got along in her pregnancy and the more her tummy showed, she let neither her stomach nor her sickness slow down her commitment to doing contact work. One day we were at a football game at Brien McMahon high school in nearby Norwalk. We had just arrived and were walking with some of the students we knew. Suddenly Carol excused herself and walked over behind a tree and promptly threw up. Then without missing a beat, she calmly pulled a Kleenex out of her pocket, wiped her mouth and re-joined the group. That's my wife, folks. As of this writing, forty-five years of marriage and still going. She's not throwing up behind trees as often, thankfully.

The Young Life office was in Stamford, the town next door. Jack was the Area Director and there were a few other guys like me who were working under Jack; the difference being that they were home-grown boys. Craig Simpson ran a club in Wilton. Paul Cowras was in Pleasantville, New York, just across the Connecticut border, and Bob Caie was in Mt. Kisco. Barbara Watt was Jack's assistant. Co Koppert, the lady I met when I was in Greenwich back in High school, had married and left staff. But she still lived in the area. In the future Co and I would become a great friends.

Sometimes in the office we'd have spiritual delibera-tions, like the time we discussed the fact that most men wore their tighty-whities underwear long after they should throw them away. This is because we have an unnatural loyalty to them. That led to who had the holiest (not, as in, most spiritual) pair. Bets were placed. We summarily dismissed Barbara from the room, dropped trou and started counting holes. Rips and tears counted. If my memory serves me, I do believe that Jack won the bet. Since he was the oldest he had more time to cultivate the holes.

Paul and Craig were bachelors at the time, and they had rented a huge old semi-dilapidated house up in Vista, New York. It was a true man-cave. At one of our weekly staff meetings we were brainstorming about having an all-county club at Halloween time. There was a room at Craig and Paul's house that was large enough to hold a few hundred kids if we moved the furniture out. We then came up with the idea of inviting our urban ministry co-workers from New York City. You may recall that I mentioned meeting Bill Milliken and Bo Nixon when I was in high school. By this time Bo had taken over Bill's position, and Connecticut Young Life liked to partner with NYC Young Life for things like all-county clubs and camps. So we called Bo to invite him to join us. We hadn't realized, however, that when we crunched the numbers the all-county club wound up bringing in closer to 500 kids than the few hundred that we had predicted. I was the new kid on the block, so I figured that problem wasn't on me. I let the other guys worry about it.

There were kids everywhere; inside, outside, on the porch, on the lawn, in the street, even some in an old cemetery that was across the street. Apparently some kids thought the cemetery was part of the decorations for Halloween. My lasting memory from that crazy night was overhearing a conversation between a few of Bo's city kids. Keep in mind, some of these were tough kids from very rough sections of the city. But that's what Young Life was about, reaching all kids everywhere. The urban work in Young Life was in its infancy, but rapidly growing under the leadership of men like Bo Nixon. In the conversation I overheard, one guy said to his buddy, "Hey, you know we can take this whole thing over. I checked and there aren't that many of those Young Life guys here!" At first I was alarmed. But then I figured, typical high school kids could never get anything organized and wouldn't know what to do if they did. That was my hope anyway. Being so new to the whole scene, their comment, and indeed the entire evening seemed pretty wild compared to all-county clubs back in Maryland.

Legends

I have said earlier that the guys in my year of the D.C. training program were shipped out to new areas. I learned that my friend Bo White had accepted a position with the urban ministry, not in New York City, but just to the north, in the town of Yonkers. Leading that work, along with being the Regional Director, was another man who was to have a big influence on me and a lot of people in New England Young Life, Dean Borgman. I began to learn a lot about the historic legacy of three amazing families from Southern Connecticut, the Borgmans, the Carpenters and the Carleys. All three families came from the streets of Bridgeport Connecticut, and some of them were in gangs.

By the time I came on the scene their reputation was legendary in Southern New England. A lot of them had come to Christ through a church I was going to hear a lot about, Black Rock Congregational Church, then located in Bridgeport, Connecticut. That church really had to stretch the limits of their grace and love to accommodate some of the biggest hell-raisers in town. Never mind that they had become Christians, they all still had some serious craziness in them. But in the beautiful way Christ transforms people, these three families produced some of the greatest leaders that Young Life Staff had ever seen.

There was: Jack Carpenter, my boss, Dean Borgman, the Regional Director, and Jack's brother Reid, who was the Regional Director of probably the largest Young Life ministry in the entire eastern U.S., Pittsburgh. Dean's brother, Dan, was a teacher at New Canaan High School and led a Young Life club in Stamford. His wife, June, was the sister of Harv Oostdyk, the guy who spoke at Natural Bridge when I accepted Christ. David Borgman led the New Canaan club, where his brother Dan taught. Jim Guyer wasn't related, but was cut from the same cloth and background. He was the Area Director for Bethlehem, PA. The list goes on and on, and over time I got to know and appreciate every one of them. The stories that came from all of these guys were the stuff of legends. I would like to challenge one of them, anyone, to please write a book and document your antics!

It was into this scene, rich with history, that I found myself. I felt out of place, as any newcomer would, but because I wasn't from their part of the country I also felt I was able to bring some new ideas to the table that were worthwhile. Looking back, I believe I contributed to the Young Life landscape, but I did not foresee the cultural adjustments I would have to make, and how long that would take.

My job title when I arrived in Connecticut was Area Director for Greenwich. About a year later Dean Borgman, who had been the Regional Director, left Young Life to take a position at Gordon Conwell Theological Seminary. His vacancy was filled by Jack Carpenter and I was promoted from Greenwich Area Director to Fairfield County Area Director. A few years later my area grew to also include Westchester County, New York. By that time Craig Simpson and Paul Cowras had left staff.

Before moving on from the topic of legends, I've written earlier about people with enormous talent and also with extraordinary speaking skills. Dean and Jack were among that group of the finest communicators I ever heard. It was a privilege listening to either one of those guys speak to a room full of high school kids. They were masters.

Bo and Yonkers

I was glad that Bo White was close by, in Yonkers. The first opportunity I had, I drove down to see him. Bo had met a young lady, Karen, and by the time we had all relocated, he was engaged to be married. As a bachelor he was living in a large urban house in Yonkers, along with several other staff guys. There were always a lot of people around whenever I was there. They all decided to throw a bachelor party for Bo before his wedding, and as his close friend, I was invited. On Friday night, I took our car, (our only car at the time), and headed down to Yonkers. It turned out to be a memorable occasion indeed. Among the list of characters that hung out at the Yonkers house were a few guys who were, shall we say, of questionable reputation. I'm not referring to the staff guys, but some of the hangers-on. One such guy apparently thought it would be really funny to drug the drink of the engaged bachelor, Bo. And since I was his closest buddy, why not drug me too?

I had never been a big drinker. I did get drunk a few times with friends, before I became a Christian, just enough to know what it felt like. That night Bo and I just had one drink that I can recall. But all of a sudden things began to get really blurry. I was thinking, "I know I've only had one drink, but why am I feeling like this, almost drunk?" The longer we sat there the worse it got. Other than the clown that drugged us, I think the rest of the group just figured we had been tossing down drinks for hours.

The last thing I remembered was staggering down a long hall, literally bouncing off of the walls, being directed by someone into the bathroom where I promptly threw up everything that had been in my stomach for the past few days. I looked over and saw Bo doing the same thing at the sink. My very last memory was being unceremoniously tossed onto a mattress on the floor in one of the bedrooms, where I was to remain until the sun came up. I later found out that one of the other staff guys, Paul Launsbury, had called Carol. She told me this is what he said to her: "Hi Carol? It's Paul. Listen, Dick won't be coming home tonight. He's a bit under the weather." Click. He hung up right away so he didn't have to field any questions.

The next morning I woke up, still nauseated, and pretty much feeling like the floor of a New York city taxicab. I made the call to Carol. I knew it was going to be one of those, "Lucy, you got a lot of splainin' to do!" calls. Carol had to have Cindy drive her down to Yonkers, since I had our only car. All the way home I rode with a paper bag on my lap, and had to use it a few times. Carol, who thought her husband and succumbed to the evil temptations of the big city was, justifiably, livid. Even I was disgusted with myself, thinking I just had too much to drink and lost control.

About two years after this incident, I had reunited with some of the urban guys who had been at Bo's bachelor party that night. We were reminiscing about the party and I commented at how embarrassing it was to be so stinking drunk and having to have my wife come get me the next day. It was only then I really learned the truth. One of the guys said, "Drunk? You and Bo weren't drunk. Remember that guy Bernie who used to work at the fire station? He drugged your drinks that night." By then, of course, it was far too late to retro-justify my actions to my wife. Not that I didn't try.

Getting Started

Over the next few months we were hard at it doing contact work, practically pitching a tent on the campus of Greenwich High School and going to every school event we could find. Tim Ficker had started to introduce us to a few of his friends, which helped. The first guy he introduced us to was Clem Williams. There would be several others who, along with Clem and Tim, would wind up being the core group for our new club. But not quite yet.

I also found out that there had been a club lacrosse team at the high school. That year it was going to be a varsity sport and they were looking for some coaching help. Because I wasn't a full time faculty member I couldn't be the head coach, but that was fine with me. I didn't want all of the off-the-field responsibilities anyway. I met a teacher who was one of the assistant football coaches, Tony Minotti. He didn't know the first thing about lacrosse but he was keen to learn. We became a great duo, because I barely knew anything about coaching. He taught me about coaching and I taught him about lacrosse. We wound up coaching the varsity lacrosse team together for the next few years, and most importantly, in that time I got to know and befriend a whole lot of high school guys. Many of them came to club, and in time some came to Christ. A few years later Greenwich High got their first girls lacrosse team, and like me, Carol teamed with a full time teacher and together they were the first coaches for that team at GHS.

There was a camp coming up and Carol and I desperately wanted to have some kids go. It wasn't a typical weekend camp, but rather a ski weekend, at Sunapee, New Hampshire. Wow, I think I like the way Young Life does things up here in Connecticut! We managed to get Tim, Clem and a few others to sign up. It wasn't a big start, but it was a start. I tried not to compare with Bowie, but back in Bowie, by December we had already started our first club.

The camp was great. We all got to ski at a great ski resort. But just as importantly, all of the leaders I've already mentioned, and more, were working together. Tim and Clem and their friends had a great time. Bo had somehow found a way to take responsibility for the program. And I thought, "Ok, we're going to show you New England guys how we roll back in Maryland with program and humor." I knew that in Bo, they were going to see our best. He didn't disappoint. The one image that remains in my mind is seeing Bo, who had created a ridiculous character he called Captain Hippodrome, charge across a snowy field, dressed in a cape and huge top hat, driving a snow mobile. I have absolutely no recollection how it fit into the program, but Bo pulled it off and kids were talking about it for months afterward. So were the New England staff guys and leaders.

Our First Greenwich Club

Finally, in March, we had enough momentum to give our first club a try. That is, we thought we had enough momentum. Boy, were we off. About 20 kids showed up, and they definitely were not saying to themselves, "Wow, look who all's here," but rather, "Where is everybody?" I remembered a standard strategy of Young Life: get the key kids and they will bring all of the other kids. We had built good friendships with both the quarterback of the football team and the captain of the cheerleaders. Both of them were at the first club, and neither of them brought any friends. Same story with the president of the senior class. He was there too, but by himself. Tim and Clem where there and a few of the people who had gone to Sunapee, but that was it.

I always believed that it was much easier to run a club of 100 or more than it is to run a club of 25 or less. The Bowie and Woodlawn clubs illustrated this; easier to run than was the smaller Brooklyn Park club. That first night at the Greenwich club there was no energy. Kids looked tentative and even a bit embarrassed to be there. I remembered Jerry Johnson's line: the main purpose of the first club is to get kids to come back to the second club. If that was true, we were in trouble. If I was a high school kid I don't think I would have come back for a second club. Ugh, and this, after six months of intensive contact work.

I don't think you'll find this in a Young Life manual any-where: there is an unwritten but very real contract between Young Life and kids. They are putting their reputation on the line when they invite a friend to club. They honor their side of the understood contract by risking that reputation when they invite their friends. For our side, we promise never to embarrass them in front of those friends by making club unattractive. Our job is to make club good enough that when those invited guests show up the first time that they'll want to come

131

back a second time. That night I violated my side of the contract with Tim and Clem and the other core kids.

During the months leading up to that first club night, Jack and the other leaders had told us that Young Life is different in New England. Kids have a whole lot more available to them. They can be very entitled, and they aren't easily impressed. Many kids preferred smaller groups, and less "rah-rah", was the term they used to describe them. Somewhat full of myself, I would boast about the large clubs in Maryland and claimed that this could happen just as easily in Connecticut as in Maryland. Carol and I still had a lot to learn about the differences between where we had been and where we now were.

In addition to our weekly staff meetings, we also had regular leadership meetings, which consisted of our staff and volunteer leaders. And there were a few more Borgmans and Carleys in that group. One of my favorite guys was a bruiser of a man named Tony Jordhamo. According to Jack, who was the source of so much colorful history of the Bridgeport crowd, Tony was the toughest of the clan, and the best street fighter. Now a mature Christian and also Jack and Judi's next door neighbor and volunteer leader, he brought his brand of wisdom and perspective into the meetings.

We sometimes met at our church. Yes, when Carol and I first got to Greenwich, we became members of Stanwich Congregational. In our minds there really was no other choice. I was looking forward to joining the church in which I sat as a high school senior seven years before, and listened to Nate Adams preach. Nate was still the pastor, and the first time Carol and I went to church I told him about my previous visit. In time we became good friends. He remained a life-long supporter of Young Life, and was, in fact, on our Greenwich committee. I never did reveal my thoughts about him looking like Ichabod Crane. But I do believe that comment slipped out one night, dropped by one of the Carleys.

We struggled through the rest of the springtime with club, never having more than 30 kids showing up, and that was on a good night and only if I included any pets in the count. It was tough sledding and my confidence was sorely challenged, coming off of the years we enjoyed in Baltimore and in Bowie. Working side by side with the best woman Young Life leader I ever knew, Carol Bond, and having Cindy and Martine part of our leadership team was a blessing. At least they had all seen what we were capable of.

Our New Arrival

The brightest day of the year for us was April 22nd, when we celebrated the birth of our first child, a son, Matthew Taylor Bond, born at 9:59 PM at Greenwich Hospital. We would eventually have three sons. Didn't name any of them James. I just knew back in 1973 that those movie sequels weren't going to last much longer. At that time the Lamaze Natural Child Birth classes were all the rage. But Carol decided that she didn't want to take them so we never went. This somehow raised the eyebrows and suspicions of some women at our church. Carol was talking with a lady one Sunday when she said, somewhat alarmingly to Carol, "Surely you are having your baby naturally," and Carol dryly replied, "No actually, I have decided this one's going to come out of my hip."

As it turned out, the birth wasn't so natural anyway. When we got to the hospital, even though she was having regular contractions, Carol wasn't dilated enough to give birth. In 1973 the fetal heart monitor was a very new and rare piece of equipment. We were told that it was used in only three hospitals in the entire country, Greenwich Hospital being one of them. Carol was hooked up to one and we could hear our baby's heartbeat, strong and clear. We had been in the labor room for a while and nothing had progressed, so I told Carol I was going to run down to the cafeteria and get a quick snack.

When I got back, the maternity ward had been closed off for a half an hour for nursing mothers to nurse. I wasn't sure why that would cause an entire wing to close. Maybe those mothers were uber-modest. I just waited, thinking there was no problem because when I left Carol it didn't appear like anything important was going to happen soon. What I didn't know was that Matthew became entangled in his umbilical cord and his heart rate plummeted. Without the heart monitor he would have been in big trouble. But with it, alarms started going off and the doctor came in and quickly performed an episiotomy. Matthew was delivered right away. By the time I got back to the room, I had missed everything. But I did welcome my baby boy into the world, and Mommy and Matthew were doing well.

By the second year in Greenwich we had said our good-byes to Martine and Cindy, who moved back to Bowie. But not before we had Matthew baptized. Together they were Matt's Godparents, along with my brother Jack. With the Godfather movie having come out just the year before, I wanted to dress Martine up as Vito Corleone but she was uncooperative. Spoil sport. It wasn't like I asked her to dress as Fredo.

Car in a Mailbox

With me gone a lot during the day it left Carol without transportation, living far from the center of town. We had one fairly new car, a Camaro. We didn't really have money for a second one, and I can remember us praying about it. One day Carol went to the mailbox and found $200 cash from some generous, anonymous friend. Right away I knew how to use it. Pop rocks candy! But Carol suggested a used car. I realize that $200 doesn't sound like a lot of money. But in 1973 my annual salary was about $13,000. Our monthly rent was $150.

I started right away looking for a used car. But I also wanted something I could work on and learn some mechanical skills without risking our good car. I finally found an old Triumph TR4 in Pound Ridge, New York and paid $225 for it. I hadn't really thought about it, but with the Camaro as our family car, it wouldn't be a problem if I drove a little two-seater. I didn't know much about cars, and even less about sports cars. It didn't start off well. No, the car started fine. But the day I brought it home wasn't a good beginning. All the way home I was disappointed that it didn't seem very peppy. There was also a slight burning smell that I hadn't noticed when I test drove it. It wasn't until I pulled into the driveway that I finally noticed: I had driven all the way home with the emergency brake on. Thank you Mr. Goodwrench.

That car became not only a huge blessing for us, it was the start of a life-long love affair with sports cars. After having it for a few years, I fixed it up and sold it at a profit, which enabled me to buy a little better sports car. Every few years I'd sell the current one at a profit and buy a little better car. And that has continued for many years. Except for a few years of riding motorcycles, there's always been a sports car in our family.

The IRA Guy

A single man lived in the carriage house up the hill, next to the garage. We didn't see too much of him, and he gave the impression of a mysterious and perhaps even a sinister character. His name was Dan. He was from Ireland and had a thick Irish accent. At one point someone told me that he had been involved with the Irish Republican Army and fled Northern Ireland. I never knew if that was true, but it wouldn't have surprised me. He was intimidating, and the few encounters I had with him involved keeping club kids out of his way when they visited Carol and me.

One day Jack Carpenter called me, knowing we were about to leave for a camp, and asked if he could use our house for a few days while we were away. He was having a very special guest in town, none other than the President of Young Life, Bob Mitchell. If that name sounds familiar, Mitch was the camp speaker at Frontier Ranch back when I was in high school and on Work Crew. I thought, "Wow, the President of Young Life will be staying at our home!" By then I had reunited with Mitch and had enjoyed some great times with him as a member of the Young Life Staff. When we got back to town I called Jack and asked if Mitch enjoyed his stay. Jack told me the following story: "We pulled up to the garage and unpacked Mitch's suitcase." (Note: Jack knew about Dan, through me) "All of a sudden that big bear of a man, Dan, came running out of his place and starting yelling at us, 'What are you two doing here, unpacking all that luggage?' I quickly started explaining the situation. He finally settled down, but couldn't resist the parting shot, 'Ya, so ye got no place else to go then, have ya?'" That line was quoted back to me not only by Jack, but by Mitch, for the next few years.

Problems and Setbacks

That spring, a new problem with Young Life in Greenwich surfaced. We had gotten to the point where we were far behind in the finances, something that was never a burden back in Bowie. I had come to realize that, although the committee consisted of a great group of folks, nobody really knew how to raise money, which I thought was pretty ironic considering the amount of wealthy people living in town. Nonetheless, we had started to enter what staff folks euphemistically referred to as "The Young Life forced savings plan," that is, when we were behind on our budget our salaries weren't paid. It was the hope that eventually enough money would be raised so we would start getting paid again in addition to receiving our back pay. But there were never any guarantees. We all knew that risk going in. We were working in a faith-based ministry, dependent on the monetary support from others. Each Young Life area was financially autonomous. Young Life headquarters provided a number of vital services, but did not supply funds to local areas when there was a shortfall.

Then we were hit with another blow. Our landlord, Mary Jackson, who was quite old and had been very ill, sadly, passed away. Her son took over her estate and informed us that we would have to move out and find other housing. Even though Cindy and Martine were finished with their year-long commitment to live with us and had returned to Bowie, obviously Carol, Matthew and I needed a place to live. When we looked for housing, the cheapest place we could find was about double the rent we had been paying. It was available but we had to make a commitment and give a down payment, so the clock was ticking.

Right around the end of the school year I received a very interesting phone call. It was from our "home" church in Baltimore, the church I had joined after I became a Christian and the church in which Carol and I were married, Chapel Hill United Presbyterian. They called to offer me a job as their Youth Pastor. Their timing was good, for the obvious reasons: club was sucking, the budget was in the tank, and we had to quickly find other housing. I was beginning to doubt the wisdom of ever having moved to a place that was so different from where I grew up. I have to admit, I was down. Not George Bailey down, I but felt beaten. You would think, accepting an offer like that would have been a slam-dunk. It would eliminate all of our problems, and we could return to Baltimore where everyone knew us and liked us. But at the same time that Little Man in me kept whispering, "You can beat this. Don't give up!" On the other hand, sometimes my Little Man was an idiot.

Chapel Hill said they would send me a job description. I had a few days to think about their offer and discuss it with Carol before it arrived. I realized there were a lot

of perks that I had in Young Life, like camp assignments, freedom with my schedule, and seminary training, that I really didn't want to give up. So I decided
that I would take their job description and revise it to
suit my own tastes. When it arrived, I wrote in what I
wanted to keep. I wanted to remain closely related to
Young Life so I could still have camp assignments and
attend seminary, and I threw in a few other juicy perks
if I took the job, like housing, and a raise. I thought,
"What the heck, they probably won't go for it anyway
and that will be the end of that." I sent it back, and in a
few days I got a phone call telling me that everything I
wanted was approved and how soon could I get back to
Baltimore?

A Big Decision

Ok, so what do we do now? I thought Carol would
definitely think we should take the offer and run. But
she didn't. Instead, she kept asking me, "What do *you*
want to do?" Some mornings I'd wake up and say to
myself, "Are you crazy? This is an offer on a silver
platter. What normal person would turn this down,
especially the way this year has gone, and the finances,
and housing? Take it already." But then the thoughts
just wouldn't leave my mind: did we not believe that
God had led us to Greenwich? Was it just to teach me a
lesson in humility? Did we read His will poorly a year
ago? Carol and I had no peace no matter which side of
the choice we landed on, and we both found ourselves
flip-flopping. All the while Chapel Hill was waiting for an
answer, and the landlady on the new housing opportunity needed an answer.

This may sound excessive, but Carol and I made a list of
pros and cons on a sheet of paper, and numerically
weighed the importance of each pro and each con. We
added up the numbers, which totaled somewhere
around 70. The pros and cons added up to only one or
two points apart. Finally, I called Chapel Hill on a

Wednesday and told them we would give them an answer by Saturday at noon. I then called the landlady and told her the same thing. We gave ourselves three more days and we were going to decide, one way or another. Whichever way this went, I had a deep sense that I was at a pivotal crossroad in my career, and even in my marriage and my life.

Wednesday through Friday Carol and I basically avoided talking about the "big decision." But there wasn't a moment when it wasn't on both of our minds. We felt we had considered every possible argument, reason, variation and nuance of both staying and leaving, in great detail. So the last few days we were pretty much silent about it.

Through all of this, Carol was amazing. We had been married and best friends for several years by the time we faced this decision. We are both strong-willed by nature. She was never a pushover when it came to hard decisions. Sometimes we would disagree about a family matter, or something financial, and when we did we managed to resolve our different points of view and make wise choices. Occasionally that meant one of us compromising for the other person. I had learned by this time that Carol had keen and quick insights into situations and people, sometimes quicker thinking and more accurate intuition than me. Our decision making was much more collaborative than argumentative.

Over the years and as our marriage grew, it became evident to me that one of the clearest means that God used to clarify His will was through Carol. She didn't often really put her foot down about something, so when she did I paid close attention; which is why I was befuddled that nothing clear or direct was forthcoming from her. I was waiting for a strong opinion. Carol was clear, but it just wasn't what I expected. She was saying, in effect, "I trust *you* on this one. I'll move back to Maryland, or stay here. I don't know what's best. The only thing I do know is, I'll trust that God's going give you the right choice. And I can live with that."

I'll never forget Saturday morning. While neither one of us were upset in any way towards each other, we didn't utter a word. About 11 o'clock I headed up to the carriage house at the top of the hill, behind our house. There was a large garage up there that Mary Jackson had let us use, and I was fiddling with something on the car. Carol was still down at the house. Right before noon, she walked up and into the garage. I looked up from the car and our eyes met. Carol said to me, "Well, what do you think we should do?" and I replied, "I don't know. What do you think we should do?" Carol: "I'll do whatever you think is best." Silence. Right then, and not one second before, I made the decision. I said to Carol, "Well...let's stay." She looked at me for a silent second and replied, "Ok. You wanna call the church, and I'll call the landlady?" And that's exactly what we did.

I do not believe that God is in the business of sitting in heaven like some kind of divine practical joker and saying, "This is your life we're talking about. You better not miss my will here. Oops, you missed it! You really blew it this time, buddy. You should have followed the signs more clearly." Through this excruciating process, I learned something completely new about seeking God's will: sometimes God wants us to make a decision, not knowing until after the fact if the decision is the right one. And in so doing, we have to reach a different level of faith and trust. In this case, only after deciding to stay did He reveal that we made the correct decision.

Over the course of my whole life I have looked back at that decision. I have shared it with others. I have used it in talks and sermons on learning to trust God. And I know for sure our faith and trust in our Heavenly Father grew exponentially from that experience. It's been through circumstances like that, that we get precious glimpses into the character of the infinite/personal God.

The very God of the universe stoops to reach us, to make Himself knowable. And times like that he "lifts the veil" and lets us see inside hints of His personality and His style.

Sometimes it helps me to think about God's definition of His relationship with us. There's a kind of progressive nature to it. He said He is the potter and we are the clay. He also said that He is the shepherd and we are His sheep. Then He called us servants, then friends, then children, and at last we are called the very brides of Christ. There is relationship, there is intimacy. We are permitted to address the very God of the universe as *Abba*, or Daddy as it's translated from the Aramaic. Such is the character of God. He loves us, and sometimes he really gets a kick out of surprising us-giving us a shock we never saw coming. Yes, sorry if that sounds irreverent, but I think He really enjoys that.

For as long as I live, I will look back on that day and that decision as a wonderful confirmation of God's love for me and for my family. It added to an ever growing list, a life-long track record of His faithfulness to us and His provisions and blessings for us. Many times in my life I had prayed about a decision and God made it clear to me, "speaking" through scripture, or Carol, or friends, or circumstances, or any number of ways. This was the first time that I had absolutely no idea what the right decision was until after I made it.

That Saturday at 12:01 PM there was no horn blast or vision of Jesus. We made our phone calls and went about our day. In the weeks that followed we made our plans to move from Taconic Road to Orchard Street. Anyone observing us would say we were carrying on, business as usual. But looking back, it changed everything. It changed us. And from that decision forward Young Life in Greenwich began to change and grow. Every now and then I used to wonder what it would have been like if we returned to Maryland. My life would have obviously taken on a very different narrative. But we didn't return, and even though we were unsure at the time, I am confident that God was sure, and had His hands planted firmly on our shoulders, guiding us.

In 1519 the Spanish conquistador, Hernán Cortés, set out to conquer the mighty Aztec empire with 600 men, sailing on eleven ships. Some of his men were afraid of the odds and tried to seize a few of his ships and leave. When he found out, he gave the order to burn his own ships so there would be no turning back. He wanted to make sure his men were fully committed to the battle. For over 600 years men had tried and failed to colonize the Yucatan Peninsula. Cortez was the first.

When we decided to turn down that job back in Baltimore we were, in effect, burning our ship. The one easy option to solve our problems was no longer on the table. We no longer had a choice. We were committed to staying.

That was a nice Baby Boomer illustration. Here's one for you Gen Xers: We took the red pill and entered the matrix. And lastly, for fellow Fuller Seminary grads and other scholars: When you make bacon and eggs the chicken makes a sacrifice, but the pig is "all in." We were the pig.

Chapter 8

Getting Things Turned Around

First things first. If we were going to make it, we had to eat and we needed to pay the rent for the roof over our heads. And that meant raising support and getting paid. In Bowie we had a strong committee and they did most of that work. I thought my calling was kids anyway, not finances. However, in Greenwich we didn't have fund raisers on the committee. Our finance guy was a good man, but every time I spoke with him about our lack of funds he only had one strategy, "Looks like we better send out another letter." To me that seemed about as ineffective as passing around a "Save the Clock Tower" flyer. I just knew there had to be a better way. Sometimes I would ask other staff guys, and I soon learned that many of them had the same attitude that I had back in Bowie; that raising money was the job of the committee, not the staff. The only problem with that reasoning was, what if the committee didn't know how?

One day I had an epiphany. It totally changed my thinking about fund raising. All that time I had been running away from it. I admitted to myself that I was afraid of fund raising and that it intimidated me. I justified running away by claiming that it was the job of the committee whereas my call was to reach kids for Christ. But

143

that day I suddenly realized, I'm not running away any-more, I'm turning around and running straight at it. I said to Carol one day, "I don't care if not one more kid comes to club. I'm going to learn how to raise money." Of course, that wasn't true, but what was true was this: I had to become passionate about fund raising. I had to stop fearing it.

My plan wasn't all that complicated, actually. The first job was to sit down and make up a list of names: parents, donors, former donors, people on our mailing list, and any other contacts. When I came up with that list I prioritized them. The ones I thought were more approachable and more likely and able to donate went to the top of the list. I then got on the phone and started calling people. I didn't try to sell Young Life or ask them for support. The only thing I tried to "sell" was getting them to agree to meet with me face to face, for the purpose of "letting them know what we're doing in Young Life to help kids in town" and that I was going to seek their help and participation.

When I met with each of them that was my agenda. By seeking their "help and participation" I wasn't just reaching for their wallets. I gave them several options to get involved: being on the committee, checking out what it would take to be a volunteer leader, attending a summer camp as an adult guest, be an occasional chap-erone at one of our special events, inviting them to visit club one night, to name a few. And I also asked them if they would consider investing financially in the ministry.

These people weren't dumb. Everyone understood that one of our big goals was to increase our support, but I honestly made several options available. Those options weren't just window dressing. As a result I not only raised a lot of money, I discovered and then recruited some really good committee members, volunteer lead-ers and other talented people over the years.

"To Boldly Go..."

I also discovered a few important principles. Teddy Roosevelt once said, "You'll never be able to lead a cavalry charge if you think you look funny on a horse." People often ask for support with what I see as a "hat in the hand" attitude; timid, unconfident, and apologetic. Folks don't want to give money or be part of something if you give off the impression that you're a rodeo clown. I learned that it was far more effective to approach people with the attitude, "This is something so exciting, and I'm offering you the opportunity to be part of it; to invest in it."

The second important principle I learned was, I could never insult someone by asking for too much money, *but* I did insult some by not asking for enough. Learning this was blind luck. Ok, actually it was from the Lord. I'm not always the brightest bulb in the box, so sometimes God has to teach me in real-life situations. One of the first guys I approached, I knew was a very wealthy man. I'm not even sure if he was a Christian, but his son had accepted Christ at a weekend camp. While Dad probably didn't understand it spiritually, he did see that his son, who had been going in a bad direction, had turned his life around. And as any parent knows, if you have an impact on their kids, the parents are touched.

When I asked this father if he would consider investing in the ministry, I showed him a little chart that explained how many donors we were seeking in different support ranges. Suddenly I got an idea: I pointed to the top tier, and said I was looking for three donors who could give $5,000. (Keep in mind, this was in 1973.) The guy's eyes widened, and for a moment I thought I lost him. Then he said to me, "Wow, that's a lot of money. I can't really do that. But I will commit to $1,000." This, from a man who previously hadn't given so much as a dollar, yet who had received mailing after mailing for the

145

past several months asking for financial support. Not only did he give substantially, I could clearly tell that he was actually complimented. By asking him for that much support I was acknowledging not only his wealth and success, but it also said that I had judged him to be an unselfish philanthropic giver. I connected with him by speaking to the man's nobler instincts.

I didn't always hit a home run like in that example. In fact, I struck out sometimes. But over all my batting average was rising, and eventually we got out of the red and I started getting paychecks again. On top of that we were able to connect with people and engender a whole lot of good will with parents in town. Call me crazy, but I actually got to the point where I almost enjoyed fund raising. I was energized by turning people onto it. There's a Pete Rose joke in here somewhere-baseball, batting average, and money-but I just can't put my finger on it. Please add one yourself.

A Better Club

When fall rolled around and school started, Carol and I were working on our strategy for making club better. Very few regulars from the previous year had graduated because club had consisted mainly of underclass students. By then Tim and Clem were juniors and had grown their own circle of friends. Further, when we had lived in back country we tended to conveniently relate more to the kids who lived near us. But Tim and Clem and their crowd lived closer to town; Riverside, Cos Cob, and Old Greenwich. When we were forced to leave Mary Jackson's place, our new home was in Cos Cob. We realized if we targeted more kids from that part of town, they tended to be more group oriented and socially active.

That's when Tim and Clem got us into a whole new group of students. It was that core group which made the difference. It wasn't drastic, but it was significant.

146

Young Life: The Adventures of an Ex Staffer

We still keep in touch with many of the kids from that era, especially Lorain Kelley and Michele McPartland. Other key friends in that crowd were Lisa Fairchild, Teal Friedmann, Gregg Wagner, Liddy Scherer, Barb Hindman, and Diane Malinowski. Not far behind them were Sue Bodenheimer, Ellen Triolo, Andy Butters, Brenda Baker, Bob Doll, Doug Kelly, Kim McKay; Clem's younger siblings, Libby and Walt Williams, the Comack sisters, and many others.

We starting holding club closer to town rather than out in the back country where we had lived, giving a lot more kids easy access. Numbers started to climb, and kids started looking forward to coming to club. By the end of the second year we were starting to see club attendance regularly in the 50's and even sometimes into the 60's, and that's without counting the pets anymore. Even though there were plenty of large homes in that part of town, I could already foresee the need to eventually find a place bigger than a private home for club.

Something else that I noticed about Young Life in Connecticut and what I had not seen back in Maryland: the kind of kids that Jack and some of the other leaders really enjoyed attracting often had more of a counter culture disposition. I tended to gravitate more towards athletes, popular kids and social-butterfly types. That's not meant as a criticism either way, but just an observation.

Jack had developed a Christian coffee house, and a lot of the kids who frequented it were more of a "hippyish" crowd. Jack also was very interested in service projects, like Young Life Work Days. We would get our campaigner kids to volunteer on a Saturday helping people do house and yard chores, and we would use the money we earned to help kids from poorer parts of Connecticut to go to camps they may otherwise not be able to afford. Young Life in Connecticut also was heavily committed to week long work-study trips for our Christian kids, where, as the name would suggest, the agenda was a combination of work and study. These trips were to a place in Americus, Georgia, called Koinonia Farm. While I felt sure these events and strategies had their place and were meaningful in kids' lives, my Young Life experience was different. I began to think of other kinds of camps and events that might be more attractive to the kinds of kids I was more used to being around.

What if?

Greenwich had a unique school holiday schedule, one that I felt sure could be utilized in some way with camp trips. Students were given an entire week off school in February and another entire week in April; Winter Break and Spring Break. If one thing was true about Greenwich kids, many came from wealthy families and could afford a lot of recreational options. In fact, the town seemed to empty out during those two weeks. The favorite and most common holiday for people were ski trips during winter break, and someplace warm during spring break. It got me thinking...

What if we could do a week of skiing, better and cheaper than what kids could do on their own? We could have club every night and make it a real outreach event. And what if we could go, not to Vermont or New Hampshire, but somewhere far away and exotic like Colorado? Although Frontier Ranch in Colorado wasn't winterized, I knew that nearby Silver Cliff Ranch was. I called out there and found that no one was using the camp during the week of the Greenwich winter break. I reserved the whole facility. Next problem: how to get out there. If we flew it would get expensive. But I had already spent a few summers traveling from the east coast to Colorado and back for summer camps. Why couldn't we do that in the winter, from Connecticut?

Young Life: The Adventures of an Ex Staffer

Traveling by bus became our plan. I anticipated that it would be hard work selling the camp to kids, but I also knew there were a lot of kids who would be interested if we could spread the word. Even though there were a lot of kids from wealthy families, a competitive price would be an attraction. And, for Greenwich kids, skiing was second nature. It seemed like everyone skied. So why not ski with us? A lot of our regular club kids were interested. I also found that a lot of kids who had never come to club heard about the trip and were interested. All the better. One guy, Ray Chickanis, became a good friend in the process of recruiting for the trip. Ray took it upon himself to be my personal travel agent at school. He even collected money and registrations and would meet me when I got to the school and hand me the latest deposits. One day he met me with these words, "Hey I'm really sorry but I lost the envelope with all of the sign-ups and the money." He waited just long enough and then smiled with a "Gotcha!" Nobody likes a smart aleck, Ray.

I learned a lesson early on in my Young Life career. For kids, the most important question about any camp was, "Who's going?" If you could get the ball rolling by getting a few of the right kids enthusiastic and on board, that ball would start to roll downhill and gain momentum. One year I knew the key to getting a certain crowd to summer camp was getting one particular girl, a leader in her class, to sign up. Her name was Cindy. She wasn't going because she had to get a job for the summer and there was no way her employer would let her off for a week when she was only working for a few months. I said to her, "What if I could get you a job and your boss would let you off for a week?" Cindy's eyes brightened. One of our committee members owned a shop in town. I gave him a call. He gave Cindy a job, she signed up for camp, and that ball started rolling downhill. P.S. He even kept her on the job on a part time basis during the following school year. Good thing Cindy accepted Christ at camp too, because otherwise I would have had her boss fire her when she got home. Kids have to learn that life can be unfair at times, you know? (Smile)

Between Christmas and February we managed to sign up a busload of kids for our first of hopefully many ski trips. We left from the Greenwich High School parking lot on a Friday night. The coach bus had two drivers and would drive through two nights and two days to get us to Colorado and Silver Cliff Ranch by sometime on Sunday. We skied from Monday through Friday at different resorts, like Breckenridge, Copper Mountain and Vail. Friday evening we pulled out of the ski resort and headed straight back to Greenwich, arriving in town on Sunday night. If that strikes you as a rather energetic and ambitious schedule, my only defense is: I was a much younger (and dumber) man back then. The kids loved the skiing, and we wound up doing our winter break ski trips every year for 12 straight years. Our successors in Greenwich continued those trips even after Carol and I moved to Florida.

Over the years we refined and improved the trips. But as long as I was in Greenwich, we never flew. And the reason, other than the obvious money savings, was that I believed our leaders could accomplish more relationally in one bus ride than they could normally achieve in an entire year of getting to know kids, doing contact work at home. Try "living" on a coach bus with a busload of high school kids for 40 to 50 hours (depending on the weather, which got pretty hairy at times) and you can't help but become good friends. We never allowed our leaders to sit together at the front of the bus, like chaperones. They were part of the group and our leaders were trained in friendship building. On the bus ride, on a ski lift, in the ski lodge, or on a ski run; with regards to building relationships with kids, to use a military term, were target-rich environments.

Untold Stories That Probably Should Remain On the Down-Low

One of our leaders rigged up a hammock between the luggage racks and kids could sign up to sleep there in three hour increments, 24/7. Between that and other kids sleeping in the luggage rack itself, others who brought portable mesh hammocks and strung them caddy-corner from the luggage rack posts, and other kids who would stake out the floor at night, it all opened more seat space. That, in turn, gave a lot of kids two seats in which to sleep. (I can only hope the statute of limitations on code enforcement of the DMV has expired.) As anyone who has ever been on an overnight flight in coach-seating knows, it's much easier sleeping if you have two seats. Except with us the bus was smellier. And the toilet was nastier. With "creative" seating and tons of extra food everyone would pack, we looked like a bunch of traveling doomsday preppers.

Also different from a flight, our westward trek included many rest stops. "Unless it's an emergency, don't use the bus toilet!" These rest stops were also for three meals a day, and depending on our location we often had to use the truck stops. There just weren't always nicer places. And when I say nicer, I'm talking Howard Johnson. I hope since the olden days there are much nicer rest stops along the highways of our heartland. Interesting characters, those truckers. Interesting, "gift" shops at those truck stations. One day I did something bad. I noticed a barrel that was labeled "Cattle Prods". I casually picked one up and pointed it at one of our leaders. I guess I must have touched his arm with it. I never knew exactly how they operated until that day.

It Worked Once, Why Not Again?

With the success of our first ski trip under our belt, and with the buzz that it created around school when everyone returned, I felt like we were starting to get our groove back. I turned my attention to Spring Break...ski trip in the winter, and some place warm in the spring. I thought about places like Daytona Beach; far, but certainly not as far as Colorado. But I kept thinking, "Where could we go that would really have a wow-factor to it?" Puerto Rico? Hawaii? Too expensive. Like the ski trip I wanted to keep the price competitive, thinking, if they can go someplace with us and do it less expensively, then we'd have something. And that's when I thought of my friend Goose, and remembered Bermuda. True, we'd have to fly there because I couldn't find pontoon buses. But by then I had had more contact with Goose than just from our honeymoon. He was a Young Life related contact and I felt sure he could help me navigate any challenges I had to face, including housing. I made the phone call.

We took a small group the first time we went to Bermuda; about 20 kids. I wasn't as sure of myself compared to planning a ski trip. Goose hooked us up with a place called Heydon Lodge, a nice, small guest cottage. We housed the girls upstairs and the guys downstairs. From being there on our honeymoon, we knew the way to get around the island was by motorbike. Naturally the kids loved the idea that each would have their own motorbike for the week. The only problem with the accommodations was the location, which was really far out on the end of the island and away from the major town, Hamilton. But the kids didn't mind because that meant more time on the motorbikes, and the entire island is only 21 square miles anyway.

We would get up in the morning, and head to the beach; almost always the famous Horseshoe Bay. We would hang out there until mid-afternoon and then people would head off to town, for shopping or site seeing. We had a few tennis players with us, a sport that I had picked up and really enjoyed, so we would head over to the National Tennis Stadium, which also doubled as a public park, and play a few sets of tennis.

Young Life: The Adventures of an Ex Staffer

During the springtime the Bermuda Tourist Board heavily promoted colleges in the States to take their spring break in Bermuda, so the island was filled with thousands of college kids, as well as a good number of high school kids. At night we did something very "un-Young Life-ish." Bermuda has a large number of night clubs. With all of the clubs packed with people and their energy, every night we got all dressed up and went out dancing. Over the years we learned a lot from our early Bermuda trip mistakes, and revised our schedule quite a bit. But that first year we just went crazy, staying at the clubs, dancing until they closed at 3 am. By the time we got back to our guest house on our motorbikes everyone would start stuffing their faces with whatever food they had bought that day. When we'd finally get to bed every night the eastern sky was getting light. We'd sleep a few hours and do it all over again the next day. Whatever I said about the ski trips vis a vis "a younger and dumber man," may also equally be inserted at this juncture.

On that first trip, instead of running our own clubs each night we tried an alternative plan. Before going out dancing we would, with the help of Goose, locate one of the half dozen Young Life clubs on the island and go visit them as guests. It provided us with a great opportunity to get to know the island kids, and it made the trip feel more international and less touristy. The spiritual emphasis was less present compared to the ski trip and the other camps we had been running, but it turned out to be a great relationship building opportunity. It served to get kids involved in club when they got home, and many of them wound up going on the weekend and summer outreach camps. On subsequent Bermuda trips we held our own clubs and the outreach was as strong as our other trips and camps.

When we got back to Greenwich there was a buzz similar to the buzz from the Colorado ski trip. In the span of just a few months, Young Life's reputation and popularity in Greenwich sky-rocketed. We still continued with club and Campaigners, and camps; but from that year and for as long as Carol and I lived in Greenwich, ski trips and Bermuda trips became an annual fixture on our schedule. And once the momentum built, each year we were able to take larger numbers of kids and run better trips. We learned from and built upon previous years' experiences.

Travel Agents

The one side effect of adding two huge, weeklong trips to a yearly calendar that already had fall and summer camps, was that at times we felt like all we did was recruit kids to camp. Because of the variety of trip options, we knew we were reaching a whole lot of different kids and the same ones weren't signing up for every camp. But Carol and I and our growing group of volunteer leaders were stretched to our limits, and some of us were beginning to feel like part-time travel agents in addition to being leaders.

I especially liked Bermuda. Of all the trips in all the years I served on staff, there never was a trip that sold itself so easily. Often that trip would literally fill up the night we opened registration. And some years we'd take up to 75 kids. Some kids would tell their parents, as sophomores, that they wanted to go on the Bermuda trip for their graduation present in their senior year. We would start taking registrations right after club on a designated night. Kids would be jostling for position in line, and the longer the sign-ups went, the more nervous the kids near the back of the line would get, afraid that the trip would fill up before they registered. For a Young Life leader that was registration heaven. The logistics of Bermuda trips and big ski trips were crazy and time consuming, but a ton of kids were going on trips, and a large number of them were giving their hearts to Christ.

By the end of our second year in Greenwich, club had

finally begun to show some significant growth. We were seeing more kids come to Christ and Campaigners was growing. We had added two major outreach camps to our regular Connecticut lineup of fall weekend camps and summer camps to Saranac. We had made the decision not to leave. We had relocated to a new home that was situated much closer to town. Yes, the Beatles had broken up, but other than that, things were definitely starting to look up.

Dress Right for the Incarnation

When missionaries are called and travel to another country it's quite natural to visualize the many cultural adaptations that they must make. Although I've never been a missionary, I have known plenty over the years and they have told me that adapting to their new homes and cultures was a long and challenging process. Chuck Reinhold, my Young Life leader, was a missionary in Ethiopia before coming with Young Life. Years after my Young Life days I was to be part of many short-term mission trips. But long-term missionaries are a whole different kettle of fish. Missionaries must learn to adapt if they ever hope to be effective in another culture.

A most remarkable Christian missionary was a man named Hudson Taylor. He was credited with opening China to Christianity, through his mission calling to that country. Check his Wikipedia page sometime. It's really impressive. What intrigued me about Taylor is... let me quote from his page: "Taylor was known for his sensitivity to Chinese culture and zeal for evangelism. He adopted wearing native Chinese clothing even though this was rare among missionaries of that time." Before Taylor, missionaries would go to a country, immerse themselves in the lives of the people, but they remained dressed as Westerners. This simple act of wearing Chinese clothing meant all the difference in the world. There is a marvelous principle in place that applies directly to Young Life.

One of my favorite theological doctrines in the Bible is the Incarnation. It relates directly to the concept that Young Life follows in its own core belief, which is entering into the world of teenagers and reaching out to adolescents everywhere. After God created us, He was not some kind of absentee landlord. He continually engaged with mankind, reaching out by sending various kings, priests, prophets and messengers as His spokes-persons.

In the fullness of God's perfect timing, God sent his Son. God's perfect plan to reach mankind was to send his "missionary" to planet earth, to tell the Good News, demonstrate His love and accomplish our salvation. The fullness of the Godhead dwelt in the person of Jesus Christ. What the kings, priests, prophets and messen-gers could not ultimately accomplish, was accomplished by Jesus. In Christ, we have the perfect king, the perfect priest, the perfect profit, and the perfect messenger (Hebrews 1-3).

Jesus didn't come for a day or a weekend, but he was literally born and lived his entire life among us. The rich and descriptive phrase, "He dwelt among us" in the first chapter of John literally means, "He pitched his tent among us." God moved into our neighborhood. And by doing so, the message of God, and indeed God Himself was wrapped up in the person of Jesus. He was God incarnate. That word literally means "in flesh." God came to humanity, in the flesh. The book of Colossians tells us that if we want to know what God is like, all we have to do is check out the person of Jesus Christ, because Jesus is the visible expression of the invisible God.

The Incarnation and Young Life

When God gave Jim Rayburn the vision to start this ministry, the theology of the Incarnation became the methodology of Young Life. Jim believed that our greatest impact on uninformed non-Christian young people would not be in our ability to speak, or run camps or have clever programs. Our impact would be in "wrapping God's love in flesh" just as Jesus did, and by having our leaders become incarnationally involved in the culture and world of young people. That way, long before our message is spoken it is lived out in front of them. Our credibility is not in our talent. It is the fact that we have lived, or "pitched our tent," in their culture and in their lives.

Not only do we spend time in their culture, we spend time and energy learning it, immersing ourselves in it, and adapting to it. We incarnate Christ by our commitment to "going wherever kids congregate." The term was coined, simply, "contact work." It's a magnificent concept. It is more than the heart of Young Life's methodology, it's the most significant core value. People who don't understand it might come look at a club or a camp and think, "Wow these leaders are really talented," or, "They really know how to reach kids." What they don't see is the 90% of the iceberg that's under the water. Speaking, clubs, camps, programs, ski trips...these are all the visible parts of the ministry. The only reason our programs have ever worked is that the 90% of work we really concentrated on, wasn't actually visible. It was the incarnational contact work.

Two stories to illustrate my point, one from Rayburn, and not in any way to put myself on his level, but a second story is meaningful to me because I saw it firsthand.

Back in the early years of Young Life, when Frontier Ranch had just opened, Young Life started to gain a reputation in some quarters around the country. As the story was told to me, a group of pastors came to visit the ranch in order to see, first hand, what the fuss was all about. As Jim Rayburn was giving them a tour they came upon a place called the Horseshoe. This was where kids were allowed to smoke. I might add that the Horseshoe was not located in some out of the way place or behind buildings. In fact, it was right smack in the middle of the camp, in front of the dining hall. Kids loved calling it the largest ashtray in the world. Because of the dry forest and subsequent fire regulations smoking had to be restricted and this was the place chosen to allow them to smoke. But the pastors were of the mindset that it was outright heresy for a Christian camp to even permit or tolerate smoking, anywhere.

Truth be told, Frontier Ranch wasn't really just a Christian camp. It was a Christian camp designed for non-Christians. Jim could tell right away what these pastors were thinking and could see the expressions on their faces. He precluded their objections with, "Isn't that amazing that non-Christians would act like non-Christians?" He also said, "Our goal is not to make kids ex-smokers. Our goal is to introduce them to Jesus. And He'll take care of the rest of the stuff." Jim wasn't in favor of promoting smoking or any other unhealthy habit. He just didn't want someone's habit or actions to be the issue. Christ was the issue. And when kids showed up at camp and had a smoking place, it said to them, "We understand your culture, and we accept you just the way you are."

On one of our annual ski trips one of my leaders was sitting next to a kid named Jeff on that long bus ride from Colorado back to Connecticut. We had a great week, and Jeff had heard the Gospel message for the first time in his life and decided to place his trust in Christ. Our leader was curious about when Jeff, who was known as quite the party-animal back at school, had first started thinking seriously about Christ and Christianity. As he asked the question, the leader was already anticipating possible answers. For someone to see the snowcapped Rocky Mountains for the first time is such a beautiful picture of God's creation and magnificence. Maybe that's what started Jeff thinking. Also, we had a great camp speaker that week, someone who was especially gifted at articulating the Gospel. Maybe that's when Jeff first started thinking seriously about Jesus.

But the answer Jeff gave, came without a moment's hesitation and it was a shocker for the leader. He said, "When did I first start thinking seriously about Christianity? That's easy, about four months ago at school, when you first learned my name." That, my friends, is the Incarnation. That is "pitching our tent" among young people. And of course it wasn't just learning Jeff's name. It was reaching out and caring and initiating, all of the things Chuck Reinhold had done years before with me and with my friends at Woodlawn High School. For me, Jack Carpenter was another rock star and a person to emulate when I think of being incarnational with kids. He exuded relational love whenever he was among high school kids. One special example stands out: he could be speaking at a camp of several hundred kids and had a rare gift that the rest of us envied. Within a few days he had learned the names of every kid at camp.

Don't Lose It

I want to say something that may be controversial for some people. Maybe there are Young Life folks today who no longer believe this. I don't mean to offend, but for me it reflects a deep truth about what makes Young Life work: *When a Young Life leader stops doing contact work, he or she can still talk to parents about kids, but they can no longer effectively speak to kids about Christ.* Back in my day some great Area Directors got promoted to Regional Directors. Sometimes that meant their participation in club work was reduced or eliminated. It would be equivalent to promoting the best teachers into administration. Sadly (in my opinion), some of those folks still took summer speaking assignments. But without doing regular, ongoing contact work, their speaking skill was based on talent and experience, not from significant connection with adolescents. They had lost their edge. And also sadly, sometimes they were the last ones to realize it. There were times I had been offered a Regional Director's position, but I was afraid of losing connection with kids. In ministry as well as in business there's a natural tendency to want to move up the job ladder. I always felt that the Area Director was the most important job there was in Young Life.

Incarnational ministry was and is part of my DNA. And any Young Life leader would say the same. We believe in it intensely, and we've seen its effectiveness time and time again in the lives of young people. In my opinion, it's the most powerful instrument there is for reaching out to people with the love of Christ.

However, when we reach out to people and when we walk into their world, we inevitably realize that it's not *they* who have to adapt and change in order for us to communicate, it's *we* who must adapt and change for them. Young Life works because leaders not only go into the world of adolescents, it works because leaders are willing to learn someone else's world, and acclimate and adjust in order to fit in.

The apostle Paul said it beautifully, in I Corinthians 9:20 ff: *To the Jews I became like a Jew, to win the Jews. To those under the law I became like one under the law (though I myself am not under the law), so as to win those under the law. To those not having the law I became like one not having the law (though I am not free from God's law but am under Christ's law), so as to win those not having the law. To the weak I became weak, to win the weak. I have become all things to all people so that by all possible means I might save some. I do all this for the sake of the gospel, that I may share in its blessings.*

Young Life leaders are willing to learn how to reach out, to be flexible, and to be non-judgmental. Before Hudson Taylor there were plenty of missionaries who traveled the world. But what made Taylor unique, and why I like to favorably compare his approach to Young Life's, is that he learned and adapted.

Learning the Culture in Greenwich

Before going to Greenwich, I had always needed to reach out, learn and adapt. I did that at Brooklyn Park High School back in college, and also with Woodlawn. And I had done that in Bowie. But in those cases the youth culture had been very similar to where I grew up and although there were differences, I was never terribly uncomfortable. But when we got to Greenwich, one of the important lessons learned was that biggest change that needed to take place was a change in me. Our ministry was not just about reaching into the sub-culture of high school kids, it was reaching into the sub culture of *Greenwich* kids, and *Connecticut* culture. And that was significantly different than everything in our own past and our own upbringing.

We thought that "high school kids are the same every-where." We assumed that just because we knew Baltimore and Washington D.C. high school cultures, we were good to go and properly equipped to do Young Life anywhere. When Jack Carpenter and others tried to say that things were different in Connecticut, we just naively and somewhat arrogantly, thought, "Well, you haven't seen us yet!" But for the first two years we just couldn't figure out why our approach wasn't nearly as effective as we had anticipated.

Things can appear the same, even when they are very different. There are some wealthy neighborhoods in Baltimore and in Washington D.C. We had never lived in any of them, but we had seen them and even knew some people who lived in them. I grew up in a lower middle class neighborhood. The transition to middle or upper middle class neighborhoods wasn't too much of an adjustment. But we didn't know that there are some very big differences between middle class and upper class culture and values, differences that ran far deeper than the size of a person's bank account.

Greenwich wasn't just an upper class town. It was different from many other wealthy towns in that there were significant numbers of people whose wealth had been in their families for generations. The common term for that is, "old-money," as opposed to "new-money." I had to smile in a scene from the film *Titanic* when Rose's mother pointed out a passenger who was wealthy, but added disdainfully that the wealth was from new-money. There's a big difference. I'm no sociologist, but even I began to see the difference. Old-money people didn't try to impress us with their wealth. It was often very understated and not so visible. New-money could be very pretentious and showy. While old-money could sometimes be snobbish, on the whole, those people were secure with their financial wealth often had an attitude of being freer and more secure. I found that, generally, old-money upper class people were a lot nicer. For those familiar with South Florida, this example might make sense: Boca Raton: new-money. Palm Beach: old-money.

But how does all of this effect the youth culture? A lot of kids had access to exceptional prosperity and privilege. In many ways, however, they often weren't even aware of just how much their world was different. There's a saying: "If you want to know what it's like to live under water, don't ask a fish." When you grow up with extra-ordinary means and perhaps live in a mansion, only as you get older do you realize that the rest of the country, much less the rest of the world, doesn't live like you do.

Entitlement

There were certainly a lot of kids who felt entitled. If their parents didn't have a ski home in Vermont, they had plenty of friends whose parents did. If they didn't go away during winter or spring break, it was a major tragedy for some. Many kids who didn't get into a prestigious college felt that their reputation was tarnished. And pity the poor kids who didn't go to college at all after graduation. They were condescendingly referred to as, "Townies." Greenwich kids had many options available to them; extensive travel, designer brand clothes, access to social events, sailing on the Sound, memberships to elite private clubs, and choice personal transportation.

Proximity to New York City meant that kids had access to all kinds of social events, whether it was concerts, plays, pro sports, or even night clubs. For many venues like Madison Square Garden, The Letterman Show, Broadway plays, or the U.S. Tennis Open, tickets were often provided by Dad's company or someone who knew someone. Being a tennis fan I went to the U.S. Open every year and the running joke was, "Go, but you should never have to pay for your own tickets. Someone has tickets they aren't using today."

The longer I lived in that world the more entitled I found myself becoming. I would get to know people and become accustomed to utilizing their contacts. I knew a parent who was the station manager for a local TV station. The station owned a Sky-Box at the Garden. One phone call and if no one at the station was using the box, I had access to 10 free tickets in a suite. Let me tell you, we used that little perk a whole lot-The Rangers, the Knicks, concerts - Carol even had our kid's birthday parties there, watching Ringling Brothers Circus. We occasionally did skits at club that were competitive and the winner would get Sky-Box tickets. They loved the ones for a Springsteen concert. Of course we had to accompany them. It takes a village.

There was a lot of pseudo sophistication and kids wanting to act like adults. But in reality, there was also a very real sophistication, the likes of which I had never experienced before. Carol's background and mine compared with Greenwich? As the saying goes, "Same world, different universe."

Don't Blink

As we immersed ourselves where we felt God had called us to live, we started to "wear the clothes" like Hudson Taylor did. Many Christians were uncomfortable because those "clothes" were of the very affluent and privileged. I met a lot of pastors, youth workers, and even some of the Young Life Staff who, like me, did not grow up in a world of prodigious affluence. Many of them really struggled to minister to people there. I learned that a dad wanted to be treated like a regular guy when it came to his kids being involved with a ministry like Young Life, or if he was on the local committee. He wanted someone to relate to him as a peer. He wasn't hung up on his prosperity or the size or value of his home, and I had to learn neither to be intimidated, nor over impressed with his social status and his credentials.

Upper class people exude an air of exclusivity, whether it be social events, or education, or club membership, or even the charities they support and the organizations for which they volunteer. Yes Greenwich had soccer moms, and many of the same ladies would show up at the Greenwich Junior League meeting dressed like they just came off a fashion show runway. There's an atmosphere of group solidarity that can almost be compared to a caste system. The housing market itself was a filtering agent, preventing all but the top echelons of home buyers to even gain admission into "the club."

By the numbers I would have guessed that the majority of folks weren't those top-of-the-ladder people. But enough of them were, so that it permeated the culture of the town and neighboring communities. Places like Darien, Wilton, New Canaan, Westport, and nearby towns across the state line in Westchester County, New

York were all heavily influenced by this culture of wealth and privilege. A non-wealthy person could wind up adopting upper class values simply by living there. I came to understand that living there and embracing upper class values didn't have nearly as much to do with how much money was in your checkbook as it did with your outlook and perception. We knew plenty of kids whose parents weren't old-money or who weren't extremely wealthy. But they very much held upper class values.

To be effective, we had to go through that whole process. I want to emphasize, however, that all over the country the very same process was going on wherever Young Life staff people lived, and especially when they moved to parts of the country that were unlike where they grew up. Staff were doing the same thing in the South, the Midwest, California, the Pacific Northwest, Middle Atlantic, Rocky Mountain States, and so on. Other staff people had to go through the same process if they moved into urban areas, or rural areas, or ethnic areas. As Young Life grew so did the number of specialty ministries, like The Capernaum Ministry that reaches out to kids with disabilities, and YoungLives, which impacts teen moms. With each specialty ministry there was a similar learning process.

Carol and I weren't "better," nor was Greenwich. It was different. We were unfamiliar and we had to learn. If you are reading this book and are from a completely different part of the country, while the explanation of the uniqueness of the Greenwich culture was hopefully interesting to read, chances are you have gone through your own version of the process where you live. And if you successfully navigated those waters, I'm sure you could also describe the intricacies of what you had to learn and the ways in which you adapted. That's what Young Life people did. And I trust that process is still going on in the Mission and will continue as long as living the Incarnation is a top priority.

Chapter 9

Random Stories

There are many stories to tell from our years with Young Life in Greenwich and Fairfield County, Connecticut. While the intent of this book is to roughly go in chronological order, I thought it would be a fun diversion to just intersperse some of those stories, even if they might be out of sequence. This chapter is about telling stories and remembering some special people.

Ski Trip That Almost Never Was

After a few years of going to Colorado for our winter break ski trips, we decide to give Park City, Utah a try. We found a great lodge that used to be the U.S. Ski Team practice facility lodging. Its major distinction was that its location was half way up on the mountain. In the morning all you had to do was put your skis on and practically ski right out the front door. We literally had to take a tram to get to our rooms the day we arrived. After our first year there, everyone loved it, so we decided to book the same place for the following year. Several months ahead of time I called the manager, a guy named Doug, who we knew from the first trip, and made our reservations. About a month before leaving, I

166

called Doug again. He was out but I left a message, just reminding him that we were coming, and to confirm the size of our group. That year we had the Darien High School club joining us, and we had two busloads.

Doug never returned my call, but in the rush of everything I didn't think about it too much, especially since there was so much to do in preparation. But something in the back of my mind kept nagging me. I tried calling Park City again about a week before the trip, and wound up leaving another message. Finally, the night before we were supposed to leave I received a call back. The person on the other end said, "Hi. I heard your messages, and have looked for a record of your reservation. Doug no longer works here. He left suddenly and didn't communicate important information to us. He never told us about your group. So we went ahead and booked another group. I'm really sorry. We're just about full."

"You're sorry?! You're full?!" If I had heard of Xanax back then, I would have started popping them like Chiclets. I couldn't believe what I was hearing. I had 80 kids leaving the next day for a trip that I had been planning for months, and we had no housing! When the guy at the other end of the line finally heard me stop yelling for a moment to take a breath, and realized that I wasn't going to accept his apology, he jumped in quickly and tried his best to offer some possible solutions. He said that the group that was booked could (somehow) double up some rooms. Also, it turned out that they didn't have every room booked. So that meant with a little stretching, he could find rooms for about half of our 80. Ok, but that wasn't even close to what we needed.

He then offered to call every hotel in town and see if he could find enough rooms for the rest of our group, and added that he would cover the price difference if another hotel was more expensive. At least he was trying. But how soon could he let us know? The buses were pulling out of the parking lot the next afternoon. He said it would be close, but he couldn't guarantee the rooms before we left. By the next day when we were leaving, we still didn't know and I learned that we wouldn't know for sure until later than night.

The only people who knew our dilemma were Carol, the Darien leader and my committee chairman at the time, Ed Nichols. We huddled up, and here's what we decided: we would leave with both buses, and not tell a soul. By that night we'd be about half way across Pennsylvania. We would stop at a rest area, (this was long before cell phones) find a pay phone and call. If they didn't have the rooms we would just turn the buses around and come home. I know, crazy! But the only other option would have been to cancel the trip before we left.

That was the longest six hours of my life; driving west, and wondering if we were going to be heading east later that night, all the while trying to act normal and not being able to tell anyone. We finally stopped to call. We got the rooms! Relief isn't strong enough of a word for how I felt. When we got to Park City space was at a premium, and some of our group had to be at another hotel down the mountain. Not a great set up, but by far better than the alternative. Whew.

Being Entertained in Bermuda

The first place my brain goes to when I think about our Bermuda trips was the hours in the emergency room at the hospital, dealing with kids who fell off of their motorbikes. Fortunately, there weren't any real serious injuries. The second story is more adventurous, and it illustrates that fine line between giving kids a loose reign, and trying to cope with what happens when they get too wild.

On that first trip to Bermuda, after one of our very late night dancing nights, followed by an eating free-for-all, just as the eastern sky was beginning to lighten, we finally had everyone settled down; the girls upstairs and the guys down. The house was on the side of the hill, so the second floor had its own entrance. I was, of course, downstairs with the guys. Just as we were finally settling down, we heard what sounded like singing and dancing. We all got out of bed and ran to the window that looked out onto the lawn, and saw a very interesting sight.

The girls had decided that it would be really funny if they got out of the house from their upstairs door and put on a little show for us in front of our window, a chorus line. I never really found out what sort of logic made them think it would be even funnier if they did this in their underwear. (I later learned that for the sake of modesty, they wore their bikini bathing suits under the underwear. That logic also defied me.) I can tell you, it was a shocker; all of the guys looking on, as dawn was almost breaking. Other guest houses including that of the manager weren't too far away. What does the Young Life leader do when something like that happens? I knew of no manual or policy that covered contingencies like this. Put in a call? "Help me Obi-Wan Kenobi. You're our only hope."

As we stood there watching them and I was trying to figure out how to handle this, (Laugh? Go along with it? Make a fuss?) one of the guys suddenly yelled to the rest of us, "Quick! Go lock every door!" Pretty soon we had a dozen girls now running all around the outside of the house barely dressed, screaming instead of dancing. The wheels had completely gone off by then. I began to imagine conversations I might have with parents when we got home.

Finally someone let them in, but because the girls had done their outrageous stunt, the night wouldn't be over until the guys tried to top them. The plan emerged, and it wasn't going to be pretty. But because it didn't involve removing more clothing, I let it go, thinking, "Please Lord, let this night be over soon."

The plan: as soon as we knew the girls were all in their rooms and quiet upstairs, one of the guys was going to run upstairs and open the door that led outside. Another guy was going to ride his motorbike into the hallway and gun the motor really loudly and scare them. I reminded them that the motorbikes couldn't rev because they had automatic clutches and not a neutral gear, thinking that might put a damper on the plan. No problem. A third guy would meet the biker in the hallway, lift the rear wheel in the air and let the rider gun the engine and make all the noise he could while the rear wheel just spun in the air.

Everything went according to plan, right up until the rear wheel lifted off the floor in the hallway. The engine roared for sure. But the guy's bike, and specifically his rear tire, had been sitting in mud outside. Let's just say in a very short time, as girls were again screaming and running out of their rooms, the entire hallway looked as if a mud grenade had gone off. Then...it got worse.

Seeing what the guys had done, one of the girls tried to cut off the bike's escape route by slamming the upstairs door shut. The biker saw what happened, paused for a panicked second, then took the only other escape route available. He headed straight down the stairs. And he would have made it too, were it not for one small problem. Just before the bottom, the staircase made a 90 degree right turn. He didn't make the turn. Motorbike straight into the wall.

The conversation that morning with the manager may have been the greatest piece of diplomacy, tactfulness and groveling that I have ever pulled off. Walls, floors, ceilings and stairs were scrubbed cleaned, and I promised him my first born child so that we didn't have to sleep in the street for the rest of the week.

The Baddest Ski Run Ever

One year our winter ski trip was to one of my all-time favorite ski resorts: Jackson Hole, Wyoming. Jackson has a few of the scariest runs I've ever seen. It's a bit crass, but we used to call such runs "Oh S**t" runs, because when you got to the top of them and looked down, that's what you said. I must tell of my brush with infamy and the scariest ski run of them all, Corbet's Couloir. I've had the privilege of skiing all over the U.S. and a few places in Europe. I'm not the greatest skier but until the day I saw Corbet's there wasn't a run I had ever seen that I wasn't willing to at least try once.

For those interested in more details, Corbet's has its own Wikipedia page. It is a very steep and narrow gully carved into the side of the mountain. At the very top the walls are on three sides and are barely 10 feet apart. Looking at it from the tram it appeared like an inverted funnel. To enter, you must free fall 10 to 20 feet, depending on how much snow there is in the crevice. When you land, on very steep terrain, you must start making turns right away, otherwise you start bouncing off the walls. For those good enough to get it right, it must be thrilling. Unfortunately I'll never know.

I had read all about Corbet's beforehand and was really looking forward to seeing it for myself. I was reserving judgement as to whether I would actually try skiing it. On my first tram ride up the mountain I managed to wrestle my way to the front so I could get a better view. I found myself standing next to a lady a few years older than me. She was about five-foot-two and very petite. She looked like she would break if she took a hard fall. As the tram started to move I couldn't stand keeping my enthusiasm and anticipation to myself, so I told this lady how much I had been looking forward to seeing Corbet's. She smiled and said, "Yes, it's quite a run." She didn't seem nearly as taken with the fame of the scariest ski run in America, so I asked her if she was

171

visiting or a local. She replied that she lived in Jackson Hole. First clue.

There was something oddly quiet about her responses. At about that time the tram rose above a smaller ridge, and...there it was. In spite of the fact that we weren't standing at the top of it and looking down, it still elicited an involuntary "Oh S**t!" from someone. Then I realized, it was from me. Once again the lady next to me just smiled. After I got my breath, a thought suddenly occurred to me, and I turned and said, "Let me ask you something, have you ever skied that thing?" and she replied, in a subtle way that suggested she was just answering the question and not bragging, "Yes, actually, I ski it fairly often. I'm going to ski it now as a matter of fact." Ooookay...I smiled back. As soon as the tram stopped I made my way off and headed in the opposite direction from my new little friend and for the rest of the week I never got any closer to Corbet's Couloir.

Wardrobe Malfunctions

We've all had wardrobe malfunctions at times. With skiing sometimes there are equipment malfunctions. It certainly didn't help that we tended to be rather abusive with our equipment, especially when skiing with high school kids. One of their favorite pastimes was skiing off of jumps. These could range from fairly small bumps or moguls in the middle of a ski run, up to places like the well-known jump at Park City in an area known as Scott's Bowl. We had actually seen locals do full flips at Scott's Bowl, something not all that common back in the 70's and early 80's.

At Jackson that day one of the guys found what looked like a fairly harmless little jump. I looked at it and figured I could probably get some air and not destroy myself too badly. Note: when Young Life leaders go skiing with the big boys, that is, the kids on the trip who were on the high school ski team or who have been skiing all their lives, there is a palpable pressure to conform and perform. Whatever they were doing, I was still young enough and certainly competitive enough (not to mention dumb enough) to try it myself. Over the years I have gotten into some trouble thinking that way.

On this particular morning, after a number of guys had taken the jump, accompanied by a lot of "air", i.e. hang time, i.e. the number of seconds your skis are in the air and not touching the ground; along with the appropriate yelling and whooping, it was my turn. "Come on, you can do this." I told myself. I clicked my heals three times like Dorothy and headed down towards the jump. I don't think I properly calculated the hang time, nor the force with which the ground would come up and hit me. The result was not returning to Kansas, but what we affectionately called a "Yard Sale." This is where many pieces of your ski equipment and your clothing would wind up scattered all over the mountain: skis, poles, hats, goggles, gloves, and oh yes, the entire toe piece from my left ski binding.

My story ended with howling laughter from my ski buddies and me collecting my yard sale possessions. The "little" jump we took that morning was almost at the top of the mountain. Walking down the hill and carrying my injured ski, I made it back to the lodge just in time for lunch.

Bad Weather and Mountain Passes

Bad weather and driving through the mountain passes were personal nightmares on those trips. Every year, around December, I would start having dreams about riding coach buses in the mountains. And over the years I had more real life scares than a *Sharknado* movie. There were times when the accumulation of snow on some mountain passes was so high that we were actually pushing the snow with the front bumper of our bus.

One time, coming down off Hoosier Pass, the visibility was so bad that the driver was using yellow-lens ski googles (skiers use them in flat light and poor visibility.) The front door of the bus was open and I was stationed there, looking out; and the driver was basically aiming the bus between the mountain on one side, and snowplow poles (tall skinny poles that show the snow-plow drivers where the guardrails were located) on the other side of the road.

Whenever the Colorado State Police decided to declare Chain Law, it meant we had to stop and put snow chains on all of the tires in order to be allowed access to the passes. One night conditions were so bad, even with chains on, it took three quarters of an hour just to get out of a parking lot at Vail.

One of my most feared passes was called Battle Mountain Pass. To get from the Young Life camp to Vail, we had to either go over Vail Pass or Battle Mountain. Pick your poison. I hated Battle Mountain. It wasn't really even a pass. It was a road carved along the side of a mountain. It was so high that if a car or a bus were to go over the side, it would have rolled forever before getting to the bottom. I envisioned all of us inside the bus and that our faces would end up looking like a Picasso portrait, had we ever taken that plunge.

One evening we left Vail in a snow storm. When we got up on the pass the conditions were treacherous. Sitting up high inside the bus made the guardrail look mini-scule. I was thinking that if the driver lost control, there was no way that little guardrail would keep us from going over the side. Just about that time I looked out the front window and saw a car coming straight at us, completely out of control. Just as we were about to collide, he managed to swing his car around and shot past us going backwards. I ran and looked out the back of our bus just in time to see him do another 180, face forwards, and promptly smash into the snow bank on the side opposite from the guardrail. At that point I gave up all hope of sanity. I simply went to the back of the bus, sat down and closed my eyes. I think I probably sucked my thumb and rocked back and forth also.

Of all the close calls, the most dangerous one for me personally happened only a few hundred yards from camp. After another grizzly trip back from the ski slopes, tired and hungry, I was relieved to be off the passes and almost to camp. I could actually see the entrance ahead. But...something was going wrong. The bus was really slowing down. I asked the bus driver, who told me, "The road is a complete sheet of ice. It must have rained earlier and now it's frozen over." Sure enough, we kept going slower and slower as the tires lost traction. Finally we came to a stop, and then...slowly, we began to slide backwards. The hill wasn't very steep, and it was as if everything was in slow motion. But we could all tell, with absolutely no control, the bus was slowly heading downhill and across the road where a big ditch was waiting for us.

Right away I took charge. I transformed from a mild mannered Young Life leader into a combination of the Cowardly Lion and George Costanza, thinking, "Well, someone's going to have to go for help. It may as well be me." I opened the front door of the bus. We were just creeping slowly. I stepped out and put my foot on the ground. Half a second after my foot touched, my backside hit the ground, my foot having completely lost traction. I was sitting on that sheet of ice. Not only that, I also started to slide, and my speed was faster than the bus. I was literally going under the bus. I felt like I was drowning or going over a waterfall. At the very last second, just before I disappeared under steel and rubber, I felt a hand reach down and grab me. I was being pulled out from under the bus and to safety. When I looked up, it was my brother Jack, who was on the trip helping as a volunteer leader.

Last but not least, I would be remiss if I left out the stories involving, shall we say, temperature extremes. One year, as we were traveling cross country in the middle of February the heater broke down on the entire bus in the middle of Nebraska. By the time we got to the camp we had 40 frozen kid Popsicle sticks. At the other end of the temperature spectrum, one year we hit a patch of very warm and sunny weather. In reality it wasn't far above freezing, but with the intensity of the sun in the high altitude it felt like we were baking. For the next few days a lot of kids spent the afternoon skiing in shorts (they actually packed shorts?!) and at lunch they would strip down to bathing suits and sun bathe (they actually packed bathing suits?!) One of our leaders, Larry, decided to not only ski in shorts but shirtless as well. Here's a tip: never ski shirtless with a bunch of high school kids. They all know how to stop sideways and spray you with snow like a frozen tidal wave.

Who Needs a Mountain?

One of my favorite alums was a kid who was very involved in club and Campaigners. We also knew his parents well, and his Mom was our sons' kindergarten teacher. His name is Trey. Trey went on to be one of the co-hosts of a popular sports program. Carol and I see him all the time on TV, and I can't help smiling, thinking of the great times we had with Trey when he was in high school. Trey also married a young lady who was also very involved in Young Life in Greenwich, Janice.

Trey was one of the funniest and least inhibited kids I knew. One of my markers for a reputation like that would be putting kids in skits at club. I could ask Trey to do anything in a skit and he would do it enthusiastically. And with Trey, anything he did from up front was funnier because he was doing it. My favorite Trey story took place on one of our ski trips.

One year we took an extra ski trip over Christmas break to Mad River Glen ski area in Vermont. We had a great week of skiing, and Trey was on that trip. On the way home on a Sunday night, our brilliant bus driver managed to run out of gas on the highway. Fortunately, he succeeded in coaxing the bus into a rest area. What the kids didn't know was that we were in for a very long rest stop. Unlike regular gasoline engines, diesel engines, like the kind in our bus that night, not only required diesel fuel, their injectors had to be primed in order to get the engine started again. And that meant getting a mechanic on site, late on a Sunday night.

The rest stop overlooked the highway. From where we were parked, we looked down a long slope that ended right at the edge of the southbound lane. That slope was snow covered. I was sitting in my seat on the bus brooding over the long night ahead, and having to find a phone and start calling parents and telling them about our delay when all of a sudden Trey yelled, "Everyone, look at that hill. Let's go skiing!" And before I could even move, he had the entire busload pouring out of the bus and into the parking lot. The luggage storage bay doors went flying open and out came their ski equipment. Soon everyone was skiing down the hill.

Sometimes I can be a few fries short of a Happy Meal, but even I was smart enough to see a major safety issue. I said to Trey, "Great idea, but have you thought about anyone who may lose control at the bottom and ski out onto the highway?" No problem. He organized a line of guys to get down to the bottom of the hill and form a safety chain. With that issue resolved, everyone sort of took over and began the first (and only) Sunday Night Olympic Downhill Bus Stop Ski Championships. The slalom course consisted of several kids standing on the hill as slalom gates, and skiers would run the slalom course around them. Another popular event was to see how many kids could stand on one set of skis while going down the slope; some in front of the person in the bindings, and some behind. No one even got close to the highway with that event, as eight or nine kids on one set of skis usually fell over after about twenty feet.

All of this was not only great fun, it was a memory that kids talked about for a long time afterwards. Plus, it killed the few hours we otherwise would have been stuck on the bus waiting for fuel and a mechanic. And it was all because of the creative energy of Trey, who was the instigator.

Sailing on the Sound

Rob was another kid who heard the Gospel for the first time on one of our ski trips. Both he and his brother were strong skiers. During the week in Colorado we skied a lot together and became close friends, which continued when we got back to Greenwich. One day Rob called and said he had to pick up his Dad's sailboat that had been in for repairs. He asked if I wanted to go with him. I said yes and picked him up. The plan was to drop my car off at the Greenwich train station and take the train down to nearby Mamaroneck, a town in West-chester County, right on the Long Island Sound, where the marina was located that had repaired the boat. We were then going to sail the boat back up to Greenwich, to the yacht club where Rob's Dad kept it.

We got to the marina and had a launch take us out to the boat, and when I saw it I have to say, I was im-pressed. It was very sleek, and about 45 feet in length. I was only in the beginning stages of learning how to sail, something that was part of most Greenwich kid's list of talents that came from living on the Sound. Many kids we knew had taken sailing lessons since they were very young. I figured, if Rob's Dad was letting Rob take this boat out, Rob must know how to handle it, and I could just enjoy the ride.

As we were sailing the boat up The Sound, I couldn't help but notice that down below, the cabin looked really sparse. There wasn't much in the way of amenities, and what was there looked stripped down. When I asked Rob about this, he said, "Oh, yeah, well my Dad races this boat. Have to keep it lightweight." That made sense. By then I knew that there was a huge sailing community and many accomplished racers in Greenwich as well as other nearby towns along the coast.

When we got to Greenwich and took care of mooring the boat, it was a short walk to the train station to retrieve my car, and I drove Rob home. Rob lived in one of those very large homes in back Greenwich. As we were pulling into his driveway, Rob said, "Hey do you have a minute? I just got a new pair of skis and I want to show them to you." As we entered Rob's house, we walked into a large foyer. In the middle of this foyer was a glass case, a very large glass case. And in the glass case were a number of trophies, some very large trophies-very large sailing trophies. Rob was in a rush to take me to the garage to see his skis, but as I went past the case, I couldn't help but slow down and look. I said to Rob, "What are all of these?" He replied, "Oh, they're my Dad's sailing trophies. I told you he raced the boat."

Although Rob was in a hurry, I wasn't moving. I began to read the inscriptions on the trophies, and slowly came to the realization that his Dad was a very successful and renowned international sailor. There were trophies from races all over the world. The ones that really caught my eye were the famous Newport to Bermuda Yacht Race trophies. Between Rob's Dad and his grandfather and the boat I had sailed in that day, they had won that race no less than three times. "Looking good, Billy Ray!" Feeling good, Louis!"

Chapter 10

Some of My Favorite People

We're at the point in our little tale where, you, the reader, get to decide if you want to read this chapter or skip it. It's sort of like those *Choose Your Own Adventure* books. Because this chapter is written for and about Greenwich people. If you aren't from Greenwich feel free to skip to the next chapter. Or maybe use the time to watch Susan Boyle sing *I Dreamed a Dream* on YouTube.

Over the course of the twelve years that we lived in Greenwich, we made many friends. This chapter is going to be hard to complete without leaving out a ton of them, but I will try to include as many stories and shout outs as I can remember. For anyone reading this who was a part of our lives at that time and we haven't mentioned you, please accept my apology.

The Bakers

It was in the summer of 1975 that we first met George and Marabel Baker. Carol and I were on a camp assignment in Colorado, where I was Program Director for a month at Silver Cliff Ranch, located just down the side of Mt. Princeton from Frontier Ranch. We got word that a

Greenwich family was staying at nearby Trail West Lodge, so when we had some free time we drove over to meet them. When they opened the door to their room, we not only met George and Marabel, we also met their three lovely adolescent daughters, Brenda, the oldest, then Beverly, and the youngest was Paula. One of the girls had been sick, so it was only a brief meeting that day, and we promised to reconnect at the end of the summer back in Greenwich.

The Bakers had a large, beautiful home in Old Greenwich, right across the road from a little private beach on the Long Island Sound. Brenda, the oldest daughter, was old enough to attend to Young Life, which she began doing. The Bakers were also members of a church in Old Greenwich that Carol and I would eventually join, The Presbyterian Church of Old Greenwich.

It wasn't long before George and Marabel became good friends. They joined the Young Life committee and became very active. One day Marabel asked about our leadership team, and soon after decided to be one of our volunteer leaders.

The Baker family went on to be among our closest life-long friends. The girls were spread out enough in age that we enjoyed at least one Baker girl in club and Campaigners for several years in a row. It didn't hurt that they were all beautiful and very popular at the high school! Marabel was to become our best female volunteer leader ever. The Baker home also became the popular hangout for Young Life kids for several years, not just the times when we held club in their family room, but all during the week.

George and Marabel became Christian role models for countless numbers of kids over the years they were involved. Because they were about ten years older than Carol and me, they became our role models for Christian parenting and as a married couple. Carol and I attribute so many of our abilities and talents as parents to being around the Bakers and learning from their lives. Although they have lived in California for many years, to this day George and Marabel have remained among our most valued friends-for-life. The girls are now all married and have their own kids.

The Lovejoys

Earlier I mentioned Lorain Kelley as one of the core kids in club when the club finally began to grow. One of her closest friends was Michele McPartland. Both were to become close friends-for-life. Together they went off to college and were roommates. After college Lorain started dating a guy who would also become a lifelong friend as well, Allen Lovejoy. I knew Allen from his high school days because he was one of the stars of the GHS lacrosse team. He was somewhat of a hell-raiser and hung out with a party crowd. But he was, easily, the best player I ever coached in Connecticut; so he had my attention and respect as an athlete. When Allen graduated he went off to Hobart College and wound up winning two National Lacrosse Championships there.

When Allen graduated from Hobart he moved back to town, and was able to buy a home shortly after he started working on Wall Street. He also had become a Christian. About the time Lorain returned from college, they started dating. They both became volunteer leaders in club. Eventually they tied the knot, and moved into the home that Allen had bought. We attended their wedding.

Allen and Lorain have remained, over 40 years later, close and dear friends. Like the Bakers but several years later, they also had three daughters: Avery, Carrie, and Elizabeth. As the girls were growing up, Carol and I had already moved to Florida. But whenever we went back to Connecticut we stayed with the family. They still live in the same home Allen bought just after school. To this day we still visit them, and they us. The girls are now all grown, and one of the great privileges of my lifetime-three great privileges actually-has been to conduct the wedding ceremonies of all three girls.

Key Kids

Michele McPartland lived just around the corner from us and often came over to babysit our boys. After graduating from college, she eventually met her husband. Carol and I had the privilege of introducing them to each other while we were all on a summer assignment at Saranac. Carol became very close to Lorain and Michele, along with many other girls from their crowd. Carol was a role model for them as the Bakers were for us.

It's hard to mention Lorain and Michele without speaking of Tim Ficker and Clem Williams. They were all close friends in high school, and also have kept in touch over the past 40 years. At the Young Life Greenwich's 50th anniversary celebration Clem, Tim, Allen and Lorain, along with many other "kids" from their generation, attended. Although I lost touch with Clem for a while, Tim and I have always remained close over the years. Like Michele and her future husband, Scott, Tim met his wife, Claire, at Saranac while on summer assignment with us. He also served on Young Life Staff for many years. When Tim came home from college during holidays, he and I would hang out at my house half the night and catch up. I still consider him one of my closest friends.

Committee and Parents

Over the years we had many committee members who also became lifelong friends. Ed Nichols was the chairman when we took the Park City ski trip and had to leave before we knew if we had rooms, mentioned earlier. His wife, Barbara, was also on the committee, and their kids,

Valery and Dale were both active in club and Campaigners. Whitey Heist was our finance chairman for several years. (Yes, there's a cheap laugh to be had, making fun of his last name and finances, but Lord knows, I would never insert cheap jokes in the middle of my serious writing endeavors.) His wife Mary ran a weekly Bible study in her home for years, which Carol attended. Whitey was one of the top executives at International Paper in Stamford. I'll always be grateful to him for helping me take a more professional approach to the business side of Young Life. Mary and Whitey's kids were also heavily involved with Young Life. They didn't attend Greenwich High, but went to a private school in town, Brunswick Academy. The boys were: Peter, Bill and Matthew Heist. Bill would eventually marry Lisa Fairchild, one of our first generation campaigner kids. Mary Heist was a mentor and role model for Carol and for many other women over the years, and we have remained in touch to this day.

I always think of two of my favorite men and role models together. That is, when I think of one of them he always reminds me of the other; Glen Dell and Walter Baker. Both were great friends of Young Life, and both were very involved in the leadership of our church. They were not only very successful businessmen, they were also great Dads and family men. Their kids were actively involved in club. Barbara Dell and Mary Baker also became wonderful friends of ours.

Gleason Frye was one of my cherished friends. Jack Carpenter had known Gleason and Joanne before we arrived in Greenwich, and told me that although Gleason had taken a few years off, I would be wise to try and recruit him back onto the committee. I was able to do that and eventually he was our committee chairman for several years. His kids, Nanette and Jonathan, were both involved in Young Life. It's been fun in recent years to reconnect with Nanette, as well as Jonathan. They both now have kids of their own who are involved in

Young Life, and Nanette and her husband have been very involved in Young Life as parents. Nanette also went on to serve on Young Life's National Board of Directors.

Gleason became for me one of those guys with whom I could go and sit down and share my life, and also learn from him. He had a practical wisdom and down-to-earth demeanor. It was easy for us to see him after we moved to Florida because he owned a business there and came to town occasionally. And for years after we left Greenwich whenever we flew back to visit, Gleason became our designated transportation source from LaGuardia airport to Connecticut. For anyone who ever lived in Greenwich, you know what kind of sacrifice and inconvenience it is to drive from Greenwich to LaGuardia and back.

Don and Joann Kern became treasured friends over many years. Although they have moved and we don't get to see them much anymore, we still keep in touch. They were on the committee and their kids, Marti and Michael were involved in Young Life. One of the saddest days of my life, less than a year after Carol and I had moved to Florida, started with a phone call from my Young Life replacement in Greenwich, Willy Bogan. He called to tell us that Michael had been tragically killed in a car accident. At Michael's funeral I had never before witnessed, in the midst of incredible pain, such inner intimacy with God than I saw in Don and Joanne. Little did I know how much their friendship, and the road they had traveled would minister to Carol and me many years later.

Bill and Shirley Prey and Peter and Evie Huckel were next door neighbors. Both were parents of great kids who were in club and Campaigners, and both became not only Young Life supporters but also great friends. Bill Prey and I shared a love for sports cars and motor racing; and sometimes our conversations would go well into the night.

Then there was the Norwegian connection; four more parents with kids very active in Young Life, supporters and great friends-for-life. They had been close friends in Norway before moving to Connecticut: Odd and Hanna Mi Johannessen, and Ellen and Per Johansen. Today they live in Florida and from time to time we still get together.

Peer Friends

A lot of our friends, like some mentioned above, were a few years older and became guiding role models and mentors for us. There were also several couples who were our age, with whom we became very close. The three couples we most often socialized with were Steve and Sam Lanfer, Karen and Greg Morgan, and Sandy and Sandi Campbell. Yes, that's not a misprint. When Carol and I referred to them in conversation we had to say, "Boy Sandy" or "Girl Sandi." We all hung out and did things together. Sandi and Sandy had the first VCR we had ever seen. They used to invite us over on Friday nights for popcorn, a movie, and champagne, of all things.

We were all members of the same church and we all had kids at about the same time. Thanks to some creative lobbying, the Campbell's managed to leverage a "ministerial membership" to the country club in Old Greenwich where they were already members, Innis Arden. We have many wonderful memories of these three couples and their kids, all grown and married now, with their own children. Steve Lanfer and I played tennis together, as did Greg Morgan. Carol was very close to all three of the ladies. The saddest memory was that Girl Sandi passed away at age 40 from cancer not long after we had moved to Florida. Never before had we lost a friend who was so close and also so near to our age. It was my privilege to speak at Sandi's funeral. It took me a long time to get over her passing.

I had a mysterious experience involving Sandi, many years later, in 1999, when I was traveling extensively for my new job. I was asked to preach at a large Church service in Kiev, Ukraine. The service was just about to begin. There were probably about 500 people assembled. I was near the front and just looking around when suddenly I saw someone who, for a moment, I fully believed to be Sandi Campbell. They say there is a look alike for everyone somewhere in the world. This woman appeared out of nowhere, and seeing her was just... shocking. In fact, it shook me so much that I literally had to sit down for a moment. When I tried to find her again, she was gone. To this day I sometimes wonder, was it just a look alike, or was there something else going on that I didn't understand? I'm normally not one of "those guys" who claims to have unusual encounters like that, but it just felt so strange and real that it really shook me.

The Harris Families

The Harris's: two families, not related, same last name, very different and both very special. Jane and Buzz Harris and their kids: Julie, Lee and Christy. Julie eventually wound up on Young Life Staff. John and Nancy Harris, and their kids: Julie, John, and Melissa. Nancy Harris will shoot me for telling this story, but it must be told! My favorite Harris memory, (other than having the privilege of conducting the wedding for Melissa,) involved their son John, and a skit I had him do in club one night. To fully appreciate the gravity and deep significance of this most unholy event, the background must be first explained.

During one year the town of Greenwich was suffering from a severe drought. The drought got so bad and the reservoir was so low, that we were told in the newspaper, if we got down to less than ten days of water supply that the town government was prepared to turn off the tap to everyone except hospitals and emergency services. While it never reached that point, there were days when we were all seriously concerned.

As a public service, the local newspaper started publishing daily water saving tips for around the home. These tips began as obvious suggestions, like not watering your lawn or washing your car. But over time more creative suggestions appeared, like putting bricks in your toilet tank so you would use less water when you flushed. The longer the drought lasted, and with the Greenwich Time's self-imposed pressure of printing a daily tip, the suggestions gradually went from creative to comically ridiculous.

There was an old skit that some Young Life leaders would use. But it was so disgusting and gross, even for me, that I had always refused to use it. A clear glass of water was placed on a table. The first person walked out and took a sip, then left. A second person followed, and not only took a sip, but also gargled some and then spit it back into the glass, and left. A third person did the same. A fourth came out, produced a toothbrush and toothpaste and proceeded to brush his teeth, using the water in the glass, then rinsed and spit the water back into the glass. The last person came out and said in a loud voice, "Man, am I thirsty!" and promptly lifted the cloudy, toothpaste colored, half-water and half-saliva glass and drank it all.

After weeks of idiotic and comical water savings suggestions in the newspaper, the set up for this skit was just too good to pass up: "Young Life's own water saving tip: share water with friends."

My main problem was finding a guy brave enough to be the last one out, who drank everyone else's backwash. Enter John Harris. This was a kid after my own heart. He would literally do anything for a laugh. The perfect club kid. When I asked him to be the last one in the skit, he didn't even hesitate. The Robo Cop of club kids.

One other little back story: his parents, John and Nancy, were on the committee. An assignment given to every committee member was to visit club twice a year, once in the fall and once in the spring. This was to encourage them to keep in better touch with the ministry's activities. I thought it was a very good concept, except for the fact that the night of this particular skit also happened to be the same night that John's mom, Nancy, was assigned to visit club.

This is going to get even grosser than it already is, so be advised. What's the warning on TV shows? "This may not be appropriate for general audiences." By the time John came out on stage and pronounced "Man, am I thirsty," the crowd was already getting ugly from what they had seen so far. John didn't down the whole glass at once. He drank about half of it and then pulled the glass away from his mouth. This had the immediate and sickening effect of forming a looping line of saliva, running from the lip of the glass to his mouth. That's when the screams began. John saw it and quickly downed the rest of the contents of the glass, wiped the drool from this mouth, and exited.

Kids were shrieking, laughing, gagging, yelling, slapping each other; and utter chaos ensued. A few kids jumped up and ran outside. I was later told that they threw up. The last site I recall was John's mom, Nancy, in the back of the room with a horribly disfigured look on her face, jumping up and running out. Nancy quit the Young Life committee the next day. Was it worth it? You bet. She later came back. She loved us, even though I'm sure she hated me that night. Once, when Carol was in the hospital from an accident, Nancy cared for our toddler son, Adam, for two weeks. She was the one who potty-trained him. I knew she couldn't stay angry forever.

Leaders

One day a student told me that I should meet one of the science teachers at Greenwich High, who she thought was a Christian. That's how I first met Joe Wesney, and later on his wife Anita. Their kids, Doug and Tom got involved in Young Life. Joe and Anita eventually joined the Young Life committee and Joe also became a volunteer leader. In spite of a hectic schedule he was always present and had a great rapport with kids. Somehow he fell into the job of giving announcements at club. One would think that is a fairly safe and pedestrian job, but not with us. We managed to dress this well-mannered and highly respected science teacher, (and eventually the head of the entire science department), into the most absolutely ridiculous costumes. He would give the announcements completely straight-faced. The kids loved it.

Ian Cron was one of the most gifted leaders I've ever known. He was a club kid in high school and we kept in touch during his four years at Bowdoin College. When he graduated and returned to Greenwich, although he was a bit reluctant to join our leadership team I persuaded him to lead music in club. I knew he was a gifted guitar player. It wasn't long before he started helping with skits, giving talks, going on our trips, and becoming fully invested in Young Life in Greenwich as a volunteer leader. Eventually Ian decided he wanted to join the staff full time. The nearby town of New Canaan was looking for a staff person and Ian was placed there. In time he relocated one town over, to Wilton, Connecticut, where he ran a great Young Life ministry. He eventually left staff and went into fulltime church ministry.

I think the best kind of volunteer leader any Young Life Staff person could have was my close friend, Eric Broadbent. Eric and I got to know each other when I was looking for some leaders to help us with our ski trips out west. Eric was an incredible skier, but not a hot-dog type. His style was smooth and controlled. It was fun just to be on the slopes with him, and I learned to ski better every time we skied together, which was a lot. Eric was also a powder-hound, and he passed that technique and passion along to me as well. I loved skiing, but it got to the point where I would have considered giving up my first born for a good day of fresh, deep powder skiing.

Before explaining why Eric was a great leader, another ski story must to be told. A few of our annual winter ski trips were to a place where Eric had actually lived for a while, Steamboat Springs. One particular year the skiing was great, but they hadn't seen fresh snow for several days, so finding untracked powder was a challenge. Good powder-hounds have a way of finding the fluffy stuff, even if it means hiking for it, or, going into the often-feared trees. Most normal people wouldn't think of skiing in the woods amongst the trees for the obvious reason; if you make a mistake, trees are hard and unforgiving, and they hurt when you hit them. But when the powder gets beaten down on the slopes, you can still find it in the trees. Besides, Steamboat was known for some breathtaking tree and glade skiing.

Eric and I took off for the woods. We soon found some delicious fresh powder and were having a ball, whooping and yelling...right up until I made the slightest of mistakes. My skis wound up on the right side of an aspen tree and my body on the left. Normally my body and my skis would have parted company right then. However, as any powder-hound knows, when skiing the deep stuff, you had better wear the old fashion ski traps. They function like a leash on a surf board. Otherwise when you lose a ski, the normal ski brake mechanism won't stop the ski in deep snow, so it can continue down the slope, often under the surface, for as long as gravity keeps pulling it. I've seen more than a few guys walking along the bottom of a ski hill poking their ski poles into the snow like they were trying to find a dead body, looking for their lost ski.

For me and my ski straps, try to imagine the position. I wound up face down, and facing down the mountain. My feet were up closer to the trunk of the tree. The straps were wrapped around the tree and my skis were facing, like me, down the mountain. And I might add, this all happened on a very steep hill. As a result, there was absolutely no way I could extricate myself from this position without help. Good for me that Eric was skiing with me. Bad for Eric that at the time of my spill he was skiing slightly below me. By the time I could yell out and Eric stopped, he was about 25 feet further down the hill. If you have ever tried walking uphill in three feet of snow, on a 40 degree slope, you won't be surprised that it was neither a happy nor a short trip for Eric to get back up to me and free me from my ski straps. I heard about that little incident for the next year or more.

With that little Lindsey Vonn side trip I think I buried the lead regarding Eric. I loved having him as one of our leaders, for several reasons. He was one of the kindest and most compassionate persons I knew. He didn't have a pretentious or arrogant bone in his body, which made him so approachable, especially to high school kids. He had two qualities that I really appreciated: he was transparent, and he was always willing to make himself vulnerable. We had other leaders who were flashier, or more gifted up front, but no one could come alongside of kids and meet them in their environment like Eric, with the possible exception of Marabel Baker.

But what I admired most about Eric was that he wasn't dependent on the club speaker, or the camp speaker to share the Gospel. He could sit down with a kid at any time and any place and share his faith. And he could do it in a winsome and relational way. While we were blessed to see a ton of kids come to Christ through club and camps, none of us could sit down one-on- one with kids and lead them to faith, like Eric. Although I was proud to work with Eric, I have to admit that I was a little embarrassed that I, the Young Life Staff guy, wasn't as gifted or as bold as Eric when it came to sharing one-on-one with kids. I knew a whole lot of kids who would later say that they accepted the Lord when talking with Eric.

Church Friends

From our church we got to know and become close to many friends, people like Connie and Happy Pappas. Happy had been in Young Life when she attended Greenwich High School many years before we got to town. She and Connie had two wonderful daughters, Beth and Jenn, both in Young Life. At one point, after college, Beth actually worked with Young Life in Sweden. And all of them have remained dear friends to this day, even though we don't see them very often.

We didn't know a lot of folks from Greenwich Baptist Church, but our close friends and committee members from GBC were Don and Lita Holt. Over the years all four of their kids, Lisa, Brad, Dawn and Courtney were all involved with club and Campaigners. The Holt girls (ladies!) attended the Young Life Greenwich's 50th anniversary celebration in 2012.

We first met Jim and Roxanne Scarlata because their oldest son, Jeff, was in club. Over the years their younger sons, Chris and Mark, also got involved; and over time the Bonds and the Scarlatas became close friends. Years later Jim and Roxanne moved to Florida and to this day we still see and socialize with them.

Frank Starvel became an esteemed friend and to this day, whenever I get back to Greenwich I give him a call and we share a meal and fellowship together. Like Gleason Frye, Frank has always been the kind of guy that although I might not see him often, when I do I can share easily with him, and look to him for his wise insights.

Norma and Norman Webster were from Johannesburg, South Africa. They moved to Greenwich with their daughter, Cheryl, and their son, Grayden. The kids starting coming to Young Life and the Webster parents soon got involved. They joined the committee and not long after, Norma became the secretary for our Greenwich office. You may think that working for me in a tiny office and an IBM Selectric typewriter was a great gig with lots of perks and pay. In reality, Norma did it out of the love of her heart for Young Life, because her work was done completely as a volunteer.

Earlier I wrote a lot about my good friend Tom Pilsch. He was two years behind me in college, and after graduation he, too, came on full time Young Life Staff. A highlight for me in 1978 was getting Tom to move to Connecticut and take over the work in nearby Darien. I was reunited with my buddy, and we were working together in Young Life. While we each ran different clubs, there was a whole lot of collaborating for county wide events, and camps. Although initially Tom was part of our annual ski trips, in 1981 he designed his own and asked Carol and me to go with him. Our trips had been in the Rockies, knowing that places like Colorado had a lot more appeal than the more close-by ski areas in Vermont and New Hampshire. But Tom decided to go a step further. Upping the ante, he put together a trip to Europe.

Chamonix

The place he decided upon was Chamonix, France. Chamonix is a beautiful town high in the French Alps, nestled under the largest Mountain in Europe, Mont Blanc. Surrounding the town, up in the mountains were half a dozen different ski areas, all making up the ski resort known as Chamonix. Each morning we would walk out of our hotel and get on a city bus. We would ride through town with everyday commuters. The buses were equipped with ski racks and the bus routes would actually take us out to the ski areas.

The Alps are majestic and the skiing was just fantastic. We had a great group of kids from Darien High School. Each night we held club back at the hotel. Tom asked our longtime friend, Peter Moore, to speak. Peter was the founder of a ministry called FOCUS, which is an outreach to private schools, including some of New England's top boarding schools. Peter and his wife Sandy accompanied us. The hotel was pretty cheap, but we didn't really care. It was called Hotel des Lacs, and the kids started calling it "Shack de Lac." They weren't used to common bathrooms at the end of the hallway, or, instead of sinks and toilets in the room, having sinks and bidets. You know that they weren't going to walk down the hall when that bidet was available for "some things."

After the Young Life trip, Carol and I were afforded a wonderful opportunity, as a gift from a club kid's parents in Greenwich. Jacques Bulterman was from The Netherlands and was involved with a travel agency in Switzerland. He arranged for us to stay as his guests in a hotel in Davos, Switzerland. At the end of our time in Chamonix, we said goodbye to the Darien group, boarded a train and headed, first to Geneva, then across the country through Bern and then Zurich. We then turned more southeast and started to ascend into the Alps, eventually finding our way to the picturesque ski town of Davos. This all happened in March, and it was beautiful to see that Spring was just starting to break in the valleys. Flowers were blooming, and the grass was turning green. But once we were in the mountains it was still full-on, all white wintertime.

We stayed in a beautiful little hotel right in town and

skied for a few days at Davos. We also wanted to see as much of the general area as we could. We rented a car and decided to drive over to nearby Austria. On our way we passed through the marvelous little nation of Liechtenstein. It's so small you can almost see from one end of it to the other. In a fight, even Rhode Island could kick its butt.

From there we passed into Austria. This was well before the Berlin wall came down, marking the fall of the Eastern Bloc nations. Border crossings had checkpoints. Passports had to be shown. And although Austria was in the West, we had never been there before, and it was a bit intimidating to see border guards holding automatic rifles and machine guns. It reminded me of that border crossing in *Stripes*. Ok, it happened before that movie came out. Just taking a little literary license.

We were admitted and made our way into beautiful Austria. We weren't close enough to visit places like Salzburg or Vienna. Little did we know that a few years later we would have that privilege during my sabbatical. But we were close enough to visit the ski villages of St. Anton, Zurs, and Lech. The snow was piled so high on the side of the roads, in places it was as if we were rats in a maze. But when we popped out to where we could see, the views were breathtaking. By the way, you might wonder, who did the babysitting back home while we were off in Europe suffering for the Lord? Two of our favorite college girls: Lorain Kelley and Barb Hindman.

Into the Missions Field

We have long since lost count of the club kids who eventually moved on to full-time ministry or missions work, or even onto Young Life Staff. But that isn't so unusual. Any Young Life leader who's been around for more than 10 to 15 years could make a similar claim. But there are two people who stand out especially, maybe because they are living and working on the continent of Africa, a part of the world that has captured my heart like no other. Susan and Meredith Townsend were two sisters who both were involved in club all through high school. Years after we left Greenwich I learned that Meredith had married and moved to Africa with her husband, where they have remained, as missionaries, to this day. We regularly receive ministry updates from them.

Peter and Christian (pronounced Chris John) Fretheim were brothers who moved to Greenwich from Scandinavia. They lived out in back country on a large estate. I think their Dad was, at one time, a big-time ski jumper; not the kind of jumping we did on Young Life ski trips, but the kind that starts on top of a giant ramp. Believe it or not, they actually had a Nordic ski jump in their back yard. Peter and I climbed up to the top of it one day, and could see the Long Island Sound several miles away.

Peter and Christian were very much products of hanging out at the Baker's house down by the beach in Old Greenwich. Both brothers became Christians and grew strong in their faith. Like Meredith, years after we left Greenwich, Peter Fretheim got married and was called into missionary work. To this day he and his family live and work in Jos, Nigeria. I get regular ministry updates from him as well. And when he comes back to the States, one of his stops is at his home church, the same one that was to become our church home, The Presbyterian Church of Old Greenwich.

Chapter 11

Growing

In the midst of some good growth in ministry, (finally!) there were also a number of other events which shaped our lives and work. Some had nothing to do with Young Life per se, but nevertheless where impactful. We lived through the tragic murder of Martha Moxley, a Greenwich teenager who was beaten to death by Michael Skakel in 1975. Readers might remember, though, that he wouldn't be convicted until many years later, in 2002.

We also endured the infamous ice storm in the early winter of 1973. We were still living in the house on Mary Jackson's estate in back Greenwich. Matthew was a baby. The electricity went out for several days. The house had but one source of heat, a gas stove in the kitchen. We tacked a blanket over the entrance to the kitchen and pretty much lived in that one room. After a few days, as soon as the roads cleared, we packed up and drove to Baltimore until the electricity was finally restored.

In the funny-but-not-so-funny-flash-forward depart-ment: many years later, in 1997, a film came out called Ice Storm. It was a fictional story but based around that actual storm of 1973. Our son Matthew was out of college and on Young Life Staff. He was the Area Director for New Canaan, just up the road from Greenwich. The town of New Canaan was the setting of the movie. He told us that there was a huge buzz in New Canaan when people heard about the film coming out. But the buzz soon turned sour when people went to see the film. It was a dark, depressing film, filled with moral decay, and a tragic ending. New Canaanites were not happy campers. Could have been worse. They could have lived in the town where *Pompeii* was filmed.

On the Field

When we first moved to Connecticut I was hoping to continue to play lacrosse. Having played and being known was a great entrée at the high school, especially since they were looking for a coach. But I still wanted to actually play. The United Stated Club Lacrosse Association, the governing body for men's lacrosse nationally, divided the nation into a southern division and a northern one. The winner of each would play for the National Championship each year. The year before we moved to Greenwich I had played for the southern division champions that won the National title. Moving to Connecticut, I wanted to play on a good northern division team. And to play for the best team meant traveling from Greenwich down to Long Island to play for Long Island Athletic Club. Our home field was Hofstra University's football stadium, in Hempstead.

For the next six years, until I retired from playing, twice a week during the season I would make the drive from Greenwich, down across the Whitestone Bridge and out to Hempstead, for practice during the week and games on weekends. It was about 100 miles round trip, with practice running from eight to ten at night. With the "normal" New York traffic, if I left the house at seven I'd get there at eight. If I left the house at six o'clock, I'd still get there at eight. It was torturous, but it was worth it. We managed to win the National Championship in my first two years and also in my last year with the team. Sometimes I'd take some of the GHS lacrosse players with me and it was fun to expose them to some of the top players in the country. And in the sport of lacrosse that also meant some of the top players in the world. I also managed to get some of my teammates out to Greenwich occasionally to help me run lacrosse clinics at the high school-something that gave me some nice brownie points with the school's athletic department.

In the spring of 1973 I was playing a home game on an unusually cold, Easter Eve night, at the Hofstra field. Carol was very pregnant and due any day, but I forced her to go to the game anyway. I mean, she wanted to go anyway. Because she was pregnant, and it was cold, she was given permission to sit in the press box. It was the next day, Sunday, April 22nd that our first son, Matthew Taylor, was born. To this day whenever we happen to see the current professional lacrosse team, The Long Island Lizards, playing on that same field, we wait for a camera view of the press box and fondly reminisce about that night. Carol says she can still almost feel the contractions.

My Brother

Although this lacrosse story has nothing to do with lacrosse per se, it has a lot to do with an historic part of my life personally, and Young Life. In addition to holding a National Championship, each year there was an All-Star game, which pitted the top players in the north with their counterparts in the southern division. One particular year the game was held in a well-known lacrosse school in Baltimore, Severna Park High School. I traveled down from Connecticut and was looking forward not only to playing in the game but also seeing friends and relatives. Tom Pilsch was still living in Maryland and he came to the game, along with my brother, Jack. The two of them were sitting together, and another person from my past happened to be there.

You may recall me mentioning a young lady who was in my Young Life Club at Woodlawn High School, Sheryl Liphard. I hadn't seen Sheryl since we moved to Connecticut so it was great to reconnect with her after the game. It was during that game that Tom introduced Sheryl to my brother. Although Jack was several years older, both he and Sheryl were single. They hit it off and decided to keep in touch. And...the rest, as they say...is history.

When they got married, they gave me the honor of conducting their ceremony. Eventually they settled down in the community of Severna Park. In time our nephew and niece were born, Eric and Sarah. They grew up and went to Severna Park High school, the very place where their parents first met. There was also a Young Life club at the school, run by a longtime friend from my Maryland days. Eric and Sarah were involved with club and Campaigners, and Jack and Sheryl were very active on the Young Life committee for many years. Like the Kardashians, we like to keep it in the family. Sarah is currently on Young Life Staff with camp food services.

New Church Home

After worshipping for a few years at Stanwich Congregational Church, for several reasons we began to feel the need for a change. But after leaving the church, we remained close friends with Nate Adams, the pastor. One reason for the change was the arrival of a new pastor in town, Dave Phillips. Dave had a history with Young Life in Pittsburgh, and even knew my Young Life leader, Chuck Reinhold. Sometimes with a change in churches, the transition can be challenging. But for the most part we remained good friends with folks at Stanwich even though we had switched to Dave's church. For years, though, I felt guilty about stealing the candle sticks from the altar when we left.

Our new church was the Presbyterian Church of Old Greenwich, or simply, PCOG. From then on, until we moved to Florida, that was to be our church home and the place where we had and still have a number of lifelong friends. Our sons were baptized there and grew up going to Sunday school. I was occasionally asked to preach there. I officiated weddings of several friends and former club kids. Sadly, I was also part of a few funerals as well, including our beloved friend Sandi Campbell.

The PCOG parking lot also became the home racing circuit for the Bond Racing Team. I've always loved motorsports, and one day I had the opportunity to buy a pretty decent go kart. I'd like to say it was for my children, but in reality it was for me. I'd eventually let Matthew and Adam race it when they got a little older and their feet reached the pedals. But in the meantime, I had my racing program all worked out. I would take several tennis ball cans and fill them with sand (pylons) and set out a twisty course on the parking lot. Then I'd grab a bunch of club kids and we'd go racing, taking turns on the kart and timing each other. There's a great principle here, and if my memory serves me, it was from my old mentor in Baltimore, Jerry Johnson. He said, "One good way to build relationships with kids: find something you like to do and get them to do it with you."

Hospital Visits

On February 18th of 1976 we welcomed our second son, Adam Taylor Bond, into the world. He not only was a Bicentennial baby, he was also born on the birthday of Enzo Ferrari. If you have to ask...don't. Once again, we made the trip to Greenwich hospital. I'd like to say the only other trip to that hospital was for our third son, six years later. But Carol changed that. When Adam was still in diapers and Matthew was just a few years older, Carol managed to find herself in the emergency room, followed by a two week hospital stay.

Carol had been riding horses with Bonnie Caie, our good friend and wife of my co-worker, Bob Caie. By that time Bob and Bonnie had left Young Life Staff and moved back to Greenwich. Fortunately for us, they came on our committee. Not only did we have their support and friendship, but also, more than anyone on our committee, they understood what it was like to be on Young Life Staff. They could relate to our lives. Bonnie had her own horse and stabled another, the one Carol would often ride.

One day, out in back Greenwich the two of them were riding together on one of the many trails. Apparently Carol and her horse had a disagreement about the direction of the trail as it related to one particular stone wall. The horse thought the trail went to one side of the wall, and Carol insisted on the other side. The horse won. Carol, I'm told, did a perfect forward flip up and over the horse's head and wound up on the ground, on her back, several feet away. By the time Bonnie caught up, it was evident that the only remaining question was; how was an ambulance going to get all the way back into the woods? Carol's back was broken, but by God's grace there was no paralysis. The back brace she had to wear for the next six months was, however, fairly fashionable.

Sometime after the brace came off, Carol was approached by the Athletic Director at the high school. By then I had been coaching the boys' varsity lacrosse team for a few years with Tony Minotti. Back in Baltimore, guys like me who knew lacrosse and could coach the game were a dime a dozen in lacrosse circles. But Connecticut was considered the lacrosse hinterlands back then, and someone with my experience was rather rare. The same was true for Carol, who had already been coaching at a private school in town, Greenwich Country Day. The Athletic Director at Greenwich HS asked Carol if she would help start a girl's lacrosse team. The policy was the same as with me: a person who wasn't a full time employee in the Greenwich school system could not be a head coach. So, also like my situation with Tony Minotti (He was the head coach on paper; I was the X's and O's guy, on the field) Carol was paired with a teacher who didn't know the game either, but who was eager to learn and who was also accepted by school policy. The bottom line was, we both benefitted greatly by all of the kids we got to know and relationships we built. And at the same time we engendered a whole lot of good will, and good "press", for Young Life around the high school and especially in the athletic department.

The Barn

As our club work continued to grow we were finally getting to the point where our meetings were too large for houses. I was reminded of the iconic words of Amity Island Police Chief Martin Brody, "We're gonna need a bigger boat." Unlike shark hunting, it was the kind of problem that we would never complain about having, but one we still had to solve. We began to look around and consider what options might be available. There was a girl on Carol's lacrosse team, Sally Hopkins, who came to club and had heard we were looking for a bigger place. She said to Carol, "We have an art studio on our property. You should ask my Dad if you can use it for club." I soon contacted her Dad, Rich Hopkins. He and his wife Bobbi had lived in town for many years, and they were delighted that Sally was interested in Young Life, not to mention that one of the leaders was also her lacrosse coach.

When I went to visit Rich, he walked me through his home and out the back door. I looked across the driveway and saw the art studio. In my mind I was thinking, "How big can a personal art studio be? We can fit close to a hundred kids in some of our larger homes. I would love to have room for twice that many." But when Rich opened the door, I knew we had found the perfect place for club; that is, if Rich would still say yes after I told him that over 100 kids or more would be traipsing across his property every week. (We eventually grew to over 200 kids at times.) I'm not sure he envisioned just what that would look like, and how many cars would stretch down his driveway and into the front street. But to my delight he gave us the green light. His daughter Sally loved Young Life and he and Bobbi wanted to help us in any way they could.

What a memorable place! Any kid who was in club during those years can tell you stories about the nights in the "Hopkins barn." (Somehow the art studio label never took.) Being a Program Director at heart, I designed a stage area, installed curtains, a simple sound system, and my favorite...a backstage area and skit closet where we stored costumes and props. Having club at homes meant hauling everything in each night and breaking it down after club. Plus we always ran the risk of damaging personal property when we met in homes. "Sorry we broke your Faberge egg Mrs. Jones." The barn was a rustic place and the Hopkins gave us free reign to do whatever we wanted. And we did.

We soon realized that there was only one problem. The barn was neither heated nor insulated. Come winter we were going to be very uncomfortable. Actually there was a tiny space heater. I used to go over and turn it on early in the morning on club day, and by 7:30 that night the inside temperature might get up to the 40's. That was a total buzz kill. I knew if we didn't fix this problem by the time the real Connecticut winter set in, we were in trouble. It was such a shame, because I thought we had the perfect place.

The Lord provided us with a beautiful solution: a financial gift and a friend who could install a commercial, industrial sized heating unit. Our friend was Eric Broadbent's brother, Larry. As mentioned before, Eric was in our leadership team. Larry installed a monster heater, up near the ceiling. From then on we really did have the perfect place. And once we were settled in, club began growing at a more rapid rate. I was reminded of Jerry Johnson's line, one that was a bitter reminder a few years prior when we were so desperately trying to get the Greenwich club off the ground. Back then kids were saying, "Where is everyone?" Now they were saying, "Everyone is here!"

The Student Center

Between Carol and me coaching and all of the other school activities with which we were involved, we were given full access and had complete freedom around the high school. Contact work, even when properly done, never really becomes easy. But at least now it was convenient. I mentioned before that the school had been designed by a California architect and had a very open layout and feel. The showpiece of the design was what was known as the Student Center. If there ever was a dream layout for Young Life leaders this was it. It functioned as the cafeteria and much more. It was the heart of the school and the place where everyone hung out when they weren't in classes. It was actually one acre of open space, indoors, with tall ceilings and winding staircases at each end. I'm not sure if it's true, but I was told that it was big enough to hold a Boeing 747.

You could stand on one of those staircases at any time of the day between classes and see at least half of the student body. You could walk from section to section and, once you knew the territory, you could pick out the cliques and the social groups; the jocks, the music and theatrical crowd, the cool kids, the nerds, the preps, and my favorite name, "the tree people." These kids were given that name because they hung out around the base of a large tree that grew in the Student Center. In the early years, kids were actually permitted to smoke, and the tree people were the prominent smokers. They were the most counter culture in dress and attitude. Skateboards and hacky sacks were often seen. Every now and then I could hear, "Aloha Mister Hand." Some of them were also druggies, but the use of recreational drugs, while not rampant (at least as far as we knew), actually crossed over to a lot of different groups.

There was a huge center desk section right in the middle of the Student Center, where information was disseminated and where students could arrange to meet people and also to inquire about school affairs. It was almost always occupied by at least one faculty member. Kids appreciated the Student Center. And in their ever-creative minds they managed to find ways to make it memorable, even if not always in the most constructive ways.

One of their favorite stunts took place when it snowed. In a sort of twisted pre-dated "flash mob" fashion, at some hidden signal (which I never did learn) out of nowhere you'd hear "Incoming!" and hundreds of snowballs were suddenly lobbed high into the air and would reign down on the center desk. If you happened to be caught there along with the faculty members, it was not fun getting pummeled. It looked like a shootout in a Quentin Tarantino movie. But for everyone else it was hilarious. Plus, it was hard to catch any one specific perpetrator.

On the more constructive side, one year as a class project the students constructed an actual life-size version of a Monopoly board that encircled the entire perimeter of the student center. To give you an idea of the size of the game, each stop on the board was an actual four by eight piece of sheetrock, appropriately painted. The dice were gigantic cubes of white sponge with the dots painted on. To "throw" the dice, they were dropped off the top of a winding staircase. The marker charms for each player were objects like an actual wheelbarrow, kiddie race car, or a thimble made from an inverted wicker basket. There were hotels, houses, the whole works. For a whole weekend people played Monopoly against each other, and it was designed to be a fundraiser.

New Ideas

As Young Life progressed in Greenwich, we learned, and adapted and grew with it. We encountered problems and challenges and would try to meet each one with solutions that were effective. One of the problems we faced was the lack of volunteer leaders. I've mentioned a few of our stronger leaders like Eric Broadbent, Marabel Baker, Ian Cron, and Joe Wesney. But unlike a lot of Young Life areas, we had no colleges close by. Colleges traditionally were good sources of volunteer leadership, particularly club kids who graduated from local high schools. The other factor that made for the scarcity of leaders in Greenwich was simply the high cost of living. Once our best club kids graduated and then finished college, very few could afford to move back to town. We would lose them as potential volunteer leaders.

Student Leaders

One solution we came upon was to equip our brightest and best high school seniors for leadership roles. We had invested untold hours with these young friends, from all the way back before they were even Christians. We developed a team that we called, simply, Student Leadership. (I had this way of coming up with clever, snappy names.) By the time Christian kids got to their senior year, they pretty much figured out that club wasn't for them. Club was the introductory level of Young Life, to draw new kids in, to be able to share the Gospel. Seniors who had already come to Christ would often just feel like spectators. We reasoned that if we could convince those kids to see themselves in a different role in club, their enthusiasm would be renewed. We challenged key seniors to think of themselves as leaders in Young Life, and we gave them responsibilities as leaders. The result was pretty dramatic. All of a sudden they had a purpose and a sense of calling. They began to take ownership of Young Life. They realized that they were no longer there to be ministered to, but rather to minister to their classmates.

I met with that team twice a month. We learned a key principle, that if each person had a responsibility, everyone felt that they were vital. Every student was assigned a specific role in leadership. We suddenly could afford the luxury of having a group of strong students committed to making the music in club more effective, for example. We had another group working with me on skits and entertainment. With a lot more hands involved, suddenly we could think about more elaborate programming.

Another ministry opportunity we developed was taken directly from my own high school days. I never forgot that the main reason I got to Campaigners every week was because Newt Hetrick called me personally every Sunday. In Greenwich we created a phone-calling chain for weekly calls to every kid involved in Campaigners. That chain was run and maintained by a few of our student leaders.

In addition, as a group we could brainstorm about activities that would further our master plan of drawing in non-Christian friends to hear about Jesus. It never was about programming or activities merely to fill a calendar. Everything served a higher purpose. Even though it was hard for some kids to understand this initially, I had the opportunity and the platform with which to train them.

Creative activities that Student Leadership came up with included events like an all-night roller skating party at a roller rink about 45 minutes up the coast from us. At about three in the morning, with everyone in their skates, we'd sit down in the middle of the rink and have a club.

I thought one of the most creative ideas to come from our student leaders, came from addressing an annual scheduling issue we had with club. The fall semester of club ran from shortly after school started until just before Christmas. Then, because of school scheduling, holidays, and exams, we would take the month of January off and start the spring semester of club in the beginning of February. We began to wonder if we could do something during January, but only if it was exciting and different from "business as usual."

I had been sharing with them about the origins of Young Life, when Jim Rayburn based the whole "club" idea in the 1940's on the existing, and then very popular after school common interest clubs; science club, gardening club, model train club, and so on. Membership in these clubs was completely elective, yet they were very well attended. There were all kinds of clubs, reflecting a large variety of student interests. Jim copied that model and terminology, when he began the first Young Life meeting. He called it a club because that was the term for the after school meetings already in existence. Only later did Jim move the club to the evenings and at the homes of kids.

With that background, I asked our student leaders this question: "What would be the equivalent of the after school common interest clubs, in the current school social setting? In other words, what event would be really popular and well attended that kids now did socially?" It didn't take long for the answer to surface: if social clubs back in the 40's and 50's were all the rage; the thing do to, and the place to be, the most common equivalent today would be, very simply, parties! Yes, parties at kids houses in the evening on weekends. Everyone loved parties, and when you planned a party and word got out, everyone wanted to be at, and be seen at, your party.

Parties

For the month of January our Student Leadership decided that instead of clubs, we would have weekend parties. The student leaders planned everything, from finding a place, to deciding music, to arranging food and drinks; non-alcoholic of course. We knew from the beginning that we could be opening Pandora's Box with the potential of drinking and drugs, or an appearance by a Bluto Blutarsky-type. But we took our best precautions and preventative measures, and went ahead with our plans anyway.

For the very first party we were offered a special bonus. A friend of one of our student leaders played in a local band. So instead of having a D.J., we planned to have a live band. (They were called *Guns N...Flowers* or something. I can't recall. They were just starting out.) Having a live band automatically elevated the status of our Young Life party over other parties. A few of our student leaders took on the responsibility of promotion. But in all honesty, I'm not sure how much promotion was needed. The word spread pretty quickly through the high school.

We managed to get a house with a huge room where we hoped to be able to handle a potentially large crowd and a band. The parents were somewhat skeptical but willing to give it a try. Poor folks.

The big day came. The band arrived a few hours ahead of time. Student leaders pitched in and leaned on their parents to cover the cost of some party snacks and food, and by mid-evening the kids started showing up...and showing up...and showing up. At somewhere in the neighborhood of 500 we lost count. There were times when we thought the evening was about to go all Lord of the Flies. It teetered a few times, for sure. On a good day that house may have handled a few hundred, but on this occasion the party overflowed outside, and in January it wasn't exactly warm out there. The house was built with a huge wrap around covered porch. All of the windows were thrown open and the dancing grew in the house and soon overflowed to the porch.

The drinking and drugs appeared to be at a minimum and if I had to venture a guess, I felt that a lot of it was that we (Young Life) had a strong positive reputation around the school. I'd like to think that many of the hardcore party animals that showed up, held back on their usual exuberances. Whatever else it was, the party was a huge hit. The buzz it created lasted. I thought, "Somewhere in heaven I bet Jim Rayburn is smiling, or is that smile actually a grimace?"

If You Build it They Will Come

For the second party, we didn't have the luxury of the live band, so one of our student leaders said he could pass for a D.J. But we needed a new venue. We pressed our luck at the first house. The parents loved Young Life and were excited about how the party went. But I don't care how big your house is, when "500 plus" high school kids descend on your private property it can push the limits of your hospitality.

We were friends with another charming couple, the Stillmans, who were on our committee and whose son and daughter were very involved in club. They had a large multi-car garage, separate from the house, with a very large rec room right above it. That would be the site of our second party. Once again the place was packed and overflowing, which was a further confirmation that the party idea really had scratched where high school kids itched.

We thought we had everything planned, especially with the first massive party already in our rear view mirror.

But what we hadn't figured, was that the party room was not on a foundation, like our first house. It was on the second floor. As the party got underway, we could feel the floor moving and bouncing right along with the beat of the music as kids were dancing.

Bob Stillman, the Dad, and I decided to go down to the garage and check out how things looked from underneath. What we saw was a combination of shocking, alarming, and...more shocking. The ceiling beams in the garage were rhythmically bowing in ways that I'm pretty sure they were never meant to bend. I had graphic visions of the entire ceiling collapsing and a few hundred high school kids continuing their dancing in the garage, amongst the all rubble, not to mention three very destroyed cars.

Bob and I exchanged glances. I could tell he was anticipating the same calamity that was running through my mind, except that his vision probably also included ambulances, law suits and court appearances. The quickest solution, of course, would have been to run upstairs and stop the whole party. But even Bob was reluctant to make that call. Still, the beams continued to do their own version of the Macarena, and flirting with disaster.

What happened next was one of those occurrences I look back on even to this day and shake my head and think, "That really didn't happen. There is no way I can be reporting this honestly and expect people to actually believe it." But, I swear to you, the testimony I am about to give is the truth, the whole truth and nothing but the truth, so help me Frank Lloyd Wright, and the DIY network.

The only possible way that I could imagine avoiding disaster that night without stopping the party, would have been to install support construction poles between the sagging beams above and the concrete floor of the garage. These poles would roughly fit the eight feet from flooring the ceiling, and then were mechanically adjustable for the exact application. I could envision them perfectly because we had put a shed dormer in our own house and those poles were used to temporarily keep the roof in place until the new walls were constructed. They were called screw-jack poles, but equipment like that was serious commercial stuff, owned and operated by construction companies. As I was pondering this, Bob said to me, "You know what? I think I have a few adjustable poles that they used in a construction project I had done a few years ago. I wonder if we could get them to work?" I looked over at him like a man in the Sahara desert would respond to the question, "Here's a canteen full of water. You think we can use this?"

We pulled aside a bunch of garden equipment and sure enough, in this man's own private collection of tools was the exact solution. And in a short time we had several of them up and adjusted, and the ceiling beams were barely moving at all. The kids never learned how close we were to the end of the party, and possibly the end of all parties in the future, and life as we knew it.

Prayer

Another idea that came out of Student Leadership was one which began from a suggestion and another story from my high school days. We would sometimes get all of our Campaigners together and spent an entire Saturday praying together. For me as a young Christian it was at first intimidating, but it made a huge impact on my life. When I shared this with our student leaders they took it a step further and decided to make it a 24 hour prayer vigil. We held it at our church, PCOG, and when the committee heard about it they wanted to get in on the action. We began as a group and then people signed up for half hour time slots, either individually or in small groups. This too became an annual event for us.

The Presbyterian Church of Old Greenwich

I mentioned our transition from Stanwich Church to PCOG. Young Life began developing a beautiful, mutual symbiotic relationship with The Presbyterian Church of Old Greenwich. As a non-denominational ministry, we never tried to promote one church over others in our community. But the plain fact was, besides PCOG and Stanwich, precious few churches had the preaching and teaching that would help new Christians grow. When kids came to Christ and asked where they could worship, our first response was always to tell them to ask their parents. But in many cases their parents had no preference and kids easily found out where Carol and I were worshipping, and wanted to check out PCOG.

As time went on more and more Young Life kids started worshiping there, and participating in Sunday school as well as other programs. There was a time when you could walk into church on Sunday morning and see rows and rows of high school kids who came because of the influence of Young Life. And some of them even got their parents involved. To this day there are former club kids, like Allen and Lorain Lovejoy, who are still members and whose own children grew up at PCOG.

From our side, we enjoyed tremendous support from the church, both financially and with personal involvement. Many of our committee members, like the Bakers, the Dells, and the Heists were active members of the church. Plus, I found a new home for those lovely candlesticks I had stolen from Stanwich Church.

Our Committee

Student Leadership helped our volunteer adult leadership scarcity issue. We faced a similar challenge with our local committee. This group really was the lifeblood of the work. This is true not only for Greenwich but for Young Life areas anywhere. Committees are made up of a variety of people: primarily parents, but also other concerned adults, local business people, and clergy. When I first arrived in Greenwich I "inherited" a lovely group of folks from my predecessors, Bob Caie and Jack Carpenter before him. This group included our own land-lady, Mary Jackson, our Pastor, Nate Adams, and our finance chairman, Neil Hearn. Because I worked with him on our fund raising efforts, I partnered closely with Neil. We were on the phone a lot and met often to-gether. Neil owned a well-known shop in town, called The Cheese Shops International. In fact, he had several stores scattered around the country that he had fran-chised. The home store was right on Greenwich Avenue, with his executive offices just around the corner.

Although these were all great folks, over time many of them began to rotate off of the committee. As they did they began to be replaced by people I had gotten to know and eventually recruited. As the ministry grew, I was encouraged to see that more and more people expressed an interest in being part of our committee. This led me to a new and different challenge: I had the responsibility of actually training people to be Young Life committee members. While there was always a degree of formal instruction that Young Life provided for the various required tasks in my job description, the reality was that a whole lot of education was learn-as-we-go, or on the job training. I don't recall that Young Life was ever that big on using manuals. Such was the case with training committee people. Through a lot of trial and error I learned how to ensure that new committee members assimilated into the committee, how to have them feel like part of the team, and how each individual could have a stronger sense of ownership; contributing to the ministry and not just being a spectator.

Some of my committee organization methods actually grew out of the success we had seen with our Student Leadership. With that group I learned that if every member had a specific responsibility their participation was stronger. For our committee, I began to think about possible tasks that could be taken on; not busy work but vital tasks. I found it interesting that many potential committee members had it in their minds that to be a member of the committee meant one thing: fund raising. I can recall a conversation I had with a set of parents I was trying to recruit. When I asked them about joining the committee, the Dad said, "We would love to join, but frankly we have absolutely no exper-ience with fund raising." Fortunately, by that time in my recruiting approach I had a whole list of necessary jobs and positions I was trying to fill. I replied that, "We have plenty of people who specialize in fund raising already. Look at some of these other committee jobs and tell me if any of them catch your interest." On that day they chose the job as the Area Director's car washer.

The more we developed as a committee in Greenwich, I saw the need to document the training strategies I was using. As far as I knew, we produced the first committee training manual, although I imagined that other guys around the country were creating similar manuals. It reminded me when we started using guitars to replace pianos several years earlier. We thought we were the first ones to think of it, but very likely we weren't. But I still was very gratified to get a lot of requests for copies of our Young Life Greenwich Committee Manual, as the word spread to other areas and regions.

From the original committee group, Neil Hearn stayed on longer than the rest. Because we couldn't afford a copier, I remember making late night trips to his office to use his copy machine...and to steal cheese. I felt like a big mouse. It may seem inexpensive and easy to own that piece of equipment now, but back then we couldn't afford one in our Young Life office. And a stable of monk copyists was too expensive. So Neil gave me free use of his copier.

Flyers and Records

I would save up whatever I had to Xerox, and once a week I'd go make my copies. I'd go at night so I didn't interfere with Neil's secretary, and I always went the night before club. I chose that night because I began making little club promotional flyers that included a map to club, that our Campaigner kids would pass out at school on club day. Before Neil, Nate Adams would let me use the Stanwich Church old time Gestetner copy machine. Actually, I guess it wasn't that old back then. Many offices still used them. But it was a long and laborious process to make copies on one of those antiques. So Neil's offer to use his Xerox copier was a godsend. I would make a few hundred copies of our "maps", a.k.a. flyers, and then deliver them to one of our designated student leader's house and stick them in his mailbox. He would take them to school the next morning and get bunches distributed to other designated campaigner kids, who would pass them out during the day.

In order to make the maps more interesting, each week I would scribble several corny jokes on them. I would also make up bogus announcements that listed different students. It grew to be a much anticipated little publication; one that kids scrambled to see, but not to get directions to club. By then club met every week at the Hopkin's barn. They liked to read the jokes and to see what I wrote about different kids and whose names appeared on the flyer each week. I began to keep meticulous lists and records, not only of the jokes I used, but also the names of the kids I mentioned in the flyer. That way I wouldn't use some kids too often and not include others. Kids could tell if I ever pulled favoritism.

Regarding record keeping, I formed a habit that became a valuable tool for me, and it has lasted me a lifetime. I kept a lot of records of ministry items. From the flyers I started making a list of "map jokes" that grew to be hundreds of jokes. If I kept them for three years I could recycle the jokes, knowing by then seniors would have graduated and incoming sophomores would never have seen them before. I found new jokes wherever I could; magazines, television, comics, anything funny that I could find.

I also kept records for club. This was many years before personal computers, so everything was handwritten. For club, Campaigners and leadership I would keep messages and talks on index cards. I still have every club talk I ever gave, going all the way back to Maryland. On the club cards I kept record of the songs we sang, the skits we did, the number of people who showed up, and even the clothes I wore. Why the clothes? Because I didn't think a whole lot about which shirt or pants I'd put on in the morning, and I didn't want to wind up wearing the same clothes every week or every few weeks...or worse. When you were a kid did you ever dream of accidentally going to school naked? Am I the only one? Was that TMI?

I kept every talk I ever gave on weekend camps, summer camp assignments, every church and youth group talk I gave, and every time I spoke for other Young Life area's fund raising banquets. In addition to a lot of record keeping, I became very proactive in finding new material, for talks and for humor. Here is a self-evaluative statement, and at the same time a principle in which I grew to believe strongly: I wasn't the most creative guy in the world, but I was a great stealer of other people's ideas. And steal I did, a lot, from a lot of sources. Maybe "steal" is too strong a word. I enjoyed *implementing* other people's ideas.

A Rather Creative Fund Raiser

While Neil Hearn was still on the committee he came up with a unique idea for a fund raising event. It was an idea I had never considered, and was not something I would even have thought to be acceptable within Young Life, at least in other places. But in Greenwich it turned out to fit perfectly; a wine and cheese tasting party. Neil used to put on such events for his business, and graciously offered to supply the cheese and the wine. In the back of my mind I was thinking, "There must be some kind of Young Life policy regarding the use of alcohol at events." But, the rebel in me quickly skated to the old justification, "Better to ask for forgiveness than for permission." Besides, we were over two thousand miles from Young Life headquarters, located way out in Colorado, and the Internet and emails were still years away. How fast could news travel? We must have had three or four wine and cheese parties before the word reached Colorado and the letter from on high arrived, to cease and desist. By then we had raised a lot of money and drank a lot of wine. The letter also said that there were to be no more open bars at our annual Greenwich fund raising banquets. That had been another fixture which enjoyed a degree of anonymity in Young Life circles for a while.

One of the reasons wine and cheese tasting parties, and open bars at our fund raising banquets, worked in Greenwich was that the people who were involved rarely came from conservative Christian backgrounds. A lot of them had only become Christians in recent years; some through their kids' involvement with Young Life and many through churches like Stanwich or PCOG. They didn't have restrictions about moderate alcohol use, or wonder about any religious issue, simply because they weren't familiar with the beliefs held by many con-servative Christians. This was just one more example of the fact that living and running a ministry in Greenwich, Connecticut was quite different from where I had previously lived.

Chapter 12

Should We Be Having This Much Fun?

We lived in Greenwich for a total of 12 years, from 1972 to 1984. By the mid 70's the ministry really began to hit its stride. After the early years of adjusting to a culture that was so different from our past, we were humming along. Club continued to be strong. Campaigners grew. The committee consisted of strongly committed adults who were genuinely excited about and felt ownership for the ministry. The finances were stable, and with four major trips per year, we were taking a ton of kids to camps. And on top of all that I had a smokin' hot wife, just like Ricky Bobby.

Banquets

Young Life's policy was that each area was financially autonomous. Headquarters existed for many vital services they provided to each area, but not financial support. We all lived or died by our ability to sustain ourselves financially. A new, creative fund raising idea began to emerge around the country. The idea of a fund raising banquet was certainly not new, and not unique in Young Life. However, a group of folks out in Minneapolis, under the leadership of Phil MacDonald and Dick Lowey, came up with a few twists to the concept that were to revolutionize banquets in Young Life. As a result, Young Life style banquets changed the entire fund raising landscape nationwide, with almost every area eventually utilizing them annually.

The banquets became first class affairs. The speakers were the best in Young Life, the entertainment was the best we could find. Rather than a general invitation, every guest was personally invited by a committee person. Each committee couple recruited their own table of guests and then sat with them during the banquet. The risky part was, we invited people as our guests with no charge, meaning that we were responsible for the entire cost of the banquets before we even raised a dollar. Guests were told beforehand that they would be asked to support the work financially. At the end of the banquet there was an intentional and forthright "ask." It wasn't "If you can help us, that would be great." It was more like, "We would like you to invest in this great ministry. All of us on the committee have made a financial investment into the work. Our budget is (budget amount) and we would like to raise the majority of that tonight. I don't know how much you were thinking about giving before you arrived, but, after all you've heard and experienced tonight, I would like you to consider increasing it."

Our first banquet in Greenwich was an eye-popping success, not only raising a large part of our budget in one evening, but also creating a landslide of enthusiasm among parents and guests in general. There was no question that our banquet was to become an annual event. It continued on every year and long after Carol and I left town.

As more and more Young Life areas began holding banquets, the need for more banquet speakers grew. I enjoyed speaking for banquets for other areas. In the

Fall and the Spring it wasn't uncommon for me to travel to different cities and speak as often as twice a month. And a lot of other staff were doing the same. It was a great feeling to show up somewhere, knowing how much work had gone on beforehand, having the privilege of being the selected spokesperson and knowing I was helping an area raise a substantial portion of their budget in one evening. Of course, there was a huge weight of responsibility not to screw things up for them. I often felt that my years of playing lacrosse, being competitive, and living with butterfly-stomach before big games and in front of a lot of people, helped prepare me. I think the largest banquet where I spoke was in Jacksonville, Florida. There were about 800 people in attendance and we were able to raise somewhere in the neighborhood of $100,000 in cash and pledges.

We were always on the lookout for top entertainment. Being in Greenwich, I knew the standards were set pretty high in terms of quality. You may recall that I mentioned a young lady who was instrumental in helping us with our Bowie Young Life work, Kathy Epstein. We always kept in close touch with Kathie over the years. Kathie Epstein went on to become Kathie Lee Gifford of "Regis and Kathie Lee" fame, and more re-cently, the "Kathie Lee and Hoda" TV show. In addition to being a TV personality, Kathie Lee is also a talented singer and performer. I called Kathie and asked if she would come perform at our banquet. At the time she was living in New York City and was delighted to help. Our committee was over-the-top excited to have her.

At the banquet, Kathie not only performed, she gave her own personal testimony of how she was involved in Young Life as a teenager. I had been asked by the committee to speak at our own banquet that year, something we didn't usually do. But because Kathie was performing, they knew she would talk about Dick and Carol Bond as her Young Life leaders, adding further credibility to Greenwich Young Life. I have to admit, it was a bit of an ego boost to be introduced as the speaker, by the famous Kathie Lee Gifford, with, "This man was my Young Life leader."

Speaking For Others

One of joys of being on Young Life Staff was being asked to speak for others. In addition to banquets, I had the distinct privilege to be asked to speak often on weekend camps. Similar to the need for banquet speakers, every area at some point was in need of a weekend Camp Speaker. Even though it meant weekends away from home, and sometimes traveling long distances, it was well worth the effort in terms of experience and satis-faction. I always considered it a great honor to be asked to be the speaker for an entire area of Young Life clubs. Those leaders were the ones who did all of the hard work: contact work, building relationships, getting kids to club, then to camp. For as long as I live I'll never forget the Camp Speaker at Natural Bridge, Virginia: Harv Oostdyk. It was through his messages that I first *really* heard the Gospel and where I decided to ask Christ into my life. I was being given the opportunity to be "Harv," for other kids, just like me, but a few years younger.

The highest honor in Young Life, in my opinion, was to be asked to speak at for an entire month at one of our summer camps. I had been Program Director for a number of years, and when the opening came to be the Camp Speaker and I was asked, it was a gratifying distinction. For 28 straight nights I would speak; a series of seven talks per week, for four straight weeks. Night seven would end and the next day 250 to 300 kids would leave camp. By that afternoon another group would arrive, and the entire weekly schedule would repeat itself.

My assignments, including speaking and the earlier program assignments, were mostly at Saranac Village in upstate New York. I had a few later on at Windy Gap in North Carolina, and one assignment was at Silver Cliff Ranch in Colorado. At Silver Cliff I was on the team with Jim Rayburn's son, Jim III. Jim and his wife Lucia, and Carol and I became fast friends in the month we lived and worked together. Like so many others, we remained lifelong friends, and still keep in touch even though they live in Colorado. By the way, Jim wrote a remarkable book about his life, his Dad, and Young Life. It's called "Dance Children Dance," and it remains on my own bookshelf to this day. I have read it several times and shared it with many others.

Summer Camp Memories

We have many wonderful memories from our summers on camp assignment. Our whole family went, which meant that our sons "grew up" at camp, most summers. It was a rich experience for them, even as youngsters, to spend a month in an environment like that and watching their Dad work. As amazing as the properties were, what made the months spent there so memorable were the people with whom I worked, and their families.

On one of my program assignments my assistant was supposed to be a friend named George Kennedy, who had been in my training group in the Washington D.C. training program. A few weeks before the assignment began, I received word from George that he wasn't going to be able to come on assignment. "Not to worry," he said, and told me he had a very good replacement. Knowing pretty much everyone in the east who had program experience, and having never even heard of this guy's name, much less that he wasn't even on Young Life Staff, I was concerned. From the first day I met this guy, I knew it was me who was going to have work to keep up. His name is Bob Stromberg. When you have a moment, Google him. YouTube him. I've never, before or since, worked with a person who was such a professional grade comedic talent. Bob could take the simplest of skits or program events and transform them into uproarious masterpieces. In front of a crowd he could mesmerize and entertain like no other. In addition to being a ton of fun, and non-stop laughs, it really was a privilege working with the guy, and becoming friends. We stayed in touch for a lot of years.

Rog Harlan

The guy who made me laugh the most on a daily basis was my dear friend Rog Harlan. Rog was a few years older than me. We came to be very close friends, along with our families. His wife was Marilyn and his three kids were Leslie, John and Lynn. He had done many assignments before he ever got to Saranac. In an attempt to pair older, more experienced guys with young guns, he was assigned as Program Director with another friend of mine, Tom Schultheis. Tom was the young gun. I was the Camp Speaker.

Among other gifts, Rog could adlib in front of a microphone for hours at a time. One of our events early in the week was the volleyball tournament. When I was on Work Crew, Bob Mitchell and Jay Grimstead would be the commentators of the weekly tournament, and like Rog, they both were gifted ad-libbers. The kids were so into Mitch and Jay's running commentary, which was pretty much about everything under the sun *except* volleyball that the whole tournament grew into a crazy combination of the athletic and comedic.

The moment I learned that Rog was going to be on the assignment, I knew we just had to commentate the volleyball tournament together. We learned to feed off each other. The give and take was spontaneous and natural. I always felt it was one of the funniest things I ever did in Young Life. The reality was, *we* thought we were really funny. Kids thought we were mildly humorous, and every now and then we were a bit funny. But I didn't care. We'd make up for it later in the week.

It was as much for our own entertainment and was the most enjoyable thing I ever did with program.

We're in Nuttyville and Rog is The Mayor

My favorite Rog Harlan story is one of the great legends of summer assignment folklore. As kids got off the buses when they arrived at camp, the Program Directors always concocted some kind of crazy welcome. At Saranac, Rog and Tom Schultheis dressed up as north woods trappers. They wore some actual furs that had been lying around the camp from the previous owners. And if you think rotten old furs smelled badly, try to imagine them doused in the diabolical smelling bug repellant used often in the Adirondacks, called Fly Dope.

Rog and Tom acted all ornery and cantankerous, like they had just walked out of the movie, *Deliverance*. They claimed that the bus was trespassing onto private property. To make the scene more authentic they would jump out of the woods and stop the bus, armed with shootin' irons. Tom had a big old double barreled shotgun filled with blank cartridges, which he would fire in to the air. Though safe, it sounded like a cannon going off and never failed to produce shock-and-awe with a busload of kids.

Rog took the armaments a step further and brought his very own .44 caliber western style six-shooter, which he would shoot into the air. While his gun was using blank cartridges too, apparently Roger's head was also filled with blanks on one particular bus arrival. By the time he pulled his gun out, half the kids were already off the bus. While he was clearing the gun from his leather holster, but before he got it actually pointed it up, he accidentally pulled the trigger. Unfortunately for the newly arriving camper who was walking right next to Rog, it wasn't the noise so much that bothered him. It was the wadding from the blank cartridge at close range hitting him in the head that was a real bummer. The wadding from a large caliber blank load can cause serious injury at close range, but this kid was lucky enough to only get a nasty cut.

Off to the camp first aid center, and soon after that, off to town for a doctor to place a few stitches in the kid's wound. The good news was, aside from a nasty cut, a headache and a rather tainted first impression of a Young Life camp, the kid was ok. The bad news was, the doctor was required to report any and all treatments resulting from gunshot wounds. Later that afternoon Saranac Lake's Finest arrived, and hauled our dear Program Director to jail. A few hours later Rog appeared back at camp, out on bail, and very contrite.

One of our staffers and good friend, Shawn Kuhn, had accompanied Rog to the police station for moral support. Quick-witted Shawn may have not been Rog's best choice. He quickly sized up the local Sheriff as a reincarnated Barney Fife and didn't waste any time. "Officer what would happen if the weapon had somehow mysteriously disappeared at camp?" When Mr. Fife explained the dire consequences of not being able to produce the weapon, Shawn turned to Rog and said, "You see Rog, I told you it wouldn't have been a good idea to throw the gun into the lake." Rog was not pleased. Neither was Barney. Shawn was, however.

Although it was many years pre-Internet, that story went viral in Young Life country faster than a speeding, ah, bullet. Rog never, ever, heard the end of that one.

P.S. A few days later, Tom Schultheis was sitting in his room listening to the radio when the news came on. This is what he heard: "In local news, a Pennsylvania man was arraigned in court today on a weapons charge. Forty five year old Roger Harlan, of Beaver Falls, Pennsylvania was charged with discharging a firearm, when the wading from a blank cartridge struck the head of a teenage boy. This took place at the Young Life

Camp on Upper Saranac Lake." Tom waited all day with a tape recorder to catch the news again in case the same report was made. It was, and to this day I have that recording on an old cassette tape.

Over the years since our summer assignment together we kept in close touch with Rog and his family. For those of us on staff who received his annual Christmas newsletter, it was a much anticipated publication and more like a stand-up comedy routine than Seasons Greetings. I still have my copies.

Program for Urban Weeks

I said that the highest honor in Young Life was being asked to speak at a summer camp. There was another honor that I counted as equally meaningful to me. Back in those days Young Life was growing in its presence and effectiveness in our urban landscape around the country. Earlier I mentioned meeting Bo Nixon, who went on to be the Director for Young Life in New York City's Lower Eastside. Urban Young Life began to spring up in cities all around the country. In due time a National Urban Director was appointed, a man named Verley Sangster. Verley organized a group of urban Young Life leaders from all over the country, called The Urban Primus Council. They helped Verley by advising him on urban ministry matters.

The urban leaders in the eastern half of the U.S. began gravitating towards taking their kids to Saranac in the month of August. Those four weeks eventually became known as *urban weeks*, populated largely, but not exclusively, by kids from the inner cities. When it came time to select the camp staff for the month of August, The Urban Primus Council had a big influence on who was picked.

My friend Tom Pilsch and I were Program Directors together one summer. We both had a lot of personal history in Black neighborhoods and had grown up with many African American friends. Maybe because of our music backgrounds, we both deeply appreciated Black contemporary music. This wasn't a fad or an attempt for us to reach into Black culture. It was more, our upbringing. As a result, for two suburban white guys, we were always comfortable in mixed cultural and racial settings. When it came to program and summer camps, Tom and I worked well together. Music was a big part of our programs, and a big part of our music was reflected in our own background and tastes in music.

Also, we grew up when dancing was a big part of our social life. Between music and dancing, and the fact that disco dancing had been the rage for a few years, even crossing over at times between suburban and urban youth culture; we decided to have a Saranac Disco for one of the evening program events. We knew it would be a stretch in the minds of many, but we felt the timing was right and that we could pull it off. We had to have a disco ball like in the movie, *Saturday Night Fever*, which was suspended in the air, had little mirrors all over it and reflected little dots of light all around the room. When we couldn't buy one, I figured I could make one instead. I took one of my son's old soccer balls and covered it in Plaster of Paris and embedded little squares of mirrors that I had meticulously cut from a large sheet of a bathroom mirror.

Selling the idea of a disco night at camp was a bit of a challenge for our more conservative leaders, but overall the event was a huge hit. That, and along with every-thing else we did, while not necessarily having an urban flair, was nevertheless inner-city-friendly enough to catch the attention of the guys on the Urban Primus Counsel. When the following August camp assignments were handed out for Saranac, Tom and I were given the high honor of being selected as the Program Directors. I was told that my friend Bo Nixon, who had seen Tom and me do the program the summer before, had lobbied for our appointment.

That assignment was spectacular. We really felt the support of the urban folks. Bo and Mary Nixon were on staff that month with us, as were Verley and Pearlean Sangster. With Verley as the head of the entire urban ministry, I knew we were in good hands. We first met Gene and Angela Wright that month. Like Bo and Mary Nixon, although we seldom ever seem them now, we have remained friends-for-life. In fact, some 25 years later, Carol was traveling with me in my post-Young Life job, to Africa. We had heard that Gene and Angela were living in Kampala, Uganda and working as missionaries. As that was one of our stops, we got to spend an evening with them. It was a sweet reunion, especially after all of those years going back to our summer together at Saranac.

The following August was noteworthy not only because it was urban month, but also because it was the month that we got to introduce two of our best friends to each other. Tom couldn't join me for that assignment. In his place was a longtime friend and Area Director in Philadelphia, Scott Hamilton. Michele McPartland was, by then, out of college. I lobbied successfully for her to be named as the girl's Work Crew boss. (Her male counterpart was Gene Wright.) Because we were so close to Michele, and because Scott and I were pretty much inseparable for the month, it was natural for Scott and Michele to get acquainted. And get acquainted they did. This was another couple I was privileged to marry, and because Michele was from Greenwich, they chose to have the wedding at our home church, PCOG. To this day, although they live in Virginia Beach, Virginia, where Scott is still on Young Life Staff after forty years. We see them whenever we can.

Recreation Can Be Dangerous to Your Health

As I approached my early 30's I started playing a lot of tennis. It wasn't hard on the body, plus your opponents didn't hit you with their sticks like they did in lacrosse. In Greenwich tennis was hugely popular. If you could play, or if you were a good sailor (I wasn't) then whole new social scenes opened up. There were many different tournaments but the most prestigious one of them all was the Annual Greenwich Town Tournament. The open division was usually won by people who had played some serious tennis in college. The finals always drew large crowds and people enjoyed watching very high quality tennis.

Although the town tourney was strictly amateur, for a few years there was a running joke around town. The famous tennis star Ivan Lendl lived in Greenwich, and so did one of his competitors, Matts Wilander. At one time Lendl was number one in the world, and Wilander, number two. Someone had produced a bumper sticker that said, "Matts Wilander-the #2 player in Greenwich."

You could play in the open division or the appropriate age division, or both. Even after I had been playing for a few years I knew I had no chance to win the open, but I entered anyway, just for the experience. I also entered my age division.

I got to the semi-finals, which was played on a Wednesday. It was a very hot day and I had my usual towel handy for wiping off during changeovers. It was also windy and my towel kept falling on the ground and sometimes blowing over into the nearby weeds. The match was close but I finally managed to win it. I was going to the finals! I went home that night, elated of course. I had three days until the finals on Saturday. Playing in the finals meant linesmen, ball boys, and referees, not to mention a grandstand full of people watching. I was excited with anticipation.

232

Later that night, I noticed that I began to itch a lot around my face and both wrists and arms. At the time I didn't take too much notice, other than it being a nuisance. However, when I woke up the next morning, right away I knew I was in some serious trouble. My entire face was swollen and itching like mad, as were my wrists and arms. It had not been since I was pre-adolescent that I last had a really bad case of poison ivy. Apparently my towel, lying on the ground and in the weeds, had gotten contaminated with the stuff. It transferred to my face and arms when I was toweling off. I was absolutely covered in sores, and miserable.

I kept trying to recall from my childhood how long before the poison ivy would start to diminish, but in none of my memories could I imagine that this case would be gone before the Finals on Saturday. In fact, by Friday it had gotten so bad that I had to go to the doctor and get some serious prescription medicine.

On Friday night my friend, Tom Pilsch, who was aware of my affliction as well as the upcoming finals, paid me a visit. He had a friend with him who I had heard of, but never met. His name was Don Mook. I mention him because Don was to eventually become a huge part in my life. To this day, we are still very close. He is married and lives nearby. We see a lot of each other, and I consider him one of my closest confidants. But on the day we met, he must have thought he was visiting a leper colony, entering my room and seeing me lying on the bed, smelling like calamine lotion and looking like, well...a leper. I gave them my best Rocky imitation, my swollen face looking like I had just gone ten rounds with Apollo Creed.

Yo Adrian I Did It!

They asked me what I was going to do about the town tournament. By then I had decided, because it was the most prestigious thing I had ever done in tennis, that if I could get some tennis clothes on I was going to at least show up for the coin flip and then immediately forfeit. When I got to the tournament I still looked like a leper, but at least I had a headband and hat on to help camouflage the poison ivy. I was also exhausted from barely sleeping for the past three nights.

My opponent couldn't have been more of an opposite sight than me. He was a member of the very prestigious Stanwich Club. That place's golf course would make Augusta National look like Tin Cup's driving range. It had received a degree of notoriety because it had re-fused to accept the application of the number one tennis player in the world, Ivan Lendl. I was told that you either inherited membership, or someone had to die for there to be an opening. My opponent walked onto the court dressed from head to toe with the then popular and exclusive tennis brand, Fila; shirt, shorts, shoes and even headband. I had on the equivalent of my Walgreen's specials. He took one look at me and, then did a double take when he saw my face. That second look was priceless. I mumbled something about having a bit of a rash. *All righty, then.*

The linespersons were there, as were the ball boys and umpire, ready to flip a coin. The stands were packed with people, including some of the Young Life folks. I couldn't resist. I told myself, "Just warm up and play one game, then I can retire." But I won the toss and held serve. "What the heck, may as well keep going. I can retire whenever I want." So I kept playing. I don't know if the guy was spooked because of the way I looked, but he kept making enough errors to keep me in the match, and I wound up winning the first set. No way was I going to stop after that.

By about midway through the second set, two things happened. One, it finally hit me full force that my tank was empty from poison ivy and lack of sleep and I was feeling completely spent; and two, my opponent realized it also. I had an early break but he was pressing hard. I finally got to the game where, if I held I would win the match, but if I lost, the set would be even. I knew if that happened, I was truly finished. But I did hold, and won. I still have an old photo of my opponent and me receiving our respective trophies. I still look like a leper, and he still has that same forced smile-grimace on his face, as if he was thinking, "I cannot believe I just lost this match to the elephant man."

Ch Ch Ch Ch Changes

The ministry continued to be blessed in so many ways. We tried new ideas and events and continued the ones we had created earlier that seemed to be effective. Our January parties worked, so we kept having them, but added an extra feature, thanks to the creativity of our student leaders: different themes for different parties. My two favorites were the New Wave party and the Tacky Clothes party. We continued our all night roller skating parties, but this time it was the committee's creativity that added a new element. They would meet us early the following morning at a designated place and prepare a pancake breakfast for everyone.

My boss and friend Jack Carpenter eventually moved away, and he was replaced by a man that most of the staff had never heard of before, Hal Merwald. The reason for his obscurity was that his previous position had been as the Young Life Director for Brazil. Our region was his first stop off the boat back in the U.S. At first I wasn't quite sure what to make of Hal. He seemed like a nice guy. When we talked he would absent-mindedly slip into speaking Portuguese, which cracked me up. I thought he was going all Pentecostal on me. Young Life had realigned the regions at that time and the region Hal inherited was a fraction of the size of that which Jack had directed. We joked that we could hold our regional meetings in a phone booth.

But the one thing Hal did have for me was time. Hal's eventual growth and stature in Young Life would take him close to the very top of the mission. When we first met, we hung out a lot together, and I began to really appreciate him not only as a boss and a mentor, but also a friend. He used to drive over to Greenwich from Ossining, New York, about half an hour away, and we'd spend hours playing pickup basketball at the Greenwich YMCA. It didn't take long for Young Life to realize that Hal had strong leadership skills, and his responsibilities grew commensurately.

The Olympics

One night I had a brief but regrettable, as it turned out, phone call with Hal. It was in the winter of 1980. In fact, it was a few days before February 22, 1980. I can remember it as if it was yesterday. Some readers may already have an idea where this is headed. For others, let me explain.

Young Life had owned Saranac Village since the early 70's. It was one of our prized camps. Because it was a summer camp, there was only one building at Saranac that was winterized: the staff building. The rest of the buildings were all closed off for the long winters in upstate New York. In the fall of 1979, in preparation for the Winter Olympics that were to be held in nearby Lake Placid, the Olympic Committee was working feverishly to secure enough housing for the hundreds of workers that were going to be needed to host the Olympics. Someone got in touch with Young Life and asked to rent the staff quarters at Saranac, with an "offer we couldn't refuse." No, not a horse's head in the bed. But they offered an obscene amount of money, plus a whole lot of tickets for Olympic events.

On the night of Hal's memorable call, this is the conversation that took place. Hal: "Hey! What are you doing this Friday night?" Me: "Ugh, nothin', why?" Hal: "You

236

know we've been renting out the Saranac staff quarters for the Olympics at Lake Placid? Well, I have two tickets for the USA and the Soviet Union hockey game. You want them?" By that time everyone had heard about those young kids on the USA hockey team. And everyone also knew that just a week before the start of the Olympics the Soviet team, considered by many to be the best hockey team in the history of the earth, had beaten and thoroughly humiliated the USA team in an exhibition match in Madison Square Garden. My answer to Hal was this: "Hal, if you think I'm going to get in a car and drive five hours to Lake Placid for a hockey game, and watch a professional team beat down a bunch of college kids, you're crazy. Give them to some other sucker." And the rest, as they say, is history. It lives on in my life as the greatest sports regret I've ever had. I have my own copy of the movie *Miracle* to remind me. And every time I hear Al Michaels commentating on Sunday Night Football these days, I still can hear his voice saying, "Do you believe in miracles?!"

An Amazing Gift

From time to time, magazines and newspapers used to write articles listing the most expensive places in the country to live. Greenwich always was at or near the top of those lists. Our experience was, a loaf of bread or a gallon of gas wasn't all that much more expensive than it had been for us in Maryland. What made living in Greenwich so brutally expensive was the housing. The prospect of buying a home on my salary was somewhere between impossible and fuhgeddaboudit. We had rented the house on Mary Jackson's estate, then rented our second little home in Cos Cob. Even though we were frugal with our money and kept a tight budget, the idea of getting enough money for a down payment on a house in the Greenwich market was unthinkable. We pretty much knew that going in. People earning what we earned had two choices: rent, or live in a town further up the line in Connecticut and commute. Everyone knew that. But...so did our committee.

After seven years of living in town, our committee came to us with a proposition: they wanted to help us buy a house. In their collective wisdom, they understood that no matter how deeply we were embedded into life in Greenwich, if we went from house renters to home-owners, we would really know that we belonged; that we wouldn't feel like outsiders who were "stationed" there. It was one of those life events that, while it touched us immediately, it kept on affecting us not only during process of buying the house but also for years afterwards. It was the most generous gesture Carol and I had ever experienced. It wasn't simply like giving us an expensive gift, for example. It became a long involved process. Because of that, our gratitude and appreciation had the opportunity to grow proportionally over time.

As to the details of the proposal, there were relatively few. Several people on the Young Life committee, along with a few other parents, formed a separate committee entirely, for the specific purpose of acquiring a home for the Bonds. We were purposely kept out of the loop, as they wanted their work to be as anonymous as possible. We were never told who was on the "housing" com-mittee, much less what went on at the meetings. We had a pretty good idea who served on it, but to this day we've never actually been told. We were never told who contributed or how much each couple actually gave. The usual suspects appear, I'm sure, in the chapter, "Some of my Favorite People." I did speak with George Baker a lot. I believe he was the chairman of that committee.

Our instructions were simply to start looking for a home that was as reasonably priced (by Greenwich standards) and keep the committee informed. During the years leading up to this, I would drive through town, playing a little game in my head as I looked at homes and fantasizing owning our own home. "We could live there. I could make that other house work. That one over there is small but we don't need a ton of room," and so on, never thinking that we could actually own a home. Our friends were now making that dream possible. Carol and I didn't waste any time starting our search.

We soon had a number of possible houses and were able to narrow them down, in time, to one. It was just a two bedroom, but there was a full attic which could be (and eventually was) converted into two more bedrooms. It was located in Riverside, a section of town very close to everything. The committee's specific offer was to supply money for the down payment in the form of an interest-free loan. We would be fully responsible for the purchase, the mortgage payments, taxes, and the maintenance of the house. It was to be entirely ours (and the bank's.) Should we ever move, we would then be required to return the loan. But the real kicker was, we only had to return the amount of the original loan. Any appreciation on the house was ours to keep. Initially, I'm not sure I fully comprehended the magnitude of this huge gesture of generosity and wisdom on the part of this committee. At the time we had no thought of ever leaving Greenwich anyway.

When we moved in, it marked a new era of our ministry. Seven years earlier we had moved to Greenwich and felt like we were living in a foreign country. In time we came to understand and embrace the uniqueness of Greenwich, and to appreciate it and to love it. Being in a home we truly owned made us feel part of everything and everyone, and fully connected. No longer were we Marylanders transported. We really were home.

Chapter 13

The Last Few Years, and Saying Goodbye

During the last few years living in Greenwich, we had no idea that our time there was drawing to a close. The ministry was going incredibly well. We at last had our own home. We had friends. We became part of the culture and social fabric. And we were a growing family of four, soon to be five. Matthew and Adam were in elementary school, and in addition to being the Greenwich Young Life leaders, we were Mom and Dad. For our boys, spending the early part of their lives in Greenwich would prove to be very defining years for them. Even today they both look back not only on many wonderful memories, but also with the knowledge that those years shaped and formed so much of who they are today.

In our experience, Greenwich was a great place to raise our kids. We understand that a lot of people would prefer a slower pace, or maybe somewhere not nearly as exposed to the potential temptations of a cosmopolitan area. But we loved it. And we honestly never thought a day would come when we would entertain the idea of leaving.

Looking back, one of the factors that made our last few years so deeply satisfying and rewarding was the knowledge that we had worked so hard and had "paid the price" in order to achieve the success with which we were blessed. We came so close to leaving, early on. When we began, we missed the familiarity of where we grew up, not to mention our family and all of our friends. We transitioned and metamorphosed as we learned the culture. That was a long, growing, and involved process. While we were going through it we didn't know how things would turn out. Experiencing the growth in the ministry after the early hardships made us grateful and it matured us. Although a home is only a physical commodity, the act of finally owning our home, and more importantly, the tremendous vote of confidence, validation, and belief in our worth by our committee, gave us profound empowerment.

Parenting

In February of 1982 Carol made another visit to Greenwich Hospital, this time to deliver our third son, Joshua Taylor Bond. While there was a part of us that would have loved to have a little girl, we never seemed to learn that trick, like our friends the Morgans and the Campbells. I mentioned earlier how we were all close friends, along with the Lanfers. With these couples having children close to the time Josh was born, along with a few other couples, the church nursery began to get crowded with babies. Matthew and Adam, by then ages nine and six, both in elementary school at nearby North Mianus School, were delighted to have a little brother.

By this time Carol and I were married for twelve years and had been parents for nine of those years. Like almost every parent, the transition from "two to three," that is, having your first child brings forth a significant change in your life. We worked to navigate that change while also going through all of the cultural and ministry changes when we moved to Greenwich. While a lot of the ministry adaptations were more on my shoulders, the transition into parenthood was more in Carol's capable hands. Not that I wasn't around. My schedule on staff gave me a lot more flexibility than had I been in a nine-to-five job. But I always felt that Carol was the one who helped me better understand my role as a responsible Dad. Our boys received consistent discipline and grew up to be respectful and polite. On rare occasions when they were insolent, they were placed in a burlap bag and beaten with reeds. Pretty standard parenting really. Other than that they never lacked from being showered with love and attention. Carol was, in my humble opinion, the best Mom ever.

One memory that stands out in my fathering experience, I must confess, is likely not a spiritually uplifting story. Matthew and Adam used to walk to and from North Mianus School together. I began to notice that something was going on with Matthew. He didn't act like his normal self for a number of days. When I tried to ask, he was reluctant to divulge any information. But Adam, second born, had no trouble pinpointing the problem. A kid in the neighborhood, Jeremy Brown, had been bullying Matthew at school. When this news came out, Matthew was fighting back the tears, obviously very upset, and he had no idea how to deal with the situation.

I got down on one knee, eye level with Matthew, as Adam looked closely to see what I was going to say. "Matt, give me your right hand." I took his hand in mine and slowly, deliberately, closed his fingers and formed a fist. Then I said, "The next time Jeremy Brown starts to bully you, here's what I want you to do. I want you to take your hand and make a fist like this. Then I want you to punch that kid in the nose as hard as you can." I got two responses: Matthew's eyebrows shot up as the rest of his face went into full-on surprise mode, and Adam got a big grin on his face and shouted, "Oh Yeah, Dad!"

The next afternoon at the usual time I looked up the

street, keeping an eye out for when the boys would walk into sight, and wondering if anything had transpired. For anyone having a first born and a second born, I'm sure you can relate to what I saw. As they rounded the corner at the end of our block, Matthew, the oldest, was walking calmly and deliberately. Adam, the younger, was running circles around his brother and practically doing cartwheels, doing his best Bundini Brown impersonation for his own Muhammad Ali. I knew something had happened at school. The story came mostly from Adam, who could barely let his brother get a word in. Jeremy had started his usual bullying. But this time, according to Adam's account, Matthew balled up his fist and punched the kid right smack in the nose. A very shocked Jeremy ran away crying.

Even though we were neighbors, we had very little contact with the Brown family other than an occasional event at the school. That night the phone rang and it was Jeremy's mother, Mrs. Brown. She wasted not a second to launch into a rant about her dear, sweet boy and how Matthew had assaulted him at school. As soon as I answered the phone I said, in a loud voice, "Hello Mrs. Brown," so that Matthew, Adam, and Carol would be alerted. They came running. They could only hear my side of the conversation, but this is what they heard: "Mrs. Brown, your dear, sweet son is not as sweet as you think. He has been bullying my son for weeks at school. I'm glad for what Matthew did, and if Jeremy ever tries to bully Matt again he's going to get more of the same." That was the last time Matthew was ever bullied by Jeremy or by anyone.

It was a fathering situation that I wouldn't have wanted to try to justify around our Christian friends, but I had a deep-down sense that this was an instance where dramatic action was needed. I never doubted that I had done the right thing. I fully respect the difference of opinion by anyone reading this who thinks I was the worst father ever.

In the "P.S." department, flash forward many years; Matthew was working on Young Life Staff in Orange County, California, and engaged to be married. We all flew out for the wedding. Matt gave every guy in his wedding a book entitled "Wild at Heart" by John Eldridge. He writes about teaching our sons to be Godly men. On page 78 of that book Eldridge tells almost exactly the same story about his son. Although it was many years later, I still felt a sense of validation. I just hope I can sell as many books as Eldridge. Hmmm.

Joshua

Sometimes things happen to our kids that are beyond our control or ability to correct. When Josh was seven months old he came down with a nasty flu bug, along with it a consistently high temperature. Trying all of the normal ways to control his temperature had little effect. He kept spiking a high fever for several days, despite visits to the doctor. Then one day quite suddenly his little head just began to droop. Even though his flu bug eventually passed, the drooping continued. While there were no other symptoms, Carol immediately suspected that something was wrong.

Over the coming months our anxiety grew as we kept a watchful eye on Josh. We recall observing him, unable to sit up, or roll over, as normal children would be doing at the same period of development, thinking, hoping, that these were just small delays. Yet, over time we had the sinking feeling that all was not well, but instead, that something was really wrong.

As we began to see more and more medical specialists, we gradually came to the realization that our dear son was suffering from an advanced form of cerebral palsy.

With many close friends our age, no less than four of them had children within months of Josh's birth. I mentioned before about the full nursery of our church when all of these little ones were dropped off before the morning services. Each week as we picked up Josh after the service there were the physical reminders, that is, all of the other kids were developing normally and there was Josh, seemingly not developing at all. In time it became so painful that we began skipping church altogether to avoid that personal torture. Denial is an early problem that parents in our predicament inevitably face. It is just hard to come to grips with the painful reality. Carol would avoid situations that put her in proximity of our close friends with children the same age. It only slapped her in the face with the reality that Josh was not developing.

To go further into the story of how deeply our lives were effected as we learned to cope with our disabled Joshua would take a long time and would sidetrack our story about Young Life. However, for anyone interested in knowing more, I have written a book about Josh. It's also available electronically on Amazon. Its title is: "Little Brown Eyes."

I will say, for the remaining years of our lives in Greenwich, having a special needs child had an enormous impact on our family. We learned that a large majority of couples that suffer through the trials of having a disabled child wind up divorced. It polarizes a family. They either split up or grow closer. By God's grace, we did the latter. As Josh's brothers began to understand the nature and the severity of his disability, they became even more loving and more protective. At the same time, he was their brother; part of Team Bond. He fully participated in our family activities, and those especially of his brothers. Never mind that he could only crawl, and could only speak in one word sentences.

Lack of speech never kept Josh out of the normal cacophony that was our evening mealtime. He made his presence known. Individually both boys related to their brother in ways that best suited their own personality.

Matthew was the tender, loving bother. He would sit for hours and read books to Josh, with Josh sitting in his lap. Adam, the more boisterous brother, would often engage Josh in more active ways. Adam was also the first to get Josh to smile, and then to laugh.

Brothers

Boys will be boys, disabled or otherwise. Occasionally our living room got converted into a World Wrestling Federation ring. Josh was the referee for his brothers. But somehow, like channeling a Hulk Hogan gone rogue, he would inevitably wind up at the bottom of a brother pile. If you think this treatment of their special needs brother was harsh, you only had to hear Josh's squeals of laughter to know that all was well in the ring.

Sometimes Matt and Adam would take a laundry basket and prop up one end with a stick. They would then lay a trail of goldfish crackers that led into the propped-up basket. Josh would eat his way into the baited trap, whereupon his brothers would knock out the stick and capture him. Eventually Josh would pop out of the basket and glance at his brothers, looking like the gopher in *Caddyshack.*

I boasted earlier that I thought Carol was the greatest Mom ever. Nothing prepares a mother, or a father, for raising a severely disabled child. And as with the raising of our other two boys, Carol took the reins of learning to raise Josh. She was learning, teaching me, and helping Matthew and Adam all at the same time. And on top of all that, she was dealing with the deep personal grief of knowing that Josh's condition would neither improve nor go away. He was going to be our greatest family challenge for the rest of our lives. My book, "Little Brown Eyes" is as much about Carol's story as it is about Josh.

Sabbatical

It was the policy of Young Life to provide a three month sabbatical from ministry, approximately every seven years. By 1983 we had been on staff for thirteen years and never had taken one, although Carol sometimes accused me of being on a mental sabbatical. To my defense, why do wives want to have serious conversations on Monday nights at 9 o'clock when the football game is just coming on? Real sabbaticals are the financial responsibility of the Area Director personally, and the local area. The local area also must cover a staff person's job responsibilities during their absence. Although I had been eligible sooner, it was only after several years in Greenwich that I felt that we could afford our sabbatical; and we had the quality of leadership who could carry on without us for an extended time. With the blessing of our committee, we began making plans.

Over the years I had become a C.S. Lewis fan. I devoured every book he had written, both fiction and non-fiction. I learned, however, that a lot of his writings were either out of print or never published. Many of these writings were still in existence, but in only two places in the world: one was Oxford University, in England, and the other was Wheaton College, in Illinois. Oxford had a cooperative agreement with the American college. Copies of Lewis's unpublished or out of print writings were made available to Wheaton. I decided to apply through the Young Life seminary, a.k.a. Fuller Theological, for an independent post graduate course, to study these writings. I was accepted and had two choices of where I wanted to spend my sabbatical: Wheaton or Oxford. Seriously?

We were to spend June, July and August in England. Through a realtor friend, Charlie Edgerton, we managed to rent our home. There was a polo club in Palm Beach, Florida that put on polo matches in Greenwich every summer, and were in need of housing for the horse trainers. Charlie managed to find tenants. And although our foyer smelled like a tack room from their clothes and equipment for the next year, Charlie negotiated an obscenely high rent, enough to practically cover our expenses in England.

For the next three months we were truly on our own Magical Mystery Tour. We rented a house in Oxford, along with a ten year old Volvo station wagon. I'd leave in the mornings to study at the Bodleian Library, home of the Lewis papers, while Carol and the boys got settled in. Every few weeks I took off a few days and we would travel; either around England, or Scotland, or across the Channel to France. While we saw anything and every-thing, we did have a sightseeing plan of sorts. We saw as many cathedrals as we could find, as many art museums, and to be really spiritual; as many Grand Prix circuits and races as we could. And I can report that we saw a lot of all three.

By the last four weeks my course work at Oxford was completed, slightly ahead of schedule, and we spent the month of August traveling throughout Europe. We continued our regular sightseeing with emphasis on our previously mentioned "Big Three" list. We also tried to connect with some Young Life people in Europe. We visited our friends George and Irene Thompson, who had been on staff in the U.S. but were then living in Edinburgh, Scotland. We also met a Young Life Staff man who was in Paris at the time. A few years before, when Carol and I had skied at Chamonix we met Rod and Fran Johnson. They lived for many years in the French town of Annemasse, just across the border from Geneva, Switzerland, where they ran Young Life. Our plan was to drive south through France, spend the night with the Johnson's and then to drive down to the French and Italian Riviera. Because we had visited Switzerland before, our travel plans didn't include that country.

By the time we arrived in Annemasse it was late at night

and we had been on the road for many hours. As Carol was putting Josh to bed, I said to Matthew and Adam, "Hey guys, who knows when you'll get this way again. Want to go to Switzerland?" They jumped in the car, with their passports, and we drove to the border, crossed into Geneva and took a late night tour of the city. One highlight I wanted them to see was the famous Reformation wall, depicting founders of the protestant Reformation, including John Calvin and John Knox. See? It wasn't all about Grand Prix circuits.

The next day we arrived at Aix-en-Provence, on the French Riviera, were we connected with longtime Greenwich friends, Bill and Barbara Edgar. Bill had been a highly respected teacher at a private school in Greenwich, Brunswick Academy, and had accepted a position at a reformed seminary in Aix. Bill was one of the brightest men I ever met. Over the years he has gained some distinction in academic circles. He now even has his own Wikipedia page.

One of the highlights of our time with the Edgars was the day we went to the beach at a little town called Cassis on the French Riviera. We had never been to a clothing optional beach before, but the south of France...I just figured, when in Rome...Oh no, you di-ent! No, we didn't. Well, Josh went topless. Matthew and Adam got Kermit the Frog eyes when they first saw all of the naked bodies. But fortunately, being pre-adolescent, their curiosity lasted only a few minutes. Mine on the other hand... but I managed to stifle my enthusiasm. Carol had gone all Richard Simmons after Josh was born and really got down to fighting weight. I tried to get her to buy an itsy bitsy bikini. In fact, I had been barking up that tree for a number of months. I was proud of her looks. Finally, before leaving for England she bought one, thinking Europe was a fair distance from Todd's Point in Old Greenwich. She wore it to the beach that day. She may as well have been a dressed as a nun compared to most of the ladies there. Interestingly, there was a cultural lesson. Sometimes we can enter other cultures where certain practices may seem odd or even wrong, when in fact, people simply live or act differently.

The sabbatical was an amazing experience for our family, on so many levels even above and beyond my personal study. Being alone together for three months, traveling to historic places, seeing so many sights, negotiating foreign cities, roads, language, currency, housing, food; made the kinds of memories that have lasted a lifetime. For the boys it represented a summer of education that was enjoyable. For Josh it was a time of uninterrupted fun and attention from his brothers as well as Mom and Dad. Matthew was even old enough to give us "backpack breaks," carrying Josh. Over the years and well into adulthood, both boys have referenced numerous experiences from that summer. We returned home feeling like world travelers, and very grateful.

Trouble Brewing

We got home in time for the boys to get back to school and for club to get going again. Although we continued to have a strong year of ministry, I could begin to see storm clouds forming on the horizon. The storm was in the form of government regulation, of all crazy things. In the early 80's a movement started to gain momentum that was eventually going to be nothing short of a cultural paradigm shift. It was stemming from the first amendment of the constitution of the United States, defining the relationship between the church and the state. For over 200 years the phrase "separation of church and state," used by Thomas Jefferson and others expressing an understanding of the intent and function of the Establishment Clause and Free Exercise Clause of the First Amendment to the Constitution, was clearly understood as a protection. This safeguard was to protect the church in America from ever being controlled by government. Its original resolve was to guarantee churches the freedom of religious expression without fear of government control, *not* the other way round. In a relatively brief period of time that interpretation made a 180 degree reversal, to: protecting the government from the church.

The impact on ministries like Young Life was devastating. At Greenwich High school, to name one among hundreds (and growing numbers each day) of high schools where Young Life existed, school access for our leaders was suddenly and irrevocably removed, and not nicely. With one fell swoop, my status at Greenwich High School went from "You can have an office in the student center if you want one" to, looking at me like I was the second gunman on the grassy knoll. Faculty and staff, many of whom were merely toeing the company line, no longer considered me an asset to the school. Maybe some of it was paranoia, but after being treated so deferentially for many years, I felt like a pariah. It seemed like everyone was against me and against that Christian organization, Young Life.

Gleason Frye was our committee chairman at the time and he provided some well-needed wisdom and perspective. He arranged a meeting with the School Superintendent, to protest our sudden exclusion from the high school campus and our being rear-ended by the School Board. In spite of Gleason's best efforts it did not go well. Twelve years of steadfast, consistent positive influence of our leaders at that school mattered not one iota, and no longer was wanted. I'm so grateful for Gleason's presence because I wasn't at all helpful in the meeting. I mainly wanted to jump across the desk and start choking the Superintendent. But, the die was cast. We were doomed before ever walking into the office. The meeting was nothing more than window dressing. Gleason put our best foot forward, but as soon as we walked out he knew we were fighting a lost cause.

I told Gleason I wanted to lawyer-up. But not long after that, every Young Life area in the country received a letter, instructing all of us to back away from confrontations with schools and School Boards. We were told that attorneys representing Young Life were working nationally to address the problem, and our fight would be through the legal system, so there was nothing more we could do. For anyone reading this who wasn't involved with Young Life back then, it may be difficult to comprehend how utterly defeated and hopeless we felt. Once the dust settled and I and everyone else learned to accept that the rules for us changed, it was adapt or quit. We eventually learned to adapt.

We either connected with students at public events, or even better, we eventually learned that there were ways to have campus access that did not violate their interpretation of the first amendment. For me, that meant extending my coaching responsibilities as far as I could stretch them. If anyone accused me of being at the school representing a Christian organization, I could always say I was there in the role of my responsibilities as the Varsity Lacrosse Coach.

This turned out to be rather ironic, I thought. Faculty leadership was easily influenced by the first complaint or criticism that crossed their desk. While all of this change was taking place around the country, I learned of co-workers who were kicked off campuses because of just one phone call from an irate parent. A Principal could get a hundred positive messages, but it only took one complaint to get someone booted. The irony was, as long as we could give that same Principal an acceptable reason to answer that one parent's complaint, we were covered. "He may work for Young Life in his own time, but the reason he is on this campus is because he is our lacrosse coach."

Spiritual Principle at Work

I am told that momma eagles have a creative way to get their young to fly. Apparently eaglets can get quite comfortable in their homes, or nests. I suppose the same can be said for the young of any species. Eagle nests are constructed of branches and twigs. The momma eagle constructs the nest in such a way that all of the sharp, pointed ends of the branches are pointing outward, so the young eaglets can rest against a comfortable nest floor and wall.

To encourage the eaglets to fly, the mother eagle simply turns the sharp ends of the branches towards the inside of the nest. No longer is the nest a place of comfort. For the eaglet's first time in their short lives the prospect of leaving their home suddenly has a desirability to it. And off they go soaring into the heavens.

We had no intention of ever leaving Greenwich, especially after the committee helped us with the purchase of our home. And after all the years and the work to get the ministry on solid footing, I thought I would be happy spending the rest of my life in Greenwich. I couldn't imagine anything making me actually *want* to leave. But God had other plans for me and for my family, plans that involved changes that would be, for us, as substantial as the transformation from Maryland to Connecticut. Our comfortable little nest was starting to have sharp pointy things sticking at us.

Had the church and state restrictions been in place before I arrived in Greenwich I wouldn't have known the difference, and it wouldn't have impacted me so heavily. But I had full access for eleven years. Greenwich High School was our second home. In fact, there were weeks when I was probably at the high school more than I was at my own home. And over time I grew to love it there. Of course, that was due to the people, which included a lot of the faculty like Joe Wesney, who had become close friends. In that twelfth year, even at times when I was allowed on campus because of coaching, I started having feelings I hadn't had since the first year. I felt like an outsider, an alien. The nest had become uncomfortable. And that's when, for the first time since we turned down the offer to return to our church in Maryland just after our first year in Greenwich, that I started thinking about leaving.

Where Do We Go From Here?

This whole experience I've been describing took several months. And all throughout the events that took place, Carol and I were trying to process it all. When it finally got to the point where thoughts of leaving started drifting into my head regularly, my talks with Carol began to intensify. While I loved living in Connecticut, one thing I did know: I most certainly was not in love with the winter weather. I thought, if we ever had to leave Greenwich, I hoped we could at least go someplace warm and sunny. We also realized by that time that Josh would be severely disabled and wheelchair bound. We thought it would be helpful to move someplace that was hospitable to those with disabilities.

For my age and years of experience, I was fairly marketable in Young Life terms. I thought if I could quietly make some inquiries, maybe we could get a better feel if the Lord was leading us away, or letting us know we needed to stay and tough it out. My philosophy had been: if you don't ask, the answer is always "no." That's the secular philosophy side. The Christian equivalent is, "knock on a door and see if the Lord opens it. If not, He wants you to go in another direction." With those two thoughts in mind, I pondered where I'd like to be if I could go anywhere in the country. In fact, after our sabbatical in Europe, Carol and I were even entertaining the idea of living overseas. However, the uncertainty of the situation with Josh, and not being able to foresee his medical requirements caused us to eliminate overseas as a possibility.

I knew some of the Young Life Staff in California, and began to ask around. I finally connected with the Western Divisional Director for Young Life and then the Regional Director for Southern California. I learned that there was, in fact, a possible opening available if I was interested. It just so happened that I was going to be in Orange County completing the last of my graduate school courses. While I was out there, I took the opportunity to check out the area they were offering, Palos Verdes.

By that time two of the Baker girls, Beverly and Paula, were in college at Pepperdine; and I was able to ask them about Southern California and specifically about Palos Verdes. Bev told me that, in her opinion, Palos Verdes was the closest thing to Greenwich that she had seen in California. I thought," Well, that's a good sign at least."

Unfortunately, not long after I returned home I received a call from the Regional Director telling me that they had decided to fill the Palos Verdes post with someone local. Because of some internal challenges and changes in Young Life out there, they felt it would be a risk to ask a family to move 3000 miles, in case problems should arise later on. I was offered another possibility further north, not far from San Francisco, but by then I felt that the door was closing on California and never did pursue that opportunity.

The Sunshine State?

I was disappointed, but I had already had another person in mind to call. I had met Charlie Scott a few times at staff functions and knew he was the Regional Director for the state of Florida. He was a tall man and a former college basketball star. That part of his background reminded me of Chuck Reinhold. Charlie was the kind of guy everyone liked. He had a pleasant personality and I thought, "I don't know the California staff that well, but for sure Charlie is a guy I could work for." He was a *glass is half full* kind of man, always positive and enthusiastic. So I wasn't surprised when I told him my situation that he immediately offered to bring Carol and me down to Florida and have a look at some possibilities.

Carol had been to Florida exactly one time in her life, when she was a little girl. I also had only been there once before, for a weekend Young Life function. But from the time we got there it reminded me of our first encounter with Jack Carpenter back in Connecticut. Florida seemed like a natural fit. Charlie and his wife Mary were gracious hosts, showing us around the Orlando area and even taking us over to Disney World. I told Charley, "Ok, I can see myself as the Area Director for the Magic Kingdom." He put us on a plane and flew us down to Ft. Lauderdale. There was an opening for an Area Director for Broward and Dade Counties and he wanted us to check it out and to meet the local committee.

The first couple we met and the people with whom we stayed, were Renee and Bob Kennedy. Carol and I didn't make the connection until we met, but years before, when Renee was single, she actually was part of the Washington D.C. volunteer leadership team and we had worked together. Now married, their kids, Kelli and Jason were very young. A "Where are they now" aside, Jason is a TV host on the "E!" network. Renee and Bob hosted us, showed us around Ft. Lauderdale, and introduced us to the rest of the committee. Everyone seemed friendly and enthusiastic, and in due time Carol and I began to feel that, if we decided it to leave Greenwich, this was a place where we could live and work for Young Life. In reality, I think we had already decided to leave. It just took a while for us to admit it.

Saying Goodbye

When we got back to Greenwich we decided to keep our thoughts private for a while longer, and to finish out the school year. The first people we told about leaving were our closest friends and our committee. We asked them not to pass the word, saying that we wanted to break the news to the Young Life kids and to our leaders ourselves. We eventually worked out the best way to tactfully make the announcement. I knew it would be hard on the kids. But most of them had known us for only three years or less, whereas some of our leaders had known us for much longer. We told the leaders first, and individually. We then announced it to the kids. I carefully noted any kids who were not present at that meeting, then after the meeting I tried to locate those absent kids so they didn't hear the news of our departure second hand. I felt that taking all of these precautions was necessary. I knew that *how* we brought closure was very important, even if painful. I just wanted to do it the right way.

Eventually everyone knew about us leaving. After school was out for summer break, our Norwegian friends, Ellen and Per Johansen, threw a big party in their back yard for us to officially say goodbye to everyone. We were blessed by this kind gesture, not to mention we received some very special going away gifts. It was a very emotional day. Our lives had been deeply entwined in the lives of these dear folks, and the town, for twelve years. We had relationships that would last a lifetime. We were turning a page in the story of our lives, moving forward. We were excited, but it was still difficult to say goodbye.

After telling Charlie Scott we'd come to Florida, over the summer Carol and I made another trip to Ft. Lauderdale; this time to house hunt. I described earlier what a blessing the committee had given us with the interest-free loan on our Greenwich home. By the time we sold that home, and with housing in Florida being much less expensive, we were able to purchase a beautiful four bedroom home. We thought we were really hot stuff because we were even able to buy a home with an in-ground swimming pool, a real luxury in Greenwich. Our parade was somewhat rained upon when I learned that the majority of the houses in our neighborhood also had pools. But I figured a lot of our Greenwich friends didn't know that, any more than I had known. So it was fun telling them faux-offhandedly, "We bought a nice home with an in-ground pool. Yeah, we're pretty cool."

Finally the day came when the movers arrived. Some of the club kids came over to say more final goodbyes. One of our dearest club kids—we called her our adopted daughter—Michele McBride, was there. Michele had a difficult home life and as we had gotten to know her, she would spend more and more time at our house, especially on weekends. It finally got to the point where she just moved in on many weekends. By then we had expanded our home to four bedrooms and had plenty of room. One of the new rooms unofficially became Michele's room.

As the men were loading our belongings, it broke my heart to see Michele standing in our driveway and crying her eyes out. We had become like second parents to her and I felt like we were abandoning our daughter, so dear had she become to us. I suppose there were many kids from over the years who could have been standing there that day we left, had they still been in in high school. But we understood, as did Michele eventually, that change happens. And when we seek God's will for our life, we don't have to worry about change. He has something wonderful in store for us.

At that time, it was virtually impossible to imagine a place or life that would be even close to matching our years in Greenwich. The next volume of this book, coming up, is a testimony to a few facts. God is in charge.

There is no security in this life apart from God. Any sense of being in control of our lives is an illusion. God is trustworthy. Our family has a history, a track record of His phenomenal faithfulness to us, which is at 45 years and counting. God loves surprising us. And finally: in my life, every time God takes away something really good, He replaces it with something even better, and almost always, something I never could see coming.

This chapter of our life closed that day as we said a teary goodbye to Michele. But that it was not the end of our close relationship with her. She often visited us in Ft. Lauderdale, especially at Thanksgiving. That became our special holiday with our "daughter." Eventually Michele married a great guy and they settled down in Greenwich. They have raised two wonderful children of their own, and every time we go back to Greenwich, we always try to see Michele.

From volunteer leader in college, to full time staff in Washington D.C., to twelve years in Greenwich. Some say it's the destination. Others say it's the journey. For me, I'd like to think it was both. Do I have any ragrets? Nope. Not even one letter.

Chapter 14

Humor

These last two chapters delve into some of the "whys" of Young Life, not just "what happened." My Dad's generation didn't seem to concern themselves as much with the "why" questions. That generation used to say, "Ours is not to reason why. Ours is just to do or die." Die? Seriously? He was from the *Silent Generation*, the name coined from another saying of that era, "Children are to be seen and not heard." Obviously, my grandkids have never heard that expression.

These next chapters are about two core values in Young Life. There will be methodology, philosophy, and even some theology discussed, along with the occasional cartoon for the attention deficit readers. I think a bit of a disclaimer is in order. I do not consider myself as an expert on the worldwide ministry of Young Life. I do not claim to understand or be intimately knowledgeable about programs, goals or core values at the time of this writing. My views are based on the following experience: I began my journey in Young Life when I was 16 years old, in 1964. I left staff in 1988. That's 24 years of direct involvement. I have remained sometimes in touch with Young Life and many of the staff over the years, and continued to speak at some camps and banquets for several years after leaving staff. However, I have not been actively involved for 27 years.

I will venture an opinion that, if Young Life has shifted its core values since the days when I was actively involved, and if some of the things I'm about to say are therefore no longer applicable, I think it's a shame; not because it might mean I am just out of touch, (even if I am out of touch.) It would be a shame because Young Life would have moved some degree away from its origins.

When I was younger and on staff, many of us had concerns about the future direction of Young Life. Would we lose our core values? Would we slide away from the things that made this ministry great; beliefs in which we trusted and believed that God has led us, as far back as Jim Rayburn? I hope that's not the case. Probably the best people to make that determination are those who were involved in the earlier days and who are also involved today. There are still a few, I'm told.

One last disclaimer: While I remained active in ministry, and youth ministry specifically for many years after leaving staff, I do not claim to be an expert on youth culture or youth ministry. In addition, for the past ten years I have not been in direct daily contact with young people. And in youth culture terms, like doggie years, that can be a lifetime.

Enough of covering my backside. Growing older sucks, but if there's a silver lining to that often dark cloud, it's the observations, experiences, and hopefully the wisdom gained over time. Those and the seniors breakfast at Denny's. These points I am about to make are simply my observations from my years of experience. If they are helpful to the reader, I am grateful. If not, merrily hit your closest *delete* button. Or go Tweet something.

Skills and Talent

It was a privilege getting to know a lot of very talented people in Young Life. Some, unlike yours truly, had a ton of natural gifts that grew from raw talent, which was encouraged and enhanced by being around other talented people. Every now and then a person comes along who just breaks the mold, whose natural ability has a way of making everything appear easy while everyone else around them must work hard to get anywhere near their level of competence. In sports, it's seen all the time. LeBron. Messi. Brady. It's true in other endeavors as well. It's nice to be around the natural shining stars, but sometimes it can be demoralizing, because it comes so easy for them. For most of us "normal" people, we have to work hard to develop skills in order to obtain even a certain level of proficiency. I'm one of those guys. I had the benefit of being around both naturally talented and highly skilled Young Life guys and was able to learn from the best.

The two core values of which I speak, both require a lot of skill in order to use effectively in the Young Life ministry. They are *Humor* and *Story-Telling*. I love that both humor and story-telling are deeply embedded Young Life's DNA. And since I've been around Young Life people since I was 16, I've enjoyed a whole lot of exposure to those very gifted and skilled people. Enough already. Let's get going...

Humor in Young Life

A termite walks into a bar and says, "Where's the bartender?"

A duck walks into a pharmacy and says to the clerk, "I want some ChapStick." The clerk says, "You're a duck. How are you going to pay for it?" The duck says, "Ah, just put it on my bill."

Young Life: The Adventures of an Ex Staffer

As a sophomore in high school, from the first time I started going to club laughing and humor were very central to Young Life. I was no stranger to humor before going to club. It did seem a bit unusual early on that there would be a religious meeting that had elements in it that were so much fun and so funny. But there was something else going on, and back then I couldn't put my finger on it. I knew something was different-good, different. My Young Life leader, Chuck Reinhold could go from being side-splitting hilarious to talking about the most spiritually intimate subjects within the span of a few minutes. And yet somehow it didn't appear to be incongruent.

The more involved I got, and the more Young Life people I met and started to hang around, I began to realize that the humor wasn't just about skits and planned events. Those guys just loved to laugh and loved to make each other laugh. It didn't really matter if the leaders were around kids or not. For them, humor was completely natural and organic in a way that I had never seen before among a Christian group. It made me want to be around them more. There was a light-heartedness about them that seemed spontaneous and not contrived. They were genuine. They were trans-parent. And they seemed comfortable in their own skin.

For a long time I just enjoyed the fun of it all, and appreciated the fact that it was unique compared to other Christian ministries I had seen. I never really questioned it or even thought about it too much. It wasn't until after high school when I was a volunteer leader that I really started thinking about and dissecting this "Young Life humor." What was really going on? Was it like the old *Sound of Music* song, "A spoon full of sugar makes the medicine go down," the sugar being the humor and the medicine being the Christian message? That may have been a surface observation, but by then I realized that there was some deeper meaning behind all of the funnies.

It's been said that if you try to analyze a kiss, you can ruin the experience altogether. Kisses aren't meant to be analyzed, but enjoyed. I think the same is true with humor. But in this case I'm going to give it a try, because I think it's important to understand, and I believe it to be a phenomenal gift that God gave to Young Life. Not that God gave humor exclusively to Young Life. But more than any other ministry I knew, Young Life, somewhere along the way, discovered some unique and very attractive insights about it.

I see humor as a gift. I'm not sure most people even want to go to the trouble to understand all that is going on underneath the humor when it's used in the context of ministry. Because of that, over the years, humor in ministry is not something I've seen given away very often. That is, I seldom see it appreciated or utilized to its full potential by groups other than Young Life. Humor and ministry working together in Young Life was all quite purposeful and integrated.

What's So Funny?

If Young Life is a ministry dedicated to a very serious mission, that kids everywhere deserve the opportunity to hear about Christianity, why do we even bother with humor at all? Isn't articulating the Gospel enough to keep us busy? With humor, there are several underlying principles coming into play. First off, all humor treats people in a holistic way. When communicating the Gospel, we primarily (although not exclusively) explain propositional truth through a largely linear style of proclamation. We speak, they listen. By comparison, humor can speak to one's emotions and feelings, and can do it in a way that gives credibility and validation to them. With laughter it helps us say, in effect, that we care about someone as a total person; in other words, holistically, not just what they think or believe.

Secondly, humor presents a certain light-hearted philosophy of life. It says, with regards to Christianity, that Christians can be fun. I know that's a cliché, but the stereotype of Christians who cannot enjoy life because all they know is seriousness is, unfortunately, a valid one. The ability to laugh at one's self is uplifting and healthy, and can even be healing. It didn't take me long to realize that humor in Young Life was very positive and upbeat. The people who were the brunt of any jokes were very often the leaders. When it was the kids who were the target, it was done in such a way that they actually felt complimented, and certainly never put down or insulted. The funniest and most talented leaders seemed always careful not to use put-down humor or sarcasm.

Thirdly, humor in Young Life had the ability to bring people together. It could unite a fragmented group. Once I began examining closely, I found the sociological dynamics of a Young Life club to be absolutely fascinating. Regarding the atmosphere in a room at the beginning of club, consider this: kids all come together for an hour. They come from a variety of circumstances and experiences. Some kids may have left a dysfunctional situation at home that night to come to club. Others may have been yelled at or criticized that day by a teacher, or a coach, or an employer. Others may have had very uplifting experiences. Kids arrive at club with all sorts of "baggage", both negative and positive.

The point is, at the beginning of a club leaders are addressing a fragmented group. For me, the purpose of the elements of club was to draw kids together and unite that fragmented group of individuals. In addition to "baggage handling," the various elements of club: (music, skits, run-on's, announcements, media and so on), if done well, moved kids from feeling threatened, uncomfortable, or intimidated, to being open, relaxed, and receptive. Why did we sing in club, for example? Was it just something fun to do? The philosophy and use of music in Young Life is a topic for another day, but music was, at least, a tool that united people. And that's what humor did. I believe that in the first 45 minutes of a Young Life club, uniting and defragmenting is the most important task. Everything we do should contribute to that effort.

And why is that? Because it sets up or prepares kids to hear the message. If a club was run well, the last fifteen minutes were what I like to call, the most *hyper-prepared moments* in an entire week of a kid's life, to be open to hearing the Gospel message. There would be a build-up in club, a uniting, and at the end, a relaxation and openness. And with that came the atmosphere where kids intently listened to a message. In my own high school experience I couldn't figure out why everyone in club would sit with rapt attention and listen to Chuck speak. He was a great speaker, but it was more than that. Everything done before he started his talk had prepared those last few moments. Humor was a significant part of that preparation process. It's been said that humor doesn't necessarily communicate, but it can sure open the door for communication. By the way, this whole preparation I have been describing, with elements like music, program and humor to prepare the hearing of the message; that process was also integral to the Young Life camping program on a much larger scale and over a period of a weekend or a week. The process was designed with the same goal in mind. That will be discussed later.

Fourthly, humor actually becomes an expression of service and even an expression love to kids. Offering humor, in its many forms, expresses care. Kids may not be able to articulate this. I sure couldn't when I was in high school. But they can sense it. Every now and then I've overheard a kid say something like, "Wow, I can't believe they went to all that trouble to set that up, just for us!" Receiving humor is a kind of like receiving a love gift.

Over the years, through media, multiple technologies and social media, kids' expectations to be entertained have grown exponentially. Even back when I was still on staff, I knew there was no way we could compete with Saturday Night Live, for example. Why did humor and other components of Young Life still work? Because we could give, in the midst of a multitude of options available, something that technologies, TV, movies, entertainment and video games couldn't provide: we could love kids incarnationally. We could wrap the message of Christ in a person, in the form of Young Life leaders and staff. We could live among them and offer unconditional love. Humor, among other "gifts", communicated that.

The fifth principle may be the most important. Young Life's style of humor was effective because it reflected the giving, non-judgmental nature of our relationships with kids. Humor says, "No strings attached," that is, it is a totally unselfish gift. It says, "Here, this is for you. There is no purpose for it other than to be a gift for you. You don't have to do anything other than accept it and enjoy it. I am asking for nothing in return. You don't have to be good to receive and enjoy it, and you don't have to earn it." Those are exactly the attitudes with which we sought to approach kids relationally in the first place. Elsewhere I have addressed more fully, the topic of incarnational relationships; the other great tool blessed and given from God. For now, my point is that humor models incarnational love.

Who Loves Ya?

Loving kids unconditionally is a reflection of the doctrine of grace, which is defined as unearned or unmerited favor. The gospel of Christ is different from religion. All religions ask their followers to do something in order to earn favor or to be acceptable. Christianity stands alone, saying, "You can't earn it. You aren't good enough and you can never be good enough to earn it. I (God) am going to give it to you. You can't give me anything in trade or in return. It is a 100% free gift to you. It wasn't free for my son. He died on the cross to pay the price for your sins, so that it can be free for you."

There is a paradox. The "loving, giving, asking-for-nothing-in-return" nature of our humor is the very thing that allowed us to utilize it for a purpose. Because we weren't asking kids to reciprocate in any way, we actually did get something back: we saw kids who felt loved, felt safe, felt comfortable, felt relaxed, forgot about their troubles for a period of time, and therefore engaged fully in hearing the Gospel.

There is also a parallel with humor and contact work. Because our incarnational approach to relationships was unconditional and we weren't doing contact work to recruit kids to club, once they understood that, that is, once they knew we were asking for nothing in return, they often did give something else in return. They started coming to club, but not all of them and not all of the time. As any Young Life leader knows, we treated kids the same whether they came to club or not. For many kids, the moment they discovered that we weren't going to change how we treated them was when they started coming to club. But some knew it all through high school and they never once came to club. It didn't matter in terms of how we treated them.

Kids have few reference points for unconditional love from someone who isn't family. And even family members can sometimes be conditional in their love. Some parents withhold love until certain behavior or performance is achieved. Beyond the family, some teachers show partiality towards brighter or more committed students. Coaches favor kids who perform well. Employers do the same. At times when I've parented, taught, coached or employed, I've been conditional. That's not always a bad thing. In fact, there's a lot of good with it. But when we're in the ministry of telling and showing the love of God; incarnational, unconditional love is the instrument God has given us to use so that kids can better understand and receive God's love.

What Kids Experience With Humor

As a result of humor, along with the other elements of club, when a new kid sits in a Young Life club or at a camp, there are two conflicting thoughts going on at the same time. One, they sense that something different, possibly strange is taking place. "Why is all of this fun going on? Where's the catch? Something's not quite right about this whole scene. Am I being played? How can these people be so crazy and fun and uninhibited, and at the same time talk about such serious, personal and religious stuff?"

Yet, at the same time there is another thought, saying, "Something feels really good about what I'm experiencing. I'm feeling accepted, noticed, important, not alone. If I am honest with myself, I'm actually feeling love. It feels like a warm blanket in here." When kids feel that, they tune in and *hyper-listening* happens. They no longer feel threatened by a person or a group, many who may be strangers or upperclassmen, or by the situation, or by what others might be thinking of them at that moment. They feel... comfortable. They feel... safe. For a brief period of time they've managed to forget about their troubles. There were times when I was speaking at camps when the room would turn ghostly silent, and everywhere I looked, eyes were focused on me so strongly that it felt like a thousand laser beams. I had to remind myself that it was due (in part) to the preparation that had gone on, through humor and the other parts of the program.

We worked to make the humor absolutely the best it could be, and the same with the music and different parts of the program. But at the end of the day, we weren't some kind of social club. And even though these principles of humor and uniting components would work in other situations, in Young Life we deeply believed that the result of our preparation work wasn't simply socio-logical in nature; it was nothing short of the presence of God's Holy Spirit. Kids listened with rapt attention because we prepared the group, but more importantly it was the presence of God's Spirit. Any youth group can make that claim, back then or today. All I'm saying is, in 50 years of knowing Young Life, God has given the tools, the talents and the wisdom to prepare kids to *really* hear the Gospel, in what I believe is the most favorable possible conditions. And humor plays a massive part in creating those conditions.

Humor at Camps

Keeping in mind my previous comment about analyzing a kiss, I find it interesting to dissect the nature of humor a bit further, particularly as it related to the camping ministry in Young Life. As far back as my Work Crew days at Frontier Ranch with Jay Grimstead, I began to see that different styles of humor worked at different times and produced varied outcomes. I understood very little of it then, but now I have the luxury of hindsight, and Young Life training.

On the first night of camp, Jay used a lot of "pull your leg" humor. Let me explain. Kids had just arrived. For them, everything was new and different. Most kids had never been to a camp that seemed more like a resort for high school kids than a camp. Jay would use that unfamiliarity as an opportunity to throw them a curve ball. For example, after the first dinner Jay would intro-duce a lovely lady who was going to sing a song "as part of our evening, after dinner entertainment here at Frontier." She was accompanied by two backup singers. The nicely dressed woman would start singing the song, "Mockingbird Hill" and the men would chime in on the chorus, which began with "Tra-la-la," followed by the rest of the chorus.

The kids took this as serious and straightforward entertainment. Everything seemed completely normal and appropriate, until the beginning of the second chorus, whereupon the backup singers joined in with their "Tra-la-la"…just a little bit louder than after the first verse. I loved to watch the expressions on the kids' faces during this process. I'd see some initial odd glances, which I interpreted as, "What the…? Weren't those guys a little louder? Probably just not as experienced as the lady singer." After the third verse the "Tra-la-la" was almost a yell, followed by the chorus sung perfectly normally; and a puzzled glance from the lady singing, over her shoulder at her two accompanists. More kids exchanged looks at each other. They started to feel embarrassed for this poor lady who was strapped with two guys who were messing up her beautiful song.

By the chorus, after the fourth verse, the two guys ramped it up another notch and began yelling the entire chorus. They also started crowding the singer around the microphone stand, squeezing her out and moving themselves closer to the mic. The kids viewing went from embarrassment for the lady to, literally, dropped jaws at the mortifying destruction of the entertainment. By the last verse the men had just pushed the woman behind them and were singing and screaming into the mic. They finished the song with a huge flourish, while the woman sulked away. It was sometime during that last chorus that the blinders came off and the kids realized that the whole thing had been a prank from the beginning. The song was a great big, "Gotcha!"

Jay knew that if he could fool his crowd like that at the very beginning, he had them, and he had them wanting more. They went from questioning, "How cool can this camp be?" to, "Ah, you got me. You guys are cooler than I thought," and also, "What's coming next?" Kids loved being thrown off balance like that. Catch them off guard and you'd win them over. Great anticipation was built. That is just one example of how and when a particular style of humor was used to build the program.

Interestingly, many years later I watched a program at a Young Life camp that was run by a couple of young guys who didn't understand, "Why we do what we do." But they had seen the Mockingbird Hill song performed before and decided to use it the first night for their program. Here's what I saw: A lady came up to sing. Two guys came with her. The song was introduced as a "really funny" song. From the first verse on, the two guys started yelling their lines and crowding out the lady singing. And that was it. Three people pushing, crowding, singing and yelling. The total purpose and therefore the effectiveness of the skit was corrupted.

Form Follows Function

There's a well-known principle: form follows function. Take automobiles, for example. When the function of a car was simply to get from point A to point B, something as simply designed as a Model T Ford did the job. Its form or design served its function. Flash forward a few, or many years, and the function of an automobile grew from just getting from one point to another. It also functioned as a comfortable place in which to ride. It functioned as a symbol of wealth and status, or maybe it functioned as a vehicle to get from one place to another really fast, or to get there carrying a whole lot of luggage. In each case the form of the automobile changed because the function changed. You're welcome for that little History Channel moment, by the way.

In the case of humor, this is why I believed it was vital to understand the function of humor and the function of different kinds of humor; the "why's", because if you didn't, as these two young program guys obviously didn't with the case of *Mockingbird Hill*, then the form could be modified to the point where it no longer had anything to do with the function. The Mockingbird Hill

skit completely lost its effectiveness because the program guys, who didn't understand the function, changed
the form.

There are many different forms and styles of humor that
perform different functions, and get different responses:
the unexpected, incongruity, the grotesque, shocking,
slapstick, absurdity, just to name a few. (The two styles
that were avoided were sarcasm and off-color humor.)
There were skits that involved getting kids up out of the
audience. There were others that were rehearsed, and
sometimes involved props and costumes. There were
also categories like theme nights and spontaneous melo-
dramas, to name a few more. Leaders would not just
create humor, they would "steal" designs from any number of sources and were always on the lookout for new
ideas and how to apply them to a Young Life context. In
the early days some staff guys actually managed to get
original scripts from the Carol Burnett Show and other
TV productions. I've been told that producers willingly
shared their resources with Young Life.

Principles

This next rather long paragraph consists of a rapid fire
list of some principles of humor that provided helpful
guidelines: Humor needed to be universal enough to
include your whole audience. (For example, you could
make fun of something that was going on at school. But
if you had an all-county club, kids that went to other
schools would have no idea what the joke meant.) To be
in a humorous production required full commitment, and
by that we meant, reckless abandon and being totally
uninhibited. It was more important for an audience to
love you than to think you were funny. Quality humor
required sensitivity and maturity. Off-color humor was a
poor substitute and took less creativity. These high
standards made us more creative. Preparation and commitment to quality was required. "We'll wing it" was only
for the one percent of really talented people out there.

For the rest of us, winging it came off sloppy. Over-preparation of a skit freed a person to better relate to the audience. Props and costumes could contribute as much as 70 percent to the success of a skit. And if 70 percent was from props and costumes, another 70 percent of the success of a skit was found in having a great ending. I know, the percentages don't add up, but they're both really important. We paid a lot of attention to the lighting and sound. We limited the physical distance between us and our audience as much as possible. We took a modest approach, not "This is going to be the funniest thing you'll ever see", but rather, "We have something planned we think you may like." We always tried to leave the audience wanting more. And we would steal, steal, steal (borrow!) material from anywhere we could.

If you aren't particularly interested in humor, that last paragraph may have put you to sleep. If that's the case, it's time to wake up, because I saved the best principle for last. A few pages back I described what goes on in a kid's head, sitting in a club. I know it's uncool to quote myself, but this principle is so important, I want you to re-read what I wrote before. Rather than having to go back and hunt for it, permit me to re-state it, here:

"Something feels really good about what I'm experiencing. I'm feeling accepted, noticed, important, not alone. If I am honest with myself, I'm actually feeling love. It feels like a warm blanket in here." When kids feel that, they tune in and hyper-listening happens. They no longer feel threatened by a person or a group, many who may be strangers or upperclassmen, or by the situation, or by what others might be thinking of them at that moment. They feel... comfortable. They feel...safe. For a brief period of time they've managed to forget about their troubles.

From the Belly

Note especially those last two lines. The most effective way to achieve that with a person using humor, and here's the most important principle: *A belly laugh is the best laugh there is.* Let me explain. Think of different kinds of laughs. There is a *That's clever* laugh. There's a *chuckle*. There's a *sarcastic* laugh. There's a *laughter of surprise*: "Didn't see that one coming." There's even a *moan*. "Ewww, that's awful." There's a *chortle*, (but I don't even know that one is), a *guffaw*, a *giggle*, a *snicker*, a *groan* (isn't that the same as a moan?) a *smirk*, and a *cackle*. Here's my definition of a *belly laugh*. It's a rear-back, don't analyze-type laugh. It's a laugh that you don't have to think about, or measure, or wonder if you "got it." It's when you see or hear something and from deep down inside of your belly a laugh comes rolling up and out of you. You can't even control it. It's a totally spontaneous reaction. It's the purest laugh there is. There is no pretense to it. It's innocent. There is no guardedness with it and some-times you don't even control what it sounds like. It may even come out as a loud snort. You don't care, because you aren't thinking about it, you are just living it. You're so in-the-moment you don't even know where you are for a second. A few of my favorite belly laugh moments in cinema history: Indiana Jones shooting the guy with the big sabre. Del saying to Neil in bed, "Those aren't pillows!" The moment the wax strip is removed on Andy Stitzer's 40 year old chest. And for the Seinfeld TV fans in the house, Cosmo Kramer: "You're as pretty as any of those other girls. You just need a nose job."

To me, a belly laugh is one of the most beautiful exper-iences in the world. When we used humor in Young Life my goal was always to get at least one belly laugh in a skit or production. No matter how much it cost in terms of time and effort, it was worth the price. Because when a kid felt comfortable and safe, and all of those feelings I wrote about, then later on they were not going to just hear the message, they were going to feel loved, and the message would become incarnated for them. Flesh would come onto the spoken word, and the statement in John 1:14 happened all over again in the living room of a club. "The word of God became a human being and dwelt among us."

The Fourth Night

An entire week at camp was filled with humor that had specific goals and resulted in amazingly effective outcomes. One other specific example that's worth examining, took place on the fourth night at summer camp. To understand the program and humor's relationship to it, it's important to first understand the progression of the nightly messages at a week of camp. The first few talks were of introductory nature, and focused on the personality of Jesus; generally covering His humanity and His divinity. The third talk usually began to introduce the concept of a broken relationship between God and mankind, but it was the fourth talk that really broke things open. That's when the speaker fully attacked the problem of sin and separation from God. The following night was all about the cross and resurrection, which is, of course, God's saving solution to our problem of sin.

The 24 hour period between the bad news, that we have a problem of sin and we can't fix it on our own, and God's solution through the cross, was a crucial time for a high schooler at camp. We reasoned that it would be hard for them to really understand the solution to the problem (of sin) unless they understood and deeply felt the problem. But it would be awful for a kid to hear that we're lost in sin, and then not hear God's solution. Fortunately, at a camp we had a captive audience, so to speak. They weren't leaving before night five arrived. So a valuable part of sharing the Christian message was to allow kids to stew over and chew on the problem for a day. At the same time, the message of sin could be overwhelming and even depressing. But because they were a captive audience, we could also afford to divert their attention away from negative message of sin, and not have them dwell on it right away, knowing we could get their thoughts back later on. For many, including a lot of parents, this kind of logic was counterintuitive. Adults want to attack and solve a difficult problem right away. Developmentally, adolescents process problems differently. Parent: "Young man, you come back in here! We are going to talk about this right now!" Kid: "Leave me alone! I don't want to talk about it." When kids feel overloaded, often they want to check out. We let them check out for a while

How could the program and the humor assist with the Gospel presentation at this point? As soon as the speaker finished praying at the end of the night four talk, the Program Director would run in and absolutely shock the crowd. Sometimes he might fire a blank gun in the air to increase shock value. Everyone was hustled to an open area of camp, where the Work Crew and staff were assembled, motionless, in what we called a *tableau*. The tableau participants were dressed in a theme costume. At Frontier Ranch, for example, the Program Directors usually used an old west theme. At Saranac Village we often set up a circus or a nautical theme.

At the firing of the gun or a loud whistle the tableau would suddenly come to life. Characters would reenact and recreate activities for which they were dressed. If there was an old fashioned square dance, or a barroom brawl, it would suddenly spring to life. If there was a circus act with jugglers, they would launch into action. An entire area with as many as 50 actors would come alive. The effect was shockingly impressive to the campers. It looked like something right out of Disney World. The instructions were given that a special dinner and evening was planned for everyone, and the price of admission was to go back to their rooms and create a costume in theme.

The leaders were in on the surprise and would be prepared to help kids make costumes. Dinner was in theme. The entire dining hall was transformed and appropriately decorated. If the theme was the circus, for example, we would have trapeze swings up in the rafters, with Work Crew kids dressed like acrobats, swinging from them. Every person whether it was Work Crew, kitchen staff or adult guests were required to be in costume. I remember back at Frontier Jay Grimstead would make certain that there were no automobiles seen, or nothing reminding us of the 20th century. Every precaution was taken so that the magical atmosphere was preserved.

The entertainment after dinner was the most elaborate and impressive programming of the entire week. I know, because as a Program Director, we worked on the entertainment for that one night more than anything else we prepared. The heart of the evening was a musical that we performed. We called it an opera. It, too, was something that grew out of Jay Grimstead's program generation. It was a corny melodrama and the songs we sang told the story (giving it the "opera" moniker.) But, the music used was contemporary music that kids recognized. The words were changed to tell the story. Jay, and others who followed him, wrote some brilliantly creative operas over the years.

For example, and don't forget, this example is from back in the 70's: Frankie Valli sung, "You're just too good to be true. Can't take my eyes off of you. You'd be like heaven to touch. I want to hold you so much." In our opera the heroine sings to the villain, who's trying to get her to divulge the location of the gold treasure by threating her on a lumberjack's buzz saw, "You're just too gross to be true, and I will never tell you, though you may saw me in two, and make my Daddy real blue, then Dudley Do-Right will come, and set you both on the run. He'll throw your butts into jail, and virtue then will prevail." By the way, I just wrote those lines without even having to go back and look them up in my files. You're welcome.

What's Really Going On?

In the midst of all this activity, what was going on internally with kids? After the very difficult message of sin, we were giving them the opportunity to let loose, blow off steam, and to "escape" in a positive and safe way. We had the confidence to know that the spiritual message wouldn't be lost. We gave them an entire evening of escapism. We also knew that the physical act of dressing up in costume aided an emotional release and catharsis. We made sure the leaders understood that it was very important for every kid to put on at least some kind of costume, even if it was just charcoal from one of the fireplaces used as makeup. We knew some kids would be reluctant, but the act of wearing even the most minimal of costume contributed to the psychological effect of distancing themselves temporarily from the emotionally charged spiritual message. That would pay dividends once we returned to the message the next day.

The relationship between program and humor, and the presentation of the Gospel message on Night Four, was profoundly intertwined. In fact, it was in close collaboration the entire week, but on that night the program reached its peak, and the message was just getting going. From Night Four on, the program emphasis decreased rapidly. The humor and the entertainment was much lower key for the remainder of the week.

If it could be graphed, it would look something like this: at the beginning of the week the program would start out of the gate at about 80 percent and the gospel message would be down around 30 percent. From Day One to the night of Day Four, the program would increase from 80 to 100 percent. The message would ride the "launch pad" energy of the program, rising slightly behind it, but increasing, reaching about 70 percent by Night Four. From then on, everything changed. The program had effectively launched the rocket of the Gospel presentation and it could decrease. I like to picture it as the liquid fuel tanks jettisoned from a space shuttle when they emptied of fuel. Meanwhile the message would ride the momentum of the program up to 90 percent by Day Five, and eventually reach the peak by Days Six and Seven, when kids were given the opportunity to accept Christ into their lives.

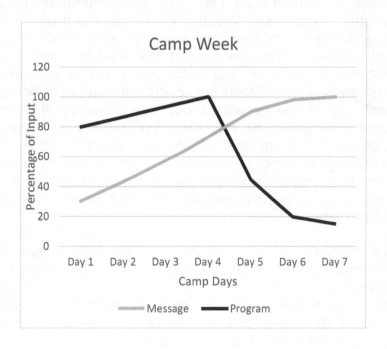

To this day I'm not sure how much of this amazing strategy was ever fully understood by those who saw it, or even experienced it as kids. I certainly didn't understand it after seeing it four weeks in a row when I was on Work Crew. But it was, and as far as I know, continues to be a powerful strategy, where humor and the program exist for the purpose of enhancing the Gospel message at camp.

Post-Young Life

In my next book I'll relate how my years in Young Life affected my life and work once I left staff. However, because we are looking into humor at this point, I thought now would be a good opportunity to pass along an example from my post-Young Life days, as it relates to humor.

For eight years I was a Youth Pastor at a large Presbyterian church in Florida. The resources and priorities of the church permitted me the luxury of taking missions trips internationally. We specifically targeted Southern Africa and Australia. The primary purpose of these trips was to train indigenous youth leaders in personal evangelism.

Wherever we went, however, I always tried to leverage our "curb appeal" (American teenagers in their country) by asking if we could conduct assemblies at their local high schools. We soon discovered that we weren't the first groups to make this request. We further learned that mission teams thought their best shot at having an attractive program in a foreign high school assembly would be to have their kids on stage, singing. It was probably the easiest, most generic and trainable talent they could use. After singing, there would be testimonies and a message. Unlike the USA, there were no restrictions regarding Christian presentations in public high schools. The national leadership which had invited us in the first place had the contacts in the school system to get us entrees to hold assemblies.

The first time I went to Africa was when I discovered African vocal music. If we all have jobs in heaven, I'm sure that the Africans' jobs will be on the welcoming committee. I had never before heard such mesmerizingly beautiful multi-layered acapella choral music in my life. So when I learned that American groups would actually stand in front of large assemblies of African kids and sing, I couldn't help but smile. Parenthetically, it also confirmed what I was learning about Africans with each visit: they were among the most gracious hosts I ever met, because apparently they never complained about Americans trying to sing to them. It would be like an American youth group having a high school assembly in Brazil and doing a Samba demonstration.

Because of my background in Young Life and my experience with humor, and considering its universal appeal, I knew we had something better to offer. Humor can cross cultural, ethnic and racial boundaries. So at the assemblies we held, we did Young Life skits. This list won't interest a reader who doesn't have the benefit of a history with Young Life, but those who do may appreciate it. We began with a skit called "I Went to Paris (and I came back with…)" It had the advantage of getting kids out of the audience and up on the stage, and sometimes a teacher as well. We then did the "Motorcycle Skit," with five of our team members on the floor being the motorcycles and the rest of our team entering to the song, *Bad to the Bone*, dressed as a motorcycle gang. They absolutely loved that one. We also inserted "No Touchy Kung Fu", and "Junior Class Play Practice" ("I am sick, you are sick, he is sick," etc). And for some cultural reason I never did figure out, the biggest hit of all was an adaption of "If I Were Not in Young Life" (We changed "Young Life" to "Gangway," the name of our youth group.) Even though some of the African kids didn't speak English, they began chanting each of our character's lines as they heard them.

Whether their reaction was due to the fact that they were used to boring assemblies, or that we were mostly White Americans, I do not know. But what I do know is that our humor did all of those things I've written about in terms of helping people become more receptive. There was an enthusiasm and electricity in the assembly halls wherever we went. One day we visited a high school in the Harare, Zimbabwe. As was typical for many of the

African schools, the assembly hall did not have seats. Kids would stand for the entire assembly. We were told there were about 1500 students. For our little team of 12 Americans, being the only pale faces anywhere in the vicinity or even that zip code, peeking out from behind the curtain before we began, was a bit intimidating. We started that assembly with "If I Were Not in Gangway" that day. By about half way through, the chanting had grown thunderous. And every time the character in the "diaper" sang, "Hello Mommy hello Daddy I love you! Pffft" (a "raspberry" his with his mouth) the place would just fall out. Kids were slapping each other and yelling. It may have been the most appreciative audience I've ever seen.

Instead of a message or sermon, we kept to the theme of skits by doing a shortened version of a presentation that had been used for years at Young Life camps, The Sin Wall and The Reconciliation Circle. The response was outstanding. Our follow-up was left in the capable hands of our national hosts. After each assembly, the members of our team were treated like celebrities, even signing autographs. Because we had trained them for that part of the mission project, they were able to handle the ego boost and use their instant fame to point kids to Christ. Each one was trained in personal evangelism and it was thrilling to see small groups of African students huddled around our students as our kids presented the Gospel to them.

I was confident that the humor we used in Zimbabwe, South Africa and Australia would be well accepted and would open the doors to effective communication of the Gospel. While Zimbabwe and South Africa both have many similarities culturally and are quite different from the U.S., Australia is a very westernized nation. Its young people share a lot of similar traits with American high school kids. Our assemblies were equally as effective there.

A Talk About Sin in Bermuda

When I first got involved with Young Life I was blown away that people could be so funny at times when they were speaking in club talks and then transform into total seriousness, and do it in a manner that seemed so completely natural. After I better understood the use of humor in ministry it began to make sense to me and eventually became part of my speaking style. I, too, could utilize humor in the midst of the most serious portions of messages and have it enhance the entire communication process.

Although almost always brought guest speakers with us for trips, there was one Bermuda trip where I decided to give the evening club talks myself. On the third of six nights was when I spoke on sin; our broken relationship with God, and the nature and consequences of sin. At one point I was trying to drive home the seriousness of sin in God's eyes. I had been reading C.S. Lewis, who I thought made an interesting point. He actually argued that there was one sin worse than the others. I had always considered that all sins were equally wrong in God's eyes, so Lewis' point caught my interest. Had it been someone else I may have dismissed it. He felt that the sin of pride was the worst sin because that's what keeps us from acknowledging other sins and from moving towards repentance.

His reasoning was a bit involved and I'm not sure I totally agreed with it, but there was certainly some truth there. I thought I would give it a try, incorporating it into my talk as another way of defining sin. After describing the nature of our iniquity and defining it from different angles, I started to echo Lewis' statement when I said, "I've talked a lot about our sin nature, things we've done wrong, good things we've failed to do, and how these sins alienate us from God. But there actually is one sin that is the worst sin you can possibly commit." I was fully intending to nail home the point that the sin of pride is what keeps us from admitting all our sins, which keeps us from repenting of them. Normally, this talk is uncomfortable to hear anyway. After all, who wants to be told, maybe for the first time in their life that they have a major problem, a sort of spiritual cancer, and that God is ticked off at them? So it's not uncommon for kids to look down, stare at their navels, look away, and act restless; often avoiding eye contact with me.

However, on that night when I told the group that there was one sin that was the worst, I felt a sudden and tangible change in the room. Everyone looked straight at me intensely. You could hear a pin drop. It stunned me at first. I only had a few seconds to try and analyze why I got that sudden reaction. Then it came to me. It was one thing to talk about different kinds of sins in the abstract, but now they wanted to hear the number one worse sin of all because they wanted to know if they were guilty of it. In their mind, sin was about to hit home and get real personal with them, either in relief (Oh, I'm so glad I don't do that sin.) or horror (I've committed the worst sin there is. I'm in deep doo-doo.) The train was about to leave the station and they wanted to know if they were on it or if they were about to be left behind.

I had absolutely no premonition of what I was about to say next. I hadn't planned it. It was completely spontaneous, and a surprise even to me. But I know where it came from. It came from that deep sense that God has given us an insight into humor in ministry. It came from that same place that I described when my Young Life leader would at one point be side-splitting funny and at the very next moment be communicating spiritually intimate truths, and it never seemed contrived or unnatural.

I waited a few seconds. I could tell they were literally holding their breath in anticipation. Then I slowly said,

"Do you know what that worst sin is?" (Another pause. They were dying out there) The worst sin is...mastur-bation!" And I held my gaze. I didn't change my expression. And like them, I didn't breathe...for about three seconds. Then I suddenly broke into a wide grin and said, "Na, I'm just kidding." There was a slight processing pause and then suddenly the room exploded. Kids were howling, screaming, and slapping five. It was the mother of all belly laughs. Leaders who, just a moment before thought I had absolutely lost my mind, were laughing uncontrollably. It must have taken five minutes before I could continue.

Ok, what happened there? Did I just ruin the most critical part of my message in order to go for a cheap laugh? Did I totally take them away from the serious-ness of the nature and the consequences of sin? Did I bring them closer to the Gospel or further away? I'm sure some would argue that I accomplished nothing but the negatives. I would reason that, even though it was unplanned and spontaneous, whatever it may or may not have accomplished, at the very least it sprung from a deep sense that humor speaks holistically even to the most fallen of God's loved ones. And it can be used for healthy and healing purposes.

I knew that whenever I addressed sin in my talks, kids were running my points through their own moral filter as they would measure what I said against their personal understanding of their sin. And for many that often included sexuality, whether they had little or a lot of personal experience. I wasn't attempting to make light of sexual transgression. In the three seconds between my pronouncement and my grin, they were horrified to discover that their question (Have I committed the worst sin ever?) was answered and they were guilty as charged. And when I grinned and said I was just kidding their relief was intense, like I had never before witnessed intense. They knew they weren't yet out of the woods. There was still the problem of sin they must address. But their relief was knowing that the train, in fact, had not yet left the station.

They also realized I was saying that we can get hung up on one particular sin and miss the whole point of falling short of the benchmark that God has set, which is perfection. Whether we sin a lot or a little, one type of sin or another, we'll never be good enough to meet God's standard. To be right with God there has to be a completely different way. Then I could go on, of course, to communicate God's permanent solution through Christ's saving work on the cross. The penalty our sin was paid for, once and for all time.

When I finally got back to my point that pride could be the worst sin because it's the one that keeps us from looking to God for help, the illusion that any one sin, sexual or otherwise, disqualifies us, was completely shattered. They were greatly relieved that they had not irrevocably destroyed all hope of getting things right with God because of one bad sin. But on the other hand, they were equally convicted that they weren't right with God, and the one thing that would keep them from getting right with Him was being too prideful to admit they were wrong.

I was convinced that what I said that night helped kids. But I never really had enough courage, if that's the right word, to try that again. The Bermuda trip consisted only of Greenwich kids. Maybe I just felt like I had that kind of trusting relationship with them. But I never felt I could say that in a weekend camp or a summer camp message. I also felt there would have been too much controversy and that wasn't a hill worth dying on for me. But oh my, did it ever work that one time.

Chapter 15

Story Telling

In addition to learning all about humor in the context of ministry, I also learned, from very early on in Young Life, about the powerful impact that could be made from telling stories and using illustrations. I can still remember some of the stories and anecdotes that Chuck Reinhold used, even fifty years later. I can also recall some of the stories that Bob Mitchell told while speaking at Frontier Ranch when I was on Work Crew.

In recent years I have noticed a rise in the use of, and in the advocacy of, story-telling. Not too many years ago, there was a rather sudden increase in literature advocating the use of narrative to enhance the communication process, not only in Christian circles but secular as well. One of my favorite authors was Max Lucado, who is a consummate story teller and who fully appreciates the power of this tool. I would still recommend his books today. But the use of story-telling and narrative in Young Life predates the more recent trending, by decades. Of course, story-telling and oral tradition dates back as far as the beginnings of civilization. Stories were passed on orally before there were written languages, stories that preserved a culture's history and identity. But my point isn't to document its origins. I'll leave that for my anthropologist friends.

When I first got involved in leadership, as with many skills I acquired, story-telling was caught as much as it was taught. My leader, Jerry Johnson, never held training seminars on how to use illustrations. It was just that everyone used them in their talks. If a role model was credited, it was Jesus himself. He used stories, examples and parables to clarify spiritual truths.

For my message preparation, the basic outline usually consisted of: a story or illustration, a Bible passage (most often a Gospel narrative about the life of Jesus) and then an explanation and application of that Bible passage. It was a simple formula, but it worked. We never began with scripture in club talks, which were always targeted to non-Christians. Had we been speaking at Campaigners Bible study groups or to a larger group of Christians, we may very well have begun with scripture, or even a biblical principle, after which we would support that principle with scripture. I've heard Young Life clubs defined as Christian meetings for non-Christians. As such, when we gave the message we were fully aware that we were speaking to kids whose interest level varied from very curious to totally disinterested, and everything in between. We knew we were tasked with grabbing and holding their attention. And the first tool I was given for that purpose was story-telling.

Stories With Benefits

What are some benefits from using stories, illustrations, and metaphors, as opposed to the linear style of a straight lecture? I'm no expert, and for those interested, the Internet and libraries can provide much more in-depth information. My desire is to relate this narrative style communication tool to what I learned in my years with Young Life. Though not completely interchangeable, when I use the term "stories" I am referring also to illustrations, examples, anecdotes, and even metaphors. But for simplification, I'll mainly stay with the term "stories."

Stories capture the listener's attention. Duh! You think that would be obvious. Try listening to anyone, anywhere, and from the moment they launch into a story you can feel the interest level rise, in your own mind as well as those around you. And for potentially disinterested high school kids, that can be a very helpful communication tool, especially at the outset of a message.

Stories utilize something that's familiar to clarify something that's unfamiliar. When we listen to a story, we naturally want to relate it to one of our existing experiences. We don't have to put forth a lot of mental effort to do this. We do it naturally. As a result, listening is less work and more enjoyable. Our minds search for similar experiences, and while we're doing that processing, we activate parts of our brains that process information differently than when we listen to someone lecture. We also tend to think in terms of cause and effect, and if a story is broken down into the simplest form, it is a connection of cause and effect. We think in narratives all day long, whether we think about walking down the street, or going to the store, or about friends or loved ones.

Good story tellers can certainly capture an audience. They can build suspense. They create drama. They have a way of drawing someone into their drama just by being a listener. Without even thinking about it, you are drawn in. "What's going to happen next? Is there a solution? What will it be? What would I do if I was in that situation?" Good story tellers speak in word pictures. They are word-crafters and know how to paint images with their discourse. They understand timing, and can do more with a silent pause at times, than the words they've been using. They know how to appeal to the senses. They can make you feel different emotions, and sounds; even colors, and tactile stimulation. They can make you relate to someone's pain, or pleasure, or fear.

Good story tellers also understand the importance of helping the listener connect the story to the point they're trying to make in the first place. Have you ever heard a speaker tell a truly interesting story, then pause at the end, and move on? Good story tellers never assume their listeners can make essential connections, so they help them, but in a way that doesn't insult their intelligence. A great story will be remembered long after the point it's illustrating. That's why it is so important to relate the story to the point.

There's another process that goes on in people's heads when they are listening to a story. They listen to it and it's enjoyable (hopefully) but they are also aware that there is purpose and direction, even if they can't see it just yet. Part of their mind moves ahead, similar to when hearing a joke. We enjoy the story told in a joke, but part of us tries to anticipate the punch line. And like a punch line in a joke, a good story has its own "punch" line. I like to call that the "ah ha" moment, when a person first realizes why the story was told, and that it points them to the greater truth of my message.

Think of a message with three parts: introduction, body and application. My stories were a springboard into the body of the night's message. The best stories were the ones that could carry me all the way through to the end of my talk; to the explanation and application of the message. Not every story was strong enough to accomplish that, so I either left the story at the beginning of the talk, or sometimes I would add another story during the application of my talk. That had two effects: it revived the listener's interest level and it clarified my applications and conclusions. I preferred talks that had just one, or possibly two stories. I've heard speakers who like clarifying every point in their talk with a brief story, or illustration, or quote. For me that clutters up a message. I'd rather have one or two powerful stories and build my talk around that.

Another accomplishment of a good story is that it creates not only a transition into your message, it can also provide a seamless transition. Bob Mitchell (Mitch) would be telling a story, and then somehow he was talking about a biblical truth about Jesus and about the Gospel. But for the life of me I had no idea how he got from one part of his talk to the other. The transition was natural and organic. That also created another effect that surprised me. It personalized his talk so that it was as if he and I were sitting in his living room and he was only talking with me.

Bass Ackwards

I had a method of using stories that I referred to as my "backwards method." I don't think many other leaders used this strategy. Whenever I tried to explain my method I was often met with odd looks. Typically, when someone is putting together a message, whether it's a club talk, or any talk, sermon or message, spiritual or secular; they decide on their main point or points, and then go looking for stories that illustrate the points.

I did exactly the opposite. I built my messages around my stories. In other words, I would find a great story, and then I'd ask myself the question: "What biblical truth (in the case of preparing club talks) or information will this story illustrate that will help kids better understand the Gospel?" I know, it sounds a bit dyslexic. I'm not even sure how I stumbled upon this process. But I really believe it's more effective. If I matched the message to the story and not vice versa, my stories had more impact. Some speakers use stories that only partially get them to their points. They fit, but they aren't a perfect, unified match. The reason my stories always fit so well is because the story was in place first, not the body of the message.

Story First, Use it Later

After I left Young Life, my first job was as a Youth Pastor. The Senior Pastor was a great communicator and as a result, a very well-known preacher. In fact, our Sunday morning services were broadcast on TV all across the country each week. Due to my interest in the power and potency of narrative, I always listened carefully to his sermons and paid particular attention to how he used stories. We also used to play a lot of tennis together. One day at tennis, we happened to be talking about boating. I'll pass along a story he told me because there's a good point at the end, so pay attention.

When Jim (my Pastor) was a young man, he had a job as a waterski instructor. One day he was giving lessons to a young mother. The mother brought her ten year old son with her to watch, so Jim had the boy with him in the boat while mom was practicing her waterskiing, trailing along behind. At one point she fell, whereupon Jim slowed and turned to go back and retrieve her. However, as he threw the steering wheel hard over and gunned the motor, two things suddenly happened. One, a wave from another boat destabilized his boat and caused it to list to the side. Two, with the sudden increase of the throttle, combined with the sudden listing of the boat, Jim, who had been sitting high up on the gunwale, was thrown completely out of the boat and into the water. In about two seconds Jim went from piloting a powerful runabout, to treading water and being a spectator to a full throttled boat, with a ten old boy sitting in the passenger's seat, traveling away from him at a high rate of speed. Adding to the crisis was Mom, who was frantically swimming towards Jim with a panicked look on her face. Jim looked at her, then back at the boat with a little boy's head bobbing around inside. The good news was, the boat was not headed out to sea. The bad news was, it was speeding directly towards the beach.

If there was one shred of good luck, Jim noticed that at least the boat was going to miss a crowded portion of the beach. It appeared to be heading towards a grove of dune grass and mango trees. Jim and Mom began swimming frantically towards shore. As they got closer they saw the boat head full speed up onto the shore, barely slowing, and launch itself into the air, then up and over the dune grass and completely disappear. They resumed their frantic swimming, noticing a few seconds later that smoke began to rise from behind the dune grass. By the time they reached the shore, the mother was absolutely hysterical, and Jim wasn't much better. They finally completed that torturously long transition from swimming, to wading, to running through knee deep water as if it was some sort of malicious quicksand, to finally hitting terra firma, and they began sprinting towards the mango trees. They looked up and what should they see? The little boy running out of the dune grass toward them, yelling these words: "Mommy, that was so much fun, can I do it again, please?!"

When Jim finally recovered his senses and made sure Mom and boy were all right, he walked around behind the dune to find the boat and to examine the source of the smoke, fearing the worst. Because the propeller was no longer in the water, but was still spinning full throttle, the boat's motor had burned out. Other than some scratches on the hull, the boat was unscathed.

I was absolutely enthralled throughout the telling of this story. It totally captured me. When Jim was finally done, I exploded, "That was amazing! What a freaking great story!" Jim smiled. He was used to getting a lot of accolades anyway, and he had a modest, self-depreciating way of receiving compliments. But I wasn't finished. My voice was probably a bit louder than normal when I said, "Please tell me you are going to use that in a sermon soon!" He then gave me a puzzled look and said, "How could I ever use a story like that in a sermon. What on earth could it possibly illustrate?"

I think my answer totally startled him. I was practically yelling by then. I said, "Who cares?! That's the greatest story I've ever heard you tell!" His next look was one I've seen before whenever I started to tell someone my backwards method of using stories. I thought, "What the heck, I'll give it another shot, with Jim this time." So I explained my backwards method. He wasn't impressed, or so I thought. He was an accomplished, polished, nationally known preacher. I was a young Youth Pastor. I assumed my suggestion fell on deaf ears. But I should have known better.

About a month later, with no forewarning from Jim, the story appeared right in a sermon, on Sunday morning, and on national TV. And, he made it work beautifully into the body of his message. The crowd went wild! In Presbyterian terms that means that the congregation appreciated the story and easily perceived how it illustrated Jim's message that day. Afterwards I saw him in the hallway. He gave me a grin and said, "See, you can teach an old dog new tricks."

Story Collector

From my earliest days in Young Life I began collecting and cataloging stories. I got them first, but not exclusively, from my own life. If I had an experience that was unusual or interesting, or a bit crazy, I made a note of it in case I could use it in a talk. I also got stories from listening to other people, from reading, from TV-from anywhere I could find them and from any source that stimulated my creativity. The best stories were always my own, but I learned that I could use a story "once removed." Over the years my story collection grew substantially. Some stories became dated over time and I could no longer reuse them. I used to have a great story about the Beatles when it was rumored that Paul McCartney had been killed in an accident. But that only had a shelf life of a few years. Some stories are as fresh and effective as the day I first used them. Though others stories faded, there were always new stories to tell, and always creative ways of using them.

With club talks I learned that I could recycle my best stories every three years. By then the youngest students would have graduated and a story would be new for the incoming classes. So I always kept meticulous records, not only of stories, but also which message points they were used to illustrate. And I naturally used my very best stories when I spoke on weekend camps, and especially at summer camps.

One of My Favorites

I cannot resist ending this chapter with one my favorite stories, a story that has survived and thrived for many years. It's said that imitation is the most sincere form of flattery. My own sons, Matthew and Adam, have both become exceptional speakers and great story tellers. Matthew served on Young Life Staff for ten years. One of the highest honors awarded to him was to be appointed as Camp Speaker at the largest Young Life camp in the country at the time, Lost Canyon, in Arizona.

Both sons have "stolen" this story from me. To be perfectly honest, I stole the story myself. I never did get to use Jim's story about the waterski lesson, once removed. Maybe I will someday. But the story I'm about to tell actually came from an impromptu discussion I had with a bunch of staff guys at a Regional meeting. One guy, Steve, shared the story, and I don't even think he realized what a gem of a story it was. Later on, I went back to him and got more background and details. I don't know if any of the other staff felt the same way about what I had heard, but I saw awesome potential. Eventually it became a regular part of every summer camp and weekend camp wherever I spoke. It's one of those stories "once removed," since it was my friend's story first. I'll tell it in first person. Reading it isn't the same as hearing and watching it, but hopefully you'll get the flavor. Sharing it verbally takes about seven minutes-a long time in a talk. But the payoff, in my opinion, makes every second worth it.

I had a friend, Steve, who moved out to California after college graduation. He wound up taking a summer job on a construction site with a few friends. They rented an old house at an inexpensive rate. The main reason it didn't cost them much is because it backed up to a major highway, called the Hollywood Freeway. (My note: for anyone familiar with highways around Southern California, it's part of the 101) *Every day after work Steve and his buddies would come home all tired and sweaty, grab a beer and sit out on the back porch on a dirty old sofa, and pass the time watching the traffic on the freeway. They soon noticed that on the southbound side of the freeway, directly across from them, was a factory that made cardboard boxes. Some of the larger boxes, the kinds that would be used for boxing stoves or refrigerators for example, would often be temporarily piled up outside behind the fence. When it was windy it wasn't uncommon for boxes to occasionally blow over the fence, down the embankment and into the southbound lanes of the Hollywood Freeway. Therein lies some of the afternoon, post-work entertainment for Steve and his buddies; watching cars negotiate boxes on the highway.*

A few hundred yards to the north of the box factory was a bend in the road, so drivers weren't permitted much of a warning before the boxes appeared in front of their path. Fortunately, there were never any accidents, and it was an amusing diversion for Steve and his buddies to watch cars swerving all over the road trying to avoid the boxes. After all, the drivers had absolutely no idea what Steve knew; that the boxes were completely empty.

The Hollywood Freeway was also used by truck traffic. And Steve soon realized that the truckers who used the route regularly knew about the box factory and that the boxes were empty. The entertainment, whenever a truck appeared around the corner, was quite different. Many truckers developed their own game. They actually would try to hit the boxes. Steve noticed that some trucks would even switch lanes to line themselves up for a good hit. The best hit, they felt, was when a truck could get lift under a box and actually cause it to rise into the air upon impact. The perfect "10" was a box that, when struck, would fly high into the air, and do a lazy somersault over top of the truck as the truck sped by underneath and landed on the ground after the truck had passed. One of Steve's buddies actually made score cards for everyone, making them look like Olympic ice skating judges. After a truck passed, they would all hold up their numbered cards and argue over each other's scores. Of course, the truckers had absolutely no knowledge of all of this horseplay. They were far away on the other side of the freeway and quickly out of site, heading south. It didn't matter to Steve's buddies. It was just something fun to do.

One day they got home, grabbed some beers and headed out to the back porch. As they sat down they noticed that a box had made its way into the outside lane of the freeway. It wasn't especially large, maybe large enough to hold a small cabinet or a nightstand. But it was sure large enough to get the "ole' truck field goal boot." It didn't take long before they saw it: off to the north, coming around the bend, was a huge eighteen wheeler. Due to the bend in the road, they could judge just when the trucker saw the box, because he moved immediately from the center lane to the outside lane where the box was sitting. He also appeared to be speeding up. They reached for their score cards and leaned forward with anticipation.

Suddenly, the whole scene changed shockingly and drastically. From a high rate of speed, the driver slammed on any and all air brakes he had, and the eighteen wheeler started pouring blue brake smoke from every wheel. Under braking the trailer started to change lanes by itself, prompting the driver to fight desperately to maintain control. Smoke everywhere, trailer swaying dangerously, and the truck's cab bouncing up and down under extreme wheels-locked braking. Right away Steve and his friends knew what was happening, even though they had only seen it a few times before. The truck driver didn't know about the box factory. He was like so many car drivers; he came around the corner and was confronted with what he thought was a large box full of something, and was trying to save his truck from being damaged. This was a whole lot funnier than cars or even experienced truckers. They had themselves a full-fledged rookie truck driver. And not only that, he was creating a four-alarm panic on the freeway. It got worse. When he finally got his truck under control, he actually brought it to a complete stop, only a few feet away from the box. Then, he got out of his truck! He was completely blocking the outside lane of the freeway, but he was going to remove that box.

By this time Steve and his buddies were laughing and screaming their lungs out. "Rookie! Loser! Idiot!" and holding up score cards with a big zeroes on them. The driver, who was far away and on the other side of the highway, in no way could hear the insults they were hurling his way. They stopped yelling long enough to see what the driver was going to do just as he got to the box. Instead of moving it off the road, he decided to open the box and peer inside. After looking, he reached in and started pulling something out of the box. In this case it wasn't totally empty after all.

What he pulled out took all of the air completely out of Steve and his friends. They stared in shock and disbelief in what they were seeing. A little arm appeared, attached to a little boy; a boy who had somehow apparently been playing in the box when it was on the side of the road before it slid over into the highway.

When the boy appeared and looked at the driver, and then looked around, even from a great distance Steve could see that his eyes were as big as saucers. The driver talked and motioned in what appeared to be an angry gesture. The little boy wasted no time. He got out of the box, ran over to the shoulder of the highway, up the embankment and disappeared. The driver casually kicked the box onto the shoulder, got back into his truck and drove off.

Several sets of jaws on the porch remained dropped for several seconds. What had they just witnessed? One thing for sure, it wasn't a rookie truck driver. That guy was heading towards the box with purpose. Steve had tried to yell something to the driver while he was out of his truck, pleading for an explanation. But the driver was too far away and was never even aware that anyone had witnessed what just took place. The only thing the guys could figure was, there must have been some odd movement of the box, or maybe a little hand sticking out of the box that alerted the driver to stop. One of Steve's friends best summed up what they just witnessed when he said, "You know what? It felt like I just saw the hand of God reach down out of the sky and stop that truck." They all knew what would have happened to that little boy had the truck not stopped.

Ok, that's the story. Want to see how I used it? I'm going to remain in first person for this.

You know what? You...and I...are...the little boy in the box. This week (or weekend) we've been talking about sin, and how it hurts us and destroys our spiritual lives. Sin is like that big old truck, bearing down on our lives, wanting to destroy us. We, all of us, are that little boy in the box, playing, unaware of the danger. And without something or someone to stop that truck, spiritually we would be dead. But like the story, it's the hand of God that has reached down from heaven, to say to you and me. "No, I'm not going to let that happen. I love you too much to let sin destroy you. I'm going to stop that truck, that power of sin. And here's what I'm going to do."

And that would be the introduction of the message about the substitutionary death of Jesus on the cross and His resurrection that defeated sin, once and for all.

What's Next?

There is more to my Young Life story. I look forward to writing about the next stop in our little journey, which took us from Connecticut to Florida, where I was fortunate to serve on staff for several more years. From there my intention is to write about "Life After Young Life." When I was on staff, we used to joke about what life would be like after we left staff. Maybe for some it was a bit like whistling past a graveyard. It was scary to think about. But for me at least, my life after leaving staff was and has been a wonderful journey. The reason I want to elaborate on it is because in many ways all that I learned and experienced with Young Life prepared and equipped me for that journey. But these are stories for the next book.

Young Life Ruined Me Generationally

I want to end with one last, but important point. It's sociological in nature. I've always had a fascination with how people relate to others as it pertains to their age. There are volumes of literature on the topic. In recent years my interest has led me to research the subject more thoroughly. The best book I know regarding Generational Studies is *Mind the Gap* by Graeme Codrington. I first met Graeme, who was a youth pastor in South Africa, several years ago when he attended a seminar I was teaching in Johannesburg. Since then Graeme has been the one to expose me to his area of expertise, Generational Theory. Graeme helped me put a language to many things I already understood, because of my history of working with young people. He also taught me a lot more. This last point was one that I first began to comprehend many years before but Graeme helped me to fully grasp its significance. I wanted to give a shout-out to Graeme because reading his book would be a benefit to anyone in ministry.

What, you may ask, does this have to do with Young Life and how being on staff "ruined" me generationally? Let me explain. Normally people grow up and move through their lives right along with their generation. For example, if you are a Baby Boomer you are very likely to exhibit sociological (not speaking of psychological) traits similar to your fellow Boomers. Generational experts like Graeme have examined and catalogued these traits and similarities. However, for people who spend a significant number of years working in youth ministry in general and in Young Life in particular, a very different tendency can emerge.

Picture yourself marching through life with all of the people in your age group. If you are a Gen Xer, for example, you're merrily walking along, through your 20's, 30's and into your 40's, with your chronological and sociological peers. Statistically you are very likely to react to life's stimuli as your peers do. Millennials tend to live, act and respond like other Millennials, as do Baby Boomers and so on.

However, the picture changes if you spend enough time in youth ministry. It affects you in significant ways. Instead of marching through life with your generation, part of you winds up standing still while the generations go marching past you. You actually get caught in a sociological nether world. On one hand, as a Boomer, for example, will always be a Boomer. On the other hand there is part of you that no longer fits anymore. There's a disconnect with people your age. Sometimes you feel oddly out of place, or out of step with your peers. It's a very real and often disconcerting phenomenon.

Why does that occur? Because you've invested your career, but you have emotionally invested in so much more than that. For you, Young Life just wasn't a job. You bought in at a much higher level. You drank the Kool-Aid. Do you remember my rather lengthy explanations of Incarnational ministry? Hudson Taylor not wearing Western clothing, and how metaphorically Young Life people have done the same? How Rayburn was led to the spiritual truth, that the doctrine of the Incarnation became the methodology of the Mission? Do you recall earlier where I described contact work's deeper significance and how it was the heart of the ministry? If you served in Young Life you completely and unapologetically embraced the deepest spiritual truth of the mission: incarnationally loving a younger (than you) generation for the sake of the Gospel. You immersed yourself in their culture, you pitched your tent. And while it changed a whole lot of kids for the Gospel, it also it changed you for life.

Do you doubt this is true? Let me give you a few examples and then you decide if any of these describes you. Example: do you ever look at people your age and they seem so old, in the way they talk, relate, dress; their interests, their priorities, or how they spend their leisure time? Example: you go to a multi-generational function, like a wedding reception. Do you ever find yourself gravitating or relating more easily with people who are significantly younger than you? Example: maybe you no longer work in Young Life, maybe like me you haven't in years. You get into my car and I drop you off at a Young Life club, or at a Young Life camp. Are you frightened? Do you feel out of place or intimidated? Or do you soon feel right at home? Example: you go watch a high school ball game where one of your own kids is playing. Sure, you may speak to other parents your age, but if the opportunity arises to speak with a few of the high school kids, do you shy away, or does it come naturally? And the ones who are your own kid's friends, when they hang out at your house do they like hanging out with you? Example: do you not tell certain friends which movie you went to see, and not because it was it was R rated? Lastly, are you even aware of how different these situations are compared to other people your age?

Young Life leaders are around young people all the time. They've reached the point where they are comfortable being an adult walking in a younger world. For some leaders that's the way they stay. For others, over time and for reasons I don't fully understand, they change. One could argue that they grow, or they evolve. They no longer easily relate to or identify with young people.

I always believed that when a Young Life leader no longer thought kids were cool, but were immature and uninteresting, that was the time to move on. Young Life always had that ability to make adolescents (people in the between-stage of childhood and adulthood,) feel comfortable because we treated them like adults, all the while accepting them when at times they still acted like children. When a leader could no longer tolerate the child part, it was time to leave. It was the constant contact and interaction that kept us immersed in, accepting and loving the younger generation.

Perhaps when a leader loses interest in young people, it's simply because they have begun to move forward again generationally. For others, they never leave or fully move forward. That's why I say that generationally, in a sense, my life is "ruined." There are fewer people my age I can really identify with. But at the same time I don't really fit into a younger generation. I'm more of an awkward Boomer. Carol and I often get very nice compliments by people in our generation. "You guys look and act so young." Or "Where do you get all of your energy and enthusiasm?" Or the guy at the Apple store who was helping me with i-pod and looked through my playlist and said, "This is the music you listen to?" Likewise, we are often the recipients of very nice compliments from people many years our junior, "We love hanging out with you guys" or "you have cool tattoos." Even when the complements aren't verbal, young peoples' presence and preference to be around us is a complement in itself.

It's been my observation that what Carol and I experience is by no means unique. I know a whole lot of people in my generation who had been in youth ministry, convey similar examples and histories. Although I haven't spent time with Jack Carpenter in years, I know for certain that if I put him in a room full of high school kids he could still relate, and Jack is into his seventh decade. And while I've never asked him, I think Jack would have the good kind of pride in that fact. Jack's but one example, but there are a whole lot of us out there. I've used the term "ruined me", but in truth, I'm glad for who I am. I feel privileged that my life has been irrevocably changed. You may move on. You may even catch up with your own generation. But for sure, a by-product of a portion of your life spent in Young Life will alter how you relate to people for the rest of your life. In the next book that's something I plan to cover. I hope you'll read it too.

Acknowledgements

I've received encouragement and affirmation from a number of friends during and after this project. Newt Hetrick gave valuable feedback on Part One: Maryland. Lorain Lovejoy did the same for Part Two: Connecticut. And special shout outs to my longtime close friends, Don Mook and Jim Cunningham. Both were career Young Life Staff guys. Jim is still on staff, 38 years and counting. In keeping with that wonderful Young Life Staff tradition I've stolen a lot of their ideas and suggestions without giving them credit, except for this crummy little paragraph at the end. Last and most important: Carol Hesson Bond. She is my density. Segue to...

Are you allowed to acknowledge yourself in this section? I'd like to acknowledge an annoying habit that I've had for years. I believe it began at our dinner table when Matthew and Adam were teenagers. We started using movie and sometimes TV quotes in our conversations. The trick was to incorporate them into the topic at hand. When I considered writing this book I thought it might be fun to try utilizing that otherwise worthless skill, so I took some liberties with quotes and (sometimes) obscure references. If you didn't get some of them, my apologies. Actually, consider them a challenge to determine from whence they came. Nice project for a rainy afternoon. I had some really good quotes that I had to delete. Cunningham said I shouldn't use them. Too obscure or, a few were a bit off-color. I'll leave you with a deletion that may fit both categories. When writing about how cold it was going to get in the Hopkins barn without a heater, I referenced, "Got a little nippy going through the pass, huh, Har?"

I'll close with a challenge. There are a lot of folks out there who are a lot like me, and you know who you are. People who grew up in Young Life and who could document their lives and experiences as I have done, for their part of the country: guys like Reid Carpenter or his contemporaries, about Pittsburgh, or Tom Hammon for Ohio, or Charlie Scott in Florida. And that's only some of the guys in our part of the country. Wherever you're from, I challenge you to document your history of this great ministry so that we can know the incredible creativity, energy and faith of many men and women who gave of themselves so that kids could hear the Gospel, reminding yourselves and others of how powerful our God is, and how faithful he was, is and always will be.

Next Book: Keep your eyes peeled, like you did for the sequels of *The Hunger Games,* for...Part Three and Four: *Young Life in Florida and Life after Young Life*

If you liked the book, a review on Amazon and/or a Facebook post would be much appreciated!

Friends Mentioned in Part One

Note: The number next to the names indicates the number of pages (if more than one) the person is named.

Adams, Nate

Bachelor, Jim

Bill Starr 2

Bond, Adam

Bond, Carol 27

Bond, Jack 3

Bond, Sheryl

Bonney, Larry, Diane 3

Byrd, Andy 6

Carpenter, Jack 4

Carroll, Linda

Case, Carol

Coe, Doug

Coleman, Mike 5

Collins, Candy

Corder, Lee 2

Corder, Paula Coe

Cross, Jim

Crutchfield, Jim

Dalton, Bob

Duddy, Neil 7

Eareckson, Joni 8

Eckhardt, Dick

Eggars, Roger 2

Epstein, Joan, Eppie, Michie, Dave

Epstein/Gifford Kathy

Garriet Connie

Goldbrick 4

Gosling, Goose

Green, Jimmy

Grimstead, Jay 5

Grove Don, Jean,

Gumph, Carol 3

Harlan, Rog

Terry (pilot) 4

Hetrick, Claire

Hetrick, Newt 13

Hidey, Diane

Hockstra, Daryl

Holladay, Doug 13

Holloway, Linda

Ivey, Shelley, Mary Ellen

Johnson, George 3

Johnson, Jerry 18

Kennedy, George

Ketchum, Tony, Bette

Kinberg, Greg 5

Kirkley, Bob

Klein, George, Pam

Knupp, Cindy

Knupp, Tuck 6

Koppert, Co 2

Lemons, Don 2

Linthicum, Bill

Liphard, Bob

McMahon, Tommy

Merwald, Hal

Milliken, Bill 2

Mitchell, Bob 3

Mundy, Martine 2

Nixon, Bo 2

Oliver, Steve

Oostdyk, Harv 2

Palumbo, Joey

Patkus, Lee

Patti's

Perrine, Harry

Perrine, Linda

Pilsch, Tom 13

Pitzenberger, Walt, Nancy

Plummer, Ronnie

Price Bobbi/Tim Smick

Raley, Tom 4

Rayburn, Jim 5

Rayburn, Jim III

Reardon, Bill

Reeverts, Bob 2

Reinhold, Chuck 29

Rohlfs, Dick

Rothgeb, Jill

Ryan, Skip

Rydberg, Denny

Sandbower, Betsy 2

Sangster, Verley

Schilling, Kathy 15

Scott, Charlie

Slepitza, Cindy 2

Young Life: The Adventures of an Ex Staffer

Smith, Brad 3

Steckman, Ray 2

Swift Bart, Joan

Terrell, Terry, Brett

Treichler, Gary, Kim

Ulmer, Rick

VanSant, Duke 5

White, Bo 8

Friends Mentioned in Part Two

Note: The number next to the names indicates the number of pages (if more than one) the person is named.

Friedmann, Teal

Fry, Joanne, Nanette, Jonathan

Frye, Gleason 3

Gifford, Kathie Lee

Gosling, Goose 2

Grimstead, Jay 4

Guyer, Jim

Hamilton, Scott

Hammon, Tom

Harlan, Marilyn, Leslie, John, Lynn

Harlan, Rog 3

Harris, Jane, Buzz, Julie, Lee, Christy

Harris, John, Nancy, Julie, John, and Melissa 2

Hearn, Neil 4

Heist, Mary, Whitey 2

Heist, Peter Bill, Matt

Hetrick, Newt 2

Hindman, Barb 2

Holt, Don, Lita, Lisa, Brad, Dawn, Courtney

Hopkins, Rich, Bobbie, Sally 2

Huckel, Peter, Evie and family

Johannessen, Odd, Hanna Mi

Johansen, Ellen, Per 2

Johnson, Jerry 3

Johnson, Rod, Fran

Jordhamo, Tony

Kelly Doug

Kennedy, George

Kennedy, Jim 3

Kennedy, Renee, Bob, Kelli, Jason

Kern, Don, Joann, Marti, Michael

Koppert, Co

Kuhn, Shawn

Lanfer, Steve, Sam 2

Launsbury, Paul 2

Lovejoy, Allen Avery Carrie Elizabeth

Lovejoy, Lorain Kelley 4

Lowey, Dick

MacDonald, Phil

Young Life: The Adventures of an Ex Staffer

Malinowski, Diane

McBride, Michele

McKay, Kim

McPartland, Michele 2

Merwald, Hal 2

Minotti, Tony 3

Mitchell, Bob 3

Mook, Don 2

Moore, Peter, Sandy

Morgan, Greg, Karen 2

Mundy, Martine 4

Nichols, Barbara, Valarie, Dale

Nichols, Ed 2

Nixon, Bo 3

Bo and Mary

Oostdyk, Harv

Pappas, Connie, Happy, Beth, Jenn

P. Janice

Phillips, Dave

Pilsch, Tom 5

Prey, Bill, Shirley and family

Rayburn III, Jim, Lucia

Rayburn, Jim 4

Reinhold, Chuck 6

Sangster, Pearlean

Sangster, Verley 2

Scarlata. Jim, Roxanne, Jeff, Chris, Mark

Scherer, Liddy

Schultheis, Tom 3

Scott, Charlie, Mary 2

Simpson, Craig 2

Slepitza, Cindy 5

Starvel, Frank

Stillman, Bob 2

Stromberg, Bob

Thompson, George, Irene

Townsend, Meredith, Sue

Triolo, Ellen

Wagner, Greg

Watt, Barbara

Webster, Norma, Norman, Cheryl, Grayden

Wesney, Joe 2

Wesney, Joe, Anita, Doug, Tom

White, Bo 3

Williams, Clem 4

Williams, Libby, Walt Trey 2

Wright, Gene, Angela

Photos for Part One

Chuck Reinhold at Staff Conference

August '65 Work Crew with Goldbrick

The day I met Jim Rayburn

14,000' Summit of Mt. Princeton. Jerry Johnson leading us up.

At Cal Berkely With Tom Pilsch

Baltimore Leaders Working
on Opening Saranac

The D.C. Training Program

Doing Program With Bo White

Performing in the Opera
at Saranac with Newt Hetrick

Photos for Part Two

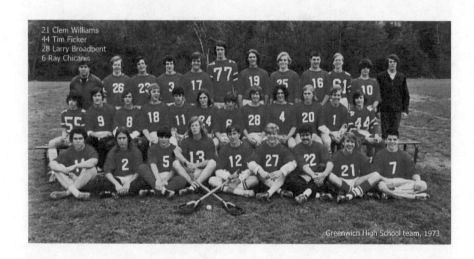

21 Clem Williams
44 Tim Ficker
28 Larry Broadbent
6 Ray Chicanis

Greenwich High School team, 1973

Wells Fargo on the Beach. Weekend Camp

Cafeteria Skit on a Weekend Camp

Dancing in Bermuda

Marabel and the Chubby Bunny Skit

Club at the Barn

Eric Broadbent giving Geek of the Week award to John Harris

The Home Our Committee Helped Us Buy

On Sabbatical

Nowadays

Made in United States
Troutdale, OR
06/01/2024

20252785R20206